ON ACCOUNT OF SEX
An Annotated Bibliography on the Status of Women in Librarianship 1987–1992

Lori A. Goetsch
Sarah B. Watstein
General Editors

Virginia Clark
Allison Cowgill
Joan Fiscella
Janice Kirkland
Jean McManus
Mary Beth Minick
Kristen L. Strohmeyer
Sandra Peterson
Mary Ellen Siflett
Mary Vela-Creixell
Contributors

for the Committee on the Status of Women in Librarianship,
American Library Association

The Scarecrow Press, Inc.
Metuchen, N.J., & London
1993

British Library Cataloguing-in-Publication data available

Library of Congress Cataloging-in-Publication Data

On account of sex : an annotated bibliography on the status of women in librarianship, 1987-1992 / Lori A. Goetsch, Sarah B. Watstein, general editors ; Virginia Clark ... [et al.], contributors.
   p. cm.
"For the Committee on the Status of Women in Librarianship, American Library Association."
Includes indexes.
ISBN 0-8108-2701-8 (acid-free paper)
  1. Women in library science--United States--Bibliography.
  2. Women in information science--United States--Bibliography.
  3. Sex discrimination against women--United States--Bibliography.
  4. Sex discrimination in employment--United States--Bibliography.
I. Goetsch, Lori A., 1954- . II. Watstein, Sarah. III. American Library Association. Committee on the Status of Women in Librarianship.
Z682.4.W65O53 1993
016.02'082--dc20   93-8164

Copyright©1993 by Lori A. Goetsch and Sarah B. Watstein
Manufactured in the United States of America
Printed on acid-free paper

CONTRIBUTORS AND ACKNOWLEDGMENTS

Virginia Clark is Editor, *Choice* magazine

Allison Cowgill is Head of Reference Services, Nevada State Library and Archives

Joan Fiscella is Professional Studies Bibliographer, University of Illinois at Chicago

Lori A. Goetsch is Head of Reference and Information Services, Michigan State University: Thanks to Marty and to the staff of Information/Reference for their support.

Janice Kirkland is Coordinator of Bibliographic Control, California State University, Bakersfield

Jean McManus is Assistant Reference Librarian and Assistant Professor, University of Illinois at Chicago: I would like to acknowledge Sarah and Lori for doing the lion's share of the work and keeping the enthusiasm for the project high.

Mary Beth Minick is Associate Librarian at Indiana University-Purdue University at Indianapolis

Sandra Peterson is Documents Librarian, Government Documents Center, Yale University

Mary Ellen Shiflett is School Library Media Specialist at the J.B. Martin Middle School, Paradis, Louisiana

Kristen L. Strohmeyer is Reference Librarian at Hamilton College: I would like to thank my husband, Bill, and my parents and sister, Anne, Bill and Amy Leimkuhler, for helping me to see what I can do and their unending love and support. I would also like to thank everyone at the Hamilton College Library.

Mary Vela-Creixell is Librarian for Fulbright & Jaworski, San Antonio, Texas

Sarah Barbara Watstein is Assistant Director for Academic Services and Head, James Branch Cabell Library, Virginia Commonwealth University: Thanks to Pam, family and friends who supported this collective endeavor to twirl the bibliographic baton once again!

TABLE OF CONTENTS

CONTRIBUTORS/ACKNOWLEDGMENTS	iii
PREFACE	vii
INTRODUCTION WOMEN IN LIBRARIANSHIP: THE RESEARCH AGENDA by Cynthia Dobson and Mary Lou Goodyear	xi
1985-86 BIBLIOGRAPHY	1
1987 BIBLIOGRAPHY	8
1988 BIBLIOGRAPHY	47
1989 BIBLIOGRAPHY	80
1990 BIBLIOGRAPHY	115
1991 BIBLIOGRAPHY	143
1992 BIBLIOGRAPHY	171
AUTHOR INDEX	203
SUBJECT INDEX	222

PREFACE

It has been almost twenty years since bibliographic work on the status of women in librarianship was initiated by the American Library Association Social Responsibilities Round Table Feminist Task Force (then Task Force on Women). The effort began in 1975 with the publication of *Women in Librarianship: Melville's Rib Symposium* (eds. Margaret Myers and M. Scarborough; New Brunswick, New Jersey: Rutgers Graduate School of Library Service). The bibliography was later expanded and indexed by the Women's Group at the University of Wisconsin (Madison) Library School. Access to information about the status of women was to advance considerably in 1979, when Kathleen Weibel and Kathleen M. Heim, with the assistance of Dianne J. Ellsworth, produced *The Role of Women in Librarianship, 1876-1976: The Entry, Advancement and Struggle for Equalization in One Profession* (Phoenix, Arizona: Oryx Press, 1979).

Material on women in libraries continued to be collected by Kathleen Weibel and Kathleen M. Heim during their consecutive tenures writing the *ALA Yearbook* article on the status of women in the profession. At the 1981 Midwinter Meeting, Kathleen Heim volunteered to continue collecting citations through 1981. With the support of the Committee on the Status of Women in Librarianship (COSWL) and the assistance of Katharine Phenix, a five-year supplement to *The Role of Women in Librarianship* was developed for the years 1977 through 1981. It was accepted for publication by the American Library Association Publishing Committee in May 1983 under the title *On Account of Sex: An Annotated Bibliography on the Status of Women in Librarianship, 1977-1981* (Chicago: American Library Association, 1984).

COSWL stated its commitment to maintain an ongoing record of resources addressing the concerns of women in librarianship in 1985. The Bibliography Clearinghouse

Subcommittee was born in that year and first noted in the *ALA Handbook 1985-86*. It is from this group, later known as the Bibliography Task Force, that work continues today with the charge to "identify published materials on the status of women in librarianship; to compile, update, and issue a bibliography of these materials on a regular basis; to alert COSWL to pertinent information on the status of women in librarianship; to provide access to ephemeral materials through ALA Headquarters." Chaired by Katharine Phenix, Lori Goetsch and Sarah Barbara Watstein, and with the assistance of Mary Ellen Landry, the Subcommittee compiled *On Account of Sex: An Annotated Bibliography on the Status of Women in Librarianship, 1982-1986* (Chicago: American Library Association, 1989).

This volume, then, constitutes the second supplement to *On Account of Sex* published by the American Library Association in 1984. As its predecessors, the bibliography is intended to be comprehensive. The scope and parameters of the bibliography have also remained essentially the same as previous ones. Included are materials that relate to the status of women in librarianship and contribute to an understanding of women's evolving status and position in the library and information science professions. Material on pay equity and comparable worth is only included as it relates to the status of women in librarianship. Included are books, articles and essays, conference reports, and pamphlets. Unpublished materials are generally not included, although there are exceptions. Material is cited in chronological order by publication date. Citations with the same date are arranged alphabetically by main entry. Author and subject indexes keyed to the citation number follow the bibliography. The subject index differs from previous editions in that it uses *A Woman's Thesaurus* (Mary Ellen S. Capek, ed., New York: Harper & Row, 1987) as a backbone. Nearly all entries are annotated with a few exceptions due to availability or language of the material.

Unlike its predecessors, this volume is the work of not one, two or three co-editors, but rather the collective work of a dozen women from different types of libraries and different regions of the country. This collaboration represents a broad range of professional and personal strengths. The Bibliography Clearinghouse roster includes women library workers from state libraries and archives, from academic libraries in both public and private institutions of higher education, and from school libraries and special libraries. Members hail from cities as diverse as Carson City, Nevada to Chicago, Illinois; from Bakersfield, California to East Lansing, Michigan; from Indianapolis, Indiana to New Haven, Connecticut; from LaPlace, Louisiana to Clinton, New York; and San Antonio, Texas to Richmond, Virginia. Over the past six years members have fulfilled individual "monitoring assignments" and met at Midwinter and Annual meetings of the American Library Association to discuss search strategies and the ongoing challenges of tracking resources addressing the concerns of women in librarianship.

Citation identification and tracking is the result of both systematic and serendipitous approaches. The major indexing and abstracting sources have been reviewed either manually or electronically. Many citations, however, were only located by an issue-by-issue analysis of periodicals and journals. Still others were identified by browsing the contents tables and indexes of books published in library science and related fields (i.e. women's studies, management, higher education, etc.). In addition to citation tracking, compilers have been responsible for annotating and indexing relevant material. The aim of the annotations is to provide enough information to enable a user to determine whether the citation is worth retrieving.

The status of women in librarianship is a complex and multifaceted issue that affects each of us in our professional and personal lives. We hope that this volume will contribute both to a greater understanding of the status of women in librarianship, and to ongoing change in the status of those who will be staffing and administering our libraries in the decade of the 1990s, the year 2000, and beyond.

Lori A. Goetsch
Sarah B. Watstein

INTRODUCTION

WOMEN IN LIBRARIANSHIP: THE RESEARCH AGENDA[1]
By Cynthia Dobson and Mary Lou Goodyear

For over a century, researchers have studied the subject of women in librarianship from a variety of viewpoints, and they have produced a considerable body of literature. The research reflects the concerns of particular eras as well as the interests of individual scholars. Consequently, there remain a number of aspects that have yet to be explored. The goal of this study is to propose a research agenda to encourage and perhaps help to focus further exploration of the subject.

This introduction analyzes research about women in librarianship by date and topic, using one of several possible outlines of vocational behavior and career development. On the basis of this examination, a research agenda is established that points to important areas that remain largely unexplored. The recommendations are divided into general, methodological, and topical areas, and studies in these areas will provide a solid foundation of information concerning women in librarianship upon which assessments of gender equity and the impact of women's issues in the profession can be based.

The research agenda developed here thus provides an example of the benefit of linking research on librarianship to another literature. Research in many professional fields is based on work done in less applied areas, achieving increased understanding by using the theories, models, and concepts of those areas. For librarianship, the literatures of vocational behavior and career development, organizational and counseling psychology, occupational sociology, and feminist studies offer helpful perspectives.

The consequence of applying a particular model, such as this one from vocational behavior literature, is a more narrow focus as well as a greater depth of understanding. This model analyzes the literature in terms of vocational studies and by definition does not examine the research from other points of view. Only in combination with other studies using a variety of perspectives will both a broad and deep understanding be achieved.

Literature Sources

Three major bibliographies of literature related to women in librarianship provide enormous assistance to anyone concerned with this topic. The first is the anthology and bibliography entitled *The Role of Women in Librarianship, 1876-1976: The Entry, Advancement and Struggle for Equalization in One Profession*, by Kathleen Weibel, Kathleen Heim, and Dianne J. Ellsworth, that examines the first one-hundred years of the profession.[2] The Committee on the Status of Women in Librarianship of the American Library Association supported the continuation of the original volume, and two updates have been published: *On Account of Sex: An Annotated Bibliography on the Status of Women in Librarianship, 1977-1981* by Kathleen Heim and Katharine Phenix;[3] and *On Account of Sex: An Annotated Bibliography on the Status of Women in Librarianship, 1982-1986* by Katharine Phenix, Lori Goetsch, Sarah Watstein and Mary Ellen H. Landry.[4] This volume provides an update for 1987 through 1992 and has been prepared by the Committee on the Status of Women in Librarianship Bibliography Clearinghouse Task Force. The scope of the bibliographies is broad, including books, chapters, articles, dissertations, government documents, and, to a limited extent, newspaper articles. The bibliographies have been compiled using *Library Literature*, *Information Science Abstracts*, *Dissertation Abstracts*, ERIC, and *American Statistics Index* as well as direct examination of various materials. The summary of research on women in librarianship in this paper is based on these bibliographies and includes material on all types of libraries, including academic, public, school, and special.

Introduction

Topical Outline for Vocational Behavior

The authors of the 1988 review of literature for the *Journal of Vocational Behavior*, Louise F. Fitzgerald and James O. Rounds, developed a topical outline for vocational studies using structural analysis.[5] They were interested in defining distinct subject areas and in determining the relations of these areas to one another. Expert raters sorted 158 vocational concepts according to similarity in meaning, and cluster analysis resulted in the fourteen clusters presented in Table 1. A multidimensional scaling procedure was used to examine the interrelationships of these clusters, leading to a two-dimension solution. As depicted in Figure 1, taken from the article, one dimension is anchored by the terms "pre-entry" and "post-entry" and focuses on processes of choice at one end and issues arising after entry into the labor market at the other.[6] The second dimension includes the two traditional perspectives in the study of vocational behavior, ranging from "counseling psychology" with its focus on individuals and their career development to "industrial-organizational" with its emphasis on the socio-organizational context and the impact of the organization. Fitzgerald and Rounds conclude that "Overall, the clustering solution represents a content analysis of the subjects and themes seen as important; as such it constitutes an empirically derived organization of what scholars view as the critical research issues in vocational behavior and career development."[7]

Both the subject indexes to the bibliographies and Fitzgerald and Rounds' outline put research on women's behavior and experience under the subject of the research itself rather than under the heading "women." For investigations specifically focused on women, however, the outline includes Cluster J: Women's Workforce Participation, and it was used by Fitzgerald and Rounds for material examining women and such topics as career issues at work, workforce participation, reactions to pay issues, and behavioral reactions to work. Because of the interest in women of the articles analyzed in this introduction, Cluster J was expanded to include topics relevant to the library science profession. Table 2 presents seven topics included in Cluster J, each containing at least twenty citations.

The summary of the literature presented in this

introduction is based on Fitzgerald and Rounds' topical outline. While the outline is a guide to the overall area of vocational behavior, the summary involves mapping specialized literature for a single occupation. Some lack of fit between the outline and the literature on women in librarianship thus is to be expected. The pattern of coverage, however, can be informative and provides the basis for the research agenda.

Methodology

The citations related to women in librarianship listed in the published bibliographies and in the 1987 through 1989 updates prepared by the Committee on the Status of Women in Librarianship Bibliography Clearinghouse Task Force comprised the database for this research. Six types of citations listed in the bibliographies were not included in this study: ads, letters, bibliographies, directories, reprints, and listings of photographs. The remaining citations were classified into Fitzgerald and Rounds' fourteen categories by reviewing the abstracts provided in the bibliographies. A citation was counted in only one category.

The citations were grouped into seven time periods. These include 1876 to 1899, 1900 to 1919, 1920 to 1939, 1940 to 1959, 1960 to 1969, 1970 to 1979, and 1980 to 1989. The first period includes 24 years, the next three periods twenty years, and the last three periods ten years. The decision to break the later years into ten-year periods was based on the social, economic, and political shifts occurring during these times, changes in the profession, and the large number of citations for these years. Statistical analysis of the last three years, 1990 to 1992, is omitted in order to maintain the ten-year periods, but an overview of the literature of these years is included in the analysis.

Findings

Tables 3 and 4 present the number and percentage of citations in the various clusters both overall and within the specific time periods from 1876 to 1989. Looking first at the "Total" line in Table 3, one finds that 1,749 citations were classified. Of this total the largest number, 621 or 36%, falls into Cluster J: Women's Workforce Participation, followed by 530 or 30% in Cluster E:

Introduction

Workplace Justice. Smaller but substantial numbers are the 267 or 15% in Cluster G: Leadership, and the 120 or 7% in Cluster D: Personnel Practices and Issues. Clusters with less than 100 but at least 15 citations include Cluster A: Decision-making Process (N=62); Cluster B: Reciprocal Work and Nonwork Relationships (N=48); Cluster M: Career Development: Life-span Perspectives (N=31); Cluster L: Vocational Choice: Person-Environment Fit Perspectives (N=17); Cluster I: Career Development Interventions (N=17); and Cluster K: Adjustment and Development in Organizations (N=15). The remaining clusters contain very small numbers of citations: Cluster C: Work-related Stress and Coping (N=7); Cluster F: Industrial-Organizational Measurement Issues (N=5); Cluster H: Assessment: Vocational Behavior (N=5); and Cluster N: Job Search (N=4). An examination of the number of citations in the clusters in terms of their locations in Figure 1 reveals an emphasis on the industrial-organizational half relative to the counseling psychology half. The larger clusters all are located below the dividing line.

The strong emphasis on women's employment issues and workplace justice is unsurprising given the nature of the bibliographies, and the small number of citations in the specialized vocational behavior topics of industrial-organizational measurement issues and assessment also is not unexpected. The large numbers related to leadership and to personnel practices and issues, however, begin to describe the current research picture.

An examination of the research within particular topical areas reveals more about the emphases and gaps in the literature. In Cluster A: Decision-making Process, the literature focuses on library school students, their attitudes toward library science, their reasons for selecting this career, and their career plans. Child care issues are the major focus of the literature classed in Cluster B: Reciprocal Work and Nonwork Relationships. Cluster D: Personnel Practices and Issues includes a number of studies on the qualifications needed by librarians, including issues such as the MLS, advanced subject degrees, and certification. On-the-job training and mentoring also are popular topics of research in this cluster. Affirmative action programs and sexual harassment have received attention, and pay equity has been extensively discussed in the literature as well as more general equity concerns. Cluster F: Industrial-Organizational Measurement Issues is a fairly new area for librarianship. Research related to assessment centers, most notably at the University of Washington, comprises most of the literature in this small cluster. Cluster G: Leadership focuses on personal characteristics of current directors as well as the strategies and experiences that assisted in their promotions. Gender differences in management and leadership also have received attention. Cluster K: Adjustment and Development in Organizations includes work on job satisfaction and career development.

Tables 3 and 4 illustrate the familiar increase in publications over time. The first five periods, from 1876 to 1969, included 358 or only one-fifth (20%) of the citations. Nearly a third (31%) of the research analyzed appeared from 1970 to 1979 (N=547), and almost half (48%) from 1980 to 1989 (N=844).

Table 4 also presents percentages within individual subject areas with at least fifteen citations. The pattern over time varies by topic. For example, citations in Cluster A: Decision-making Process occur from 1900 to 1989, with a relatively large percentage (27%) in the 1900 to 1919 period reflecting the emphasis on recruiting within the profession during this period. In contrast, citations in Cluster I: Career Development Interventions and Cluster K: Adjustment and Development in Organizations are instead concentrated in the 1980 to 1989 period.

Table 5 presents the number and percentage of citations in the subcategories of Cluster J: Women's Workforce Participation. Examination of the table reveals the debate in the late nineteenth and early twentieth centuries concerning the entry of women into the profession. In the positive category, arguments supporting the suitability of women for the profession are prevalent in the literature as well as defenses of the value women can contribute. In the negative category, arguments against women entering the profession declined with time but were replaced by discussions concerning the negative aspects of a feminized profession, a topic that continues to be a popular one with authors.

The data in Table 5 also reveal a strong emphasis on statistics concerning the number of men and women in librarianship, with 229 or 37% of the citations in this area. This emphasis began as acceptance of women in the profession was gained and awareness of the status of women in the profession became a concern. Details concerning the male/female

Introduction

composition of the profession have become well documented, and many routinely collected data sets published each year now include segregation of the data by gender. Research in the area of race has shown an increasing emphasis over time and has increased in 1990 and 1992, but remains a relatively small segment (6%) of the work related to women in librarianship. Biography and historical writing also have increased over time, but they remain a small (6% and 4% respectively) part of the literature.

Diverse interests make up the Other category. Beginning in the late 1970s and the 1980s publications in this category expanded, with researchers reporting work in areas that are of concern to the feminist scholarly community. The topics include pornography, censorship, homophobia, women as volunteers, and services to women. More recent emphases of this literature are women as library users and the information needs of women. Library science topics such as women's issues in collection development, cataloging, and reference also are subjects that have received recent attention. These areas show strong growth in the 1990s adding significant pieces to the body of knowledge.

Across the fourteen clusters, researchers have selected a variety of settings and subjects to study. More than half of the citations report on either a mixed group of libraries or do not identify the type of library investigated. In research dealing with a single type of library, the most studied is the academic library, followed by the public library. The subject group most likely to be examined is directors, particularly directors of libraries who are members of the Association of Research Libraries, with the next most common group being library school students.

Discussion

Classifying the citations gathered on women in librarianship into the topical outline developed by Fitzgerald and Rounds (1989) provided several insights into this literature. First, it is very unevenly divided among the clusters. Some areas are particularly popular while others seem to have little interest for investigators. A balanced distribution is not a goal, but the degree of unevenness is striking. Second, writing on industrial-organizational psychology topics is much more prevalent than writing focused on counseling psychology topics. The organizational setting is a more popular choice for library researchers than individual librarians themselves. Third, topics that would seem to be areas of concern for a feminized profession--career development from a life-span perspective, work and nonwork relationships, and work-related stress and coping-- have received relatively little attention. Fourth, within studies directly related to women, statistical compilations describing gender distribution rather than more substantive discussions are the most common. And finally, the emphases on particular kinds of libraries and certain kinds of subjects have a definite impact on how widely the research findings can be generalized and the level of information available concerning particular groups and types of libraries.

The Research Agenda

Research concerning women in librarianship is directed toward understanding the experience of women in the profession. An agenda for research should both point to areas in need of exploration and suggest improvements in the research process. The following recommendations therefore are divided into methodological suggestions and descriptions of subject areas in need of further study.

Methodological Recommendations

The experience of women in librarianship has both paralleled and diverged from that of men in the profession. Understanding the experience of women in librarianship requires research that explores the situation of both men and women. Thus a study of women's characteristics or career paths needs either to include both men and women as subjects or to build specifically on earlier research that did have men as its subjects. Answers to questions about the importance for women as opposed to men of factors such as decisiveness, child care responsibilities, or mentoring for any of a wide range of occupational outcomes can only be found if both men and women are studied.

Published research tends to omit statistically nonsignificant findings, but these as well as significant findings should be reported. Researchers need to provide information concerning the

Introduction

areas in which gender is not a significant variable as well as information about those where it is important. Both types of results are required to develop an understanding of the experience of women librarians and, pragmatically, to avoid studies that unnecessarily duplicate previous work.

Research on women in librarianship would be enriched by stronger links with the literature of other fields. This introduction presents an attempt to use an organizing framework from the study of vocational behavior to understand research concerning women in librarianship. A similar investigation could have used insights from the sociology of occupations or from women's studies. Such links will bring developed theoretical structures, concepts, methodologies, and measurement tools to the investigation of librarianship, and they will allow comparison of librarianship to other professions.

Topical Recommendations

The research agenda needs to be expanded to include a wider range of topical areas. As noted above, there is a stronger emphasis in the current research database on organizational topics than on those that look at the individual. This may be a result of a professional focus on libraries as organizations, a focus which is not found to the same extent in other professions where individuals often practice their professions outside of organizational settings. It also may reflect a bias toward the importance of institutions over the individuals who work within them. Many of the topical areas related to individuals and their career development, those in the top half of Figure 1, are of utmost importance to women and deserve more attention.

A related need is that of becoming more inclusive in the choice of organizational settings to study. Most of the literature deals with librarians in general, but when an organizational setting is chosen it is most often the academic library. This may be a result of academic librarians performing research due to their faculty status and the impact of promotion and tenure criteria related to research and publication. Their familiarity with academic libraries and the existence of convenient mailing lists, such as the members of the Association of Research Libraries, may explain this focus. There is a need, however, for other types of libraries--school, public, and special libraries administered within both public and private institutions--to become the setting for research studies of gender issues.

Libraries are complex organizations containing a wide variety of positions. The research on women in librarianship has stressed managerial employees, particularly library directors. Statistical studies have documented the lack of women in director positions, and so it is understandable that much research has been focused on how to improve the numbers of women in these positions. The lack of research on line employees, however, limits the profession in understanding the work experience of its varied members. There is a whole area of research--studies that examine the career paths and professional experience of men and women catalogers, reference librarians, children's librarians, and others as well as paraprofessional and clerical staff--awaiting investigation.

Specific topical recommendations may be divided into the four quadrants in Figure 1 from Fitzgerald and Rounds. Those in the top two quadrants emphasize the interests of counseling psychology and the career development of individuals. Potential research in the upper left quadrant includes the differences between women and men in career progression and job productivity and the differential effect for women and men of career counseling interventions on career planning. Gender differences in the choice of particular library specialties and the status of those specialties also is of concern. Other important research might focus on differences between men and women in navigating career transitions such as returning to the job after work interruptions, plateauing, or adjusting to retirement.

In the upper right quadrant, potential topics include how men and women may differ in job-seeking behavior and in the rate of successful job searches. Information concerning gender differences in job barriers would prove helpful in efforts to encourage the careers of women. Dual-career issues, the effect of opportunities for job sharing and part-time work, and changes in the importance of nonwork factors across the life cycle and at different points in the career path for women as opposed to men are of immediate concern. The final targets for research in this area include gender differences in burnout, factors that may moderate stress, and the relationships among stress, conditions of work, and personal characteristics.

Introduction

The lower half of Figure 1 contains topics that relate to the organizational setting. In the lower right quadrant, research that examines gender bias in currently used measures in job analysis and performance evaluation would strengthen both research and practice. Other questions of interest are the differences in recruitment and selection of men and women for library jobs, the effect of job characteristics on performance, and differences by gender in withdrawal through lateness, absenteeism, and turnover. Studies of sex differences in work-related attitudes and mentoring would be valuable, and additional research on sexual harassment, particularly harassment of library patrons by other library patrons or staff, is recommended. In the final quadrant, located on the lower left, the effect of the feminization of the profession on career decisions by men and women and the link of career plans and aspirations with other characteristics for men and women are topics of great interest. Gender bias in career guidance instruments and in tools used to assess interests and traits of prospective librarians is another important topic for research. Finally, studies of middle managers' characteristics and career paths, investigations of sex differences in librarians' concepts and use of power and authority, and the applicability of feminist perspectives on management and leadership in libraries are of particular interest.

Conclusion

This analysis of the literature of women in librarianship from 1876 to 1989 presented in this introduction has revealed past concentrations in some areas of Fitzgerald and Rounds' topical outline, particularly those related to organizational subjects. This analysis led to recommendations for further research in both methodological and topical areas. The research agenda points to topics in need of further study, including those related to employment issues and to feminist analysis of the profession.

In the first anthology and bibliography, Weibel looked to the future and noted that the women's movement might impact librarianship in any of three different contexts: "1) as *a women's profession* in which females make up the majority of the work force; 2) as *a feminized profession* with the 'negative' connotations of characteristics labeled female, such as passivity, emotionalism, and intuitiveness; and 3) as *a feminist profession* operating on a feminist value system wherein traditional roles based on sex and power are no longer extant and life choices and ability determine functions."[8] At that time she concluded that projections of librarianship as a feminist profession were highly speculative. The research of the intervening years has begun to address feminist issues, and future studies of women in librarianship may well take a more feminist perspective than has been the case thus far. Two recent works provide examples of this point of view. In one, Hildenbrand argues that if research establishes a relationship between those areas of librarianship that have a higher percentage of women and inferior conditions of employment within librarianship, then it is time to expand the feminist agenda and concentrate on female-intensive specialties in library work.[9] In the other, Baum examines 250 articles written between 1965 and 1985 that met her criteria of having been written by American women about women in librarianship. Analyzing these works as well as women's programming at American Library Association annual conferences during this same period, she concludes that a liberal rather than radical feminist ideology is evident in both library literature and programming. She also notes that there has been a failure of women in librarianship to identify with and cite feminist authors outside of library literature. Baum does not provide a specific research agenda, but she indicates that "library women should strive to make active and continuing contact with the various streams of the feminist movement--to mandate a dialogue between library women and feminists generally."[10]

Researchers will be better able to access gender equity in the profession with the information that will result from further research on women in librarianship. Linking the research to other perspectives, including feminism, will enrich their understanding of the experience of women in this profession.

Figure 1. Two-dimensional scaling solution of 14 vocational behavior clusters.

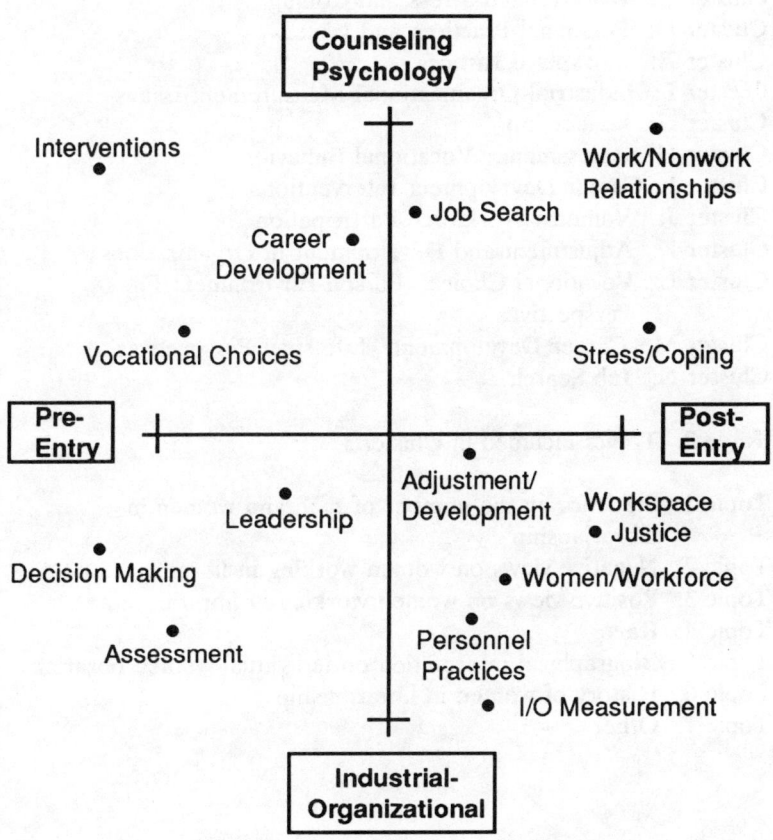

Reprinted from Louise F. Fitzgerald and James O. Rounds, "Vocational Behavior, 1988: A Critical Analysis," *Journal of Vocational Behavior* 35 (October 1989):105-163. Reprinted by permission.

Table 1. Clusters obtained by Fitzgerald and Rounds (1989).

Cluster A: Decision-making Process
Cluster B: Reciprocal Work and Nonwork Relationships
Cluster C: Work-related Stress and Coping
Cluster D: Personnel Practices and Issues
Cluster E: Workplace Justice
Cluster F: Industrial-Organizational Measurement Issues
Cluster G: Leadership
Cluster H: Assessment: Vocational Behavior
Cluster I: Career Development Interventions
Cluster J: Women's Workforce Participation
Cluster K: Adjustment and Development in Organizations
Cluster L: Vocational Choice: Person-Environment Fit Perspectives
Cluster M: Career Development: Life-span Perspectives
Cluster N: Job Search

Table 2. Topics included in Cluster J

Topic 1: Statistics on the number of men and women in librarianship
Topic 2: Negative views on women working in libraries
Topic 3: Positive views on women working in libraries
Topic 4: Race
Topic 5: Biographical information on individual women librarians
Topic 6: History of women in librarianship
Topic 7: Other

Table 3. Number of citations in the 14 clusters by date of publication.

	A	B	C	D	E	F	G	H	I	J	K	L	M	N	Total
1876-1899	0	0	0	2	7	0	2	0	0	53	0	0	0	0	64
1900-1919	17	1	1	10	34	0	7	0	0	41	0	1	0	0	112
1920-1939	1	0	0	6	18	0	13	0	0	23	0	0	0	0	61
1940-1959	8	0	0	1	12	0	9	0	0	22	0	0	0	0	52
1960-1969	7	5	0	2	14	0	15	0	0	21	0	0	5	0	69
1970-1979	6	23	5	60	171	5	86	0	5	170	1	6	9	0	547
1980-1989	23	19	1	39	274	0	135	5	12	291	14	10	17	4	844
Total	62	48	7	120	530	5	267	5	17	621	15	17	31	4	1749

Table 4. Percentage of citations in the 14 clusters by date of publication.

	A	B	C	D	E	F	G	H	I	J	K	L	M	N	Total
1876-1899	0	0	--	2	1	--	1	--	0	9	0	0	0	--	4
1900-1919	27	2	--	8	6	--	3	--	0	7	0	6	0	--	6
1920-1939	2	0	--	5	3	--	5	--	0	4	0	0	0	--	3
1940-1959	13	0	--	1	2	--	3	--	0	4	0	0	0	--	3
1960-1969	11	10	--	2	3	--	6	--	0	3	0	0	16	--	4
1970-1979	10	48	--	50	32	--	32	--	29	27	7	35	29	--	31
1980-1989	37	40	--	33	52	--	51	--	71	47	93	59	55	--	48
Total	100	100	na	100	100	na	100	na	100	100	100	100	100	na	100

Table 5. Number and percentages of citations in Cluster J subtopics by date of publication.

Number

Date	Stat	Neg	Pos	Race	Biog	Hist	Other	Total
1876-1899	7	5	34	0	0	0	7	53
1900-1919	5	13	17	0	0	0	6	41
1920-1939	7	5	8	1	0	0	2	23
1940-1959	12	7	1	0	1	0	1	22
1960-1969	6	12	0	0	2	1	0	21
1970-1979	74	21	0	11	15	11	38	170
1980-1989	118	21	1	28	20	14	89	291
Total	229	84	61	40	38	26	143	621

Percentage

Date	Stat	Neg	Pos	Race	Biog	Hist	Other	Total
1876-1899	3	6	56	0	0	0	5	9
1900-1919	2	16	28	0	0	0	4	7
1920-1939	3	6	13	3	0	0	1	4
1940-1959	5	8	2	0	3	0	1	4
1960-1969	3	14	0	0	5	4	0	3
1970-1979	32	25	0	28	39	42	27	27
1980-1989	52	25	2	70	53	54	62	47
Total	100	100	101	101	100	100	100	101

Notes

1. An earlier version of this introduction was presented at the Research Forum of the Library Research Round Table, American Library Association Annual Conference, San Francisco, June, 1992.
2. Kathleen Weibel and Kathleen M. Heim with the assistance of Dianne J. Ellsworth. *The Role of Women in Librarianship, 1876-1976: The Entry, Advancement and Struggle for Equalization in One Profession*. Phoenix, AZ: Oryx Press, 1979.
3. Kathleen Heim and Katharine Phenix. *On Account of Sex: An Annotated Bibliography on the Status of Women in Librarianship, 1977-1981*. Chicago: American Library Association, 1984.
4. Katharine Phenix, Lori Goetsch, Sarah Watstein, and Mary Ellen H. Landry. *On Account of Sex: An Annotated Bibliography on the Status of Women in Librarianship, 1982-1986*. Chicago: American Library Association, 1989.
5. Louise F. Fitzgerald and James O. Rounds. "Vocational Behavior, 1988: A Critical Analysis." *Journal of Vocational Behavior* 35 (October 1989):105-163.
6. Ibid., p. 113.
7. Ibid., p. 108.
8. Kathleen Weibel. "Towards a Feminist Profession," in Weibel, Heim, and Ellsworth, *The Role of Women in Librarianship*, p. 287.
9. Suzanne Hildenbrand. "'Women's Work' Within Librarianship: Time to Expand the Feminist Agenda." *Library Journal* 114 (September 1, 1989):153-155.
10. Christina D. Baum. *Feminist Thought in American Librarianship*. Jefferson, NC: McFarland, 1992, p. 126.

1985-86 BIBLIOGRAPHY

1986-01 *Academic and Public Librarians: Data by Race, Ethnicity, and Sex*. Jeniece Guy, Project Director. Chicago: American Library Association, Office for Library Personnel Resources, 1986.
    Provides update to the 1981 publication *The Racial, Ethnic, and Sexual Composition of Library Staff in Academic and Public Libraries*. Data collected include race, ethnicity, and sex of librarians as well as three levels of positions: directors, assistant, associate, deputy directors; department or branch heads; and entry level. Discusses the advancement of women and minorities. (See also **1991-04**)

1986-02 Artemeeva, E. B. and T.A. Zhdanova. "The Socio-Psychological Aspect of Library Management in the USA [Sotsialno-psichologicheskie Aspekty Rukovodstva Bibliotechnymi Kadrami v SSA]." *Bibliotekovedenie i Bibliografia za Rubezhom* 107 (1986):59-72.
    Discusses problems of library management including the status of women in the profession and suggestions for its improvement.

1986-03 Association of Theological Schools in the United States and Canada. *Fact Book on Theological Education for the Academic Year 1985-1986*, edited by William L. Baumgaertner. Vandalia, Ohio: [The Association], 1986.
    Includes sex distribution of faculty and administrative personnel including librarians, changes in employment of women and blacks by position held, and trends in salaries for administration, faculty, and librarians.

1986-04 *Characteristics and Trends of Illinois Public Community College Faculty and Staff, Fall Terms 1983-1985*. Springfield, IL:

Illinois Community College Board, 1986. ERIC, ED 275 362

Includes librarians as academic support personnel and provides data by sex for degrees earned, service years, and age.

1986-05 *Characteristics of Illinois Public Community College Faculty and Staff, Fall Term 1984.* Springfield, IL: Illinois Community College Board, 1985. ERIC, ED 262 841

Includes librarians as academic support personnel and provides statistics by sex for degrees attained, years of service, and age.

1986-06 Coady, Reginald. "An Analysis of State Library Job Application Forms for Compliance with EEOC Guidelines." *Journal of Library Administration* 7 (Spring 1986):49-59.

Analyzes the job application forms of the 50 state libraries for compliance with federal equal employment opportunity guidelines for pre-employment inquiries. Notes that nine states asked the applicants to identify their sex; four asked about the applicants' marital status.

1986-07 Dewey, Barbara. "Job Evaluation Systems in Academic Libraries: Current Issues and Trends." *Journal of Library Administration* 6 (Winter 1985-86):23-31.

Discusses the need for academic libraries to look at the job evaluation process more thoroughly in order to address issues of pay equity and comparable worth. Cites two sex discrimination cases.

1986-08 Fields, Jacqueline P. *Career Transitions of Women in Professions.* Working Paper No. 155. Wellesley College, Massachusetts Center for Research on Women, 1985. ERIC, ED 282 123

Analyzes librarianship in section on career transitions in female intensive occupations. Indicates that transitions for librarians are few, partly due to limited opportunity to move from one type of library to another. Identifies expected shortages in highly specialized areas and the most promise for jobs in non-library information positions.

1986-09 Hannon, Natalie Rodkin. "The Influence of Individual Factors, Economic Sector, and Sex Stereotyping on Women's Occupational Mobility and Status Attainment." Ph.D. diss., Fordham University, 1986.

Uses data from the National Longitudinal Surveys to study the impact of various factors on women's occupational mobility and status. One finding is that women in female intensive occupations such as librarianship have lower status and less upward mobility than women in male intensive occupations.

1986-10 "Historian Says Role of Women's Groups Ignored in Writing of Public Library History." *American Libraries* 17 (November 1986):782.

Summarizes "Women and Libraries" by Anne F. Scott, *Journal of Library History, Philosophy, and Comparative Librarianship* 21 (Spring 1986):400-405.

Letters:

Carmichael, James V. "Honoring Our Heritage." *American Libraries* 18 (February 1987):120.
Heim, Kathleen M. "Recognizing Women's Associations." *American Libraries* 18 (February 1987):120.

1986-11 Koichi, Mori. "Melvil Dewey and His Feminism" [in Japanese]. *Toshokan-kai* 38 (November 1986):169-175.

Discusses Dewey's role in recruiting women to librarianship at the School of Library Economy at Columbia University and his encouragement of various women's careers.

1986-12 Morrison, Louise E. et al. "The Profession." *ALKI: The Washington Library Association Journal* 2 (December 1986):91-123.

1986-13 Murphy, Marcy and Martha J. Bailey. *An Investigation of the Managerial Competencies of Research Librarians: A Preliminary Report of a Council on Library Resources Grant, 1983-85.* Washington, DC: Council on Library Resources, 1986. ERIC, ED 277 372

Includes figures on sex of middle managers and assistant

directors: 60-70% of middle managers are women, but much fewer are reported at the Assistant Director level. Tables include breakdown by sex.

1986-14 Okko, Marjatta. "Characteristics of Class 1985 in Library and Information Science at University of Tampere" ["Kirjastotieteen ja informatuekan opiskelun Tampereen yliopistossa v. 1985 aloittaneiden karakteristuekkaa."] *Kirjastotiede ja Informatiikka* 4 (1985):83-88.

Surveys 60 students starting the Library and Information Science program. Notes that females make up 75% of the students surveyed.

1986-15 Phenix, Katharine. "Women in Librarianship: Research." *WLW Journal* 10 (1985):27-28.

Criticizes a paper presented by Michael Harris at the 1985 winter meeting of the Association for Library and Information Science Education which includes a critique of the role of feminists in librarianship as "only interested in getting to the top."

1986-16 Ramer, James D. et al. "Recruitment of Library School Faculty." *Journal of Education for Library and Information Science* 27 (Fall 1986):100-104.

Discusses typical means of recruitment including contacts with individuals and published position announcements and reports results of survey of library schools and their recruitment practices. Includes data regarding sex of the faculty members recruited and type of initial contact; the difference was not determined to be statistically significant.

1986-17 Rothstein, Samuel. "Professional Staff in Canadian University Libraries." *Library Journal* 111 (November 1, 1986):31-34.

Bemoans what the author sees as stagnation among Canada's academic librarians which he attributes to an aging workforce and lack of professional development and motivation. While not directly addressing gender, the following letters reflect an outrage with Rothstein's article from a decidedly female perspective.

Letters:

Gill, Molly. "Don't Trust Anyone Over 30." *Library Journal* 112 (January 1987):6.
Nelson, Veneese C. "Ask Not What Your Profession...." *Library Journal* 112 (April 1, 1987):6.

1986-17a Smith, Catherine. "Behavioral Implications of Ambiguous Information and its Temporal Placement in the Library Employee Selection Process." Ph.D. diss., University of Pittsburgh, 1986.

Identifies differences in interviewers' judgments of a hypothetical job applicant based on a letter of reference read before or after reading excerpts from a simulated interview. One survey element is sex of subject.

1986-18 Solomon, Barbara M. *In the Company of Educated Women*. New Haven, CT: Yale University Press, 1986.

Makes brief historical mention of librarianship as one of the "so-called semiprofessions" because it was considered suitable work for women. Includes librarians in a table entitled "Women in Selected Professional Occupations, 1910-1982, as a Percentage of All Workers in Those Fields." Title was well reviewed; the list below is representative but not comprehensive.

Reviews:

Antler, Joyce. *Signs* 12 (Winter 1987):386-390.
Baker, Therese L. *Contemporary Sociology* 15 (January 1986):95.
Berlin, Miriam H. *Change* 18 (March-April 1986):50-53.
Blair, K.J. *Choice* 23 (September 1985):177.
Brown, Cynthia Farr. *Journal of Interdisciplinary History* 18 (Fall 1987):381-382.
Burstyn, Joan N. *Journal of Higher Education* 58 (January-February 1987):110-113.
Carter, Patricia Anne. *Educational Studies* 17 (Winter 1986):568.
Chambers-Schiller, Lee. *American Historical Review* 91 (April 1986):454-455.
Klingberg, Susan. *College and Research Libraries* 50 (September 1989):587.

Lefkowitz, Mary. *Times Literary Supplement*, 21 November 1986, 1301.
Leonardi, Susan J. *Women's Studies* 13 (September 1986):398-402.
McFeely, Mary Drake. *Library Journal* 110 (April 15, 1985):72.
Ritvo, Harriet. *Psychology Today* 20 (January 1986):80.
Simmons, Adele. *New York Times Book Review* 90 (October 6, 1985):34.
Sochen, June. *Journal of American History* 72 (December 1985):667-668.
Spacks, Patricia Meyer. *New Republic* 193 (July 1, 1985):30-34.
Walsh, Margaret. *History* 71 (October 1986):458.

1986-19 Tallman, Johanna E. *Check Out a Librarian*. Metuchen, NJ: Scarecrow Press, 1985.

Describes stories and experiences of various librarians to introduce the reader to the profession. Includes history of the author's career.

Reviews:

AB Bookman's Weekly 77 (June 23, 1986):2956.
Borko, Harold. *Library Journal* 111 (April 15, 1986):62.
Library Science Annual 2 (1986):152.

1986-20 Trelles, O.M. and J.F. Bailey. "Autonomy, Librarian Status, and Librarian Tenure in Law School Libraries: The State of the Art, 1984." *Law Library Journal* 78 (Fall 1986):605-681.

1986-20a U.S. Congress. House. Select Committee on Children, Youth, and Families. 99th Congress. *Work in America: Implications for Families: Hearing...April 17, 1986.* Washington, DC: U.S. Government Printing Office, 1986.

Table entitled "Median weekly earnings of wage and salary workers who usually work full time by detailed (3-digit census code) occupation and sex, annual averages, 1985" includes librarians.

1986-21 Walters, Daniel L. "The Wounded Psyche of the Professional Librarian." *ALKI: The Washington Library Association Journal* 2 (December 1986):95-97.

    Argues that "vocation" is a more appropriate term than "profession" for librarianship. Suggests that one indication of librarians' second class citizenship is the greater number of men in upper administration in an occupation primarily for women.

1986-22 Webreck, Susan J. "The Effects of Personality Type and Organizational Climate on the Acquisition and Utilization of Information: A Case Study Approach Involving the Professional Staff of Four Academic Libraries." Ph.D. diss., University of Pittsburgh, 1986.

    Attempts to identify relations among personality type, organizational climate, and "information richness" through four case studies. Refers to gender differences in communication styles in the literature review and provides data on respondents by sex but does no analysis based on gender.

1987 BIBLIOGRAPHY

1987-01 "Actions of the Board of Directors Oct. 23-24, 1986." *Special Libraries* 78 (Winter 1987):54.
Notes motion against child care provision at annual conference due to concern over association's liability.

1987-02 "Actions of the Board of Directors, June 5, 6, and 12, 1987." *Special Libraries* 78 (Fall 1987):308.
Notes creation of a $6000 affirmative action scholarship to replace two $3000 minority stipends.

1987-03 *Activism in American Librarianship, 1962-1973*, edited by Mary Lee Bundy and Frederick J. Stielow. Westport, CT: Greenwood, 1987.
Includes a chapter on the impact of the women's rights movement during the 1960s and early 1970s. (See also **1987-29**)

Reviews:

Berman, Sanford. *Library Journal* 113 (June 1, 1988):88.
DeLoach, Marva L. *RQ* 28 (Fall 1988):127.
Editor. *Journal of Academic Librarianship* 14 (May 1988):110-111.
Flagg, Gordon. *American Libraries* 19 (April 1989):321-322.
Smith, Eldred. *Journal of Academic Librarianship* 14 (September 1988):240.
Stevens, Norman. *Wilson Library Bulletin* 62 (April 1988):85.
Trezza, Alphonse F. *Libraries and Culture* 25 (Spring 1990):288-289.

1987-04 "Affirmative Action Plan for Montgomery County, Md."
Library Journal 112 (September 1, 1987):120.
Announces that an affirmative action plan was published and distributed to employees of the Montgomery County Department of Public Libraries, Maryland, and summarizes the reasons it was developed.

1987-04a "ALA Officers & Awards." *Library Journal* 112 (August 1987):36.
Announces Kathleen Heim as winner of the ALA Equality Award.

1987-05 American Library Association. Committee on Minority Concerns. "Report of the Minority Concerns Committee to the ALA Council 1987 Midwinter Conference." In *ALA Council Minutes* Vol. 28 (January 1987), 7-8; exhibit #5, 58-66. Chicago: American Library Association, 1987.
Includes exhibit which enumerates recommendations of *Equity at Issue* (ALA Council, 1985) with implementations. Recommends that the American Library Association Office for Library Personnel Resources broaden its survey of racial, ethnic, and sexual composition of library personnel to include data collection from all association committees and affiliated groups.

1987-06 American Library Association. Office for Library Personnel Resources. *Academic and Public Librarians: Data by Race, Ethnicity and Sex.* Chicago: American Library Association, 1987.
Results include finding that 75.1% are female and that the largest minority group is black women. Includes 15 tables. (See also **1987-89**)

1987-06a "American Library Association Selected Awards." *School Library Journal* 34 (September 1987):102.
Announces Kathleen Heim as winner of the ALA Equality Award.

1987-07 Anderson, A.J., Sandra Collins, and Catherine Doyle. "The Flashy Fellow." *Library Journal* 112 (October 15, 1987):45-47.

Part of the "How Do You Manage?" series. Creates a hypothetical situation concerning an academic library director's decision to hire a male for the position of assistant director for public services and the staff's subsequent displeasure with the decision and the process.

1987-08 Anderson, A.J., Anne M. Galler, and John N. Koch. "Watch Your #*!!X&#*!* Language." *Library Journal* 112 (May 15, 1987):51-53.

Part of the "How Do You Manage?" series. Creates a hypothetical situation concerning the use of profanity at the workplace, specifically a male assistant librarian who complains to his female supervisor about the frequent use of obscenities by other staff members.

Letter:

Sanders, Thomas R. "Managing to Do What's Right." *Library Journal* 112 (October 1, 1987):6.

1987-09 "Annual ARL Salary Survey." *The Innocent Bystander* (A Weekly Newsletter for the University of Connecticut Libraries) 18 March 1988, 1.

Highlights of the survey are noted, including the average salary of female vs. male library directors.

1987-10 "Annual Report: 1987 was a Landmark Year." *FLICC Newsletter* 143 (Winter 1987/88):4.

Notes hiring of a consultant to study feasibility of developing recommended classification and qualification standards for the 1410 and 1411 series.

1987-10a *ARL Annual Salary Survey 1986*, compiled by Gordon Fretwell. Washington, DC: Association of Research Libraries, 1987.

Includes data on salaries and years of experience of ARL university librarians, ARL minority university librarians, and medical and law librarians.

The Bibliography

1987-11 Association of College and Research Libraries. New England Chapter. *1986/87 Salary Survey of New England College Libraries*. Worchester, MA: [The Association], 1987.
    Includes data on number, average salaries, and average years of experience by sex for four-year undergraduate institutions in six New England states.

1987-12 Association of Theological Schools in the United States and Canada. *Fact Book on Theological Education, 1986-87*, edited by William L. Baumgaertner. Vandalia, Ohio: [The Association], 1987.
    Includes sex distribution of faculty and administrative personnel (including librarians), changes in employment of women and blacks by position held, and trends in salaries for administrators, faculty, and library staff.

1987-13 Avi. "All That Glitters." *The Horn Book* 53 (September/October 1987):569-576.
    Discusses children's librarianship from a man's perspective, noting that "children's literature is ill-recognized, ill-supported, considered uninteresting because it is a world created in large measure by women for a readership which in large measure is female" and that this attitude extends to librarianship.

1987-14 "Bad News for Equal Opportunity Revealed in Study of Ohio Public Libraries." *Library Journal* 112 (May 15, 1987):25.
    Announces study released by Ohio Women Librarians which shows that "serious sex-based inequities" have affected the hiring and wages of public library directors there. Men run more public libraries than women and receive substantially higher salaries than their female counterparts. (See **1987-114**)

1987-15 Barefoot, Martha Bagby. "Legislative Efforts in North Carolina for Women and Minorities." *North Carolina Libraries* 45 (Spring 1987):7-9.
    Reviews the history of employment and civil rights legislation in the state and notes issues of current legislative interest: child support, job training, and flextime.

1987-16 Barkman, Donna. "An Experience in Peer Leadership." *School Library Media Quarterly* 15 (Summer 1987):211-216.
Discusses women's leadership styles based on a description of the activities of a group of female media professionals, librarians, and educators responsible for planning and operating a school library system as part of the New York State library network.

1987-17 Baum, Christina D. "The Impact of Feminist Thought on American Librarianship, 1965-1985." Ed.D. diss., University of Kentucky, 1987.
Examines the contents of 250 books and articles about library women written between 1965 and 1985, the citations in these works with regard to feminist authors outside librarianship, and the contents of women's programming at ALA annual conferences. The 250 items reveal an "overwhelming liberal feminist focus" with the top two issues being wage discrimination and sexist terminology. Only 20 of the 250 cited feminist authors outside librarianship. The content analysis of ALA programs found a total of 91 programs at 21 conferences. Concludes that (1) 250 works over 20 years from 100,000 librarians 80% of whom are women is a small showing demonstrating indifference, lack of authorship by library women, and male editorial control in publishing and (2) the literature is primarily descriptive in content without proposing agendas for action. Published as *Feminist Thought in American Librarianship*. Jefferson, NC: McFarland, 1992. (See **1992-16**)

Review:

Hildenbrand, Suzanne. *Library and Information Science Research* 11 (October-December 1989):388-390.

1987-18 Becker, Louis. "Job Ads Accused of Bias." [letter] *American Libraries* 18 (April 1987):246.
Criticizes *American Libraries* for accepting job ads which encourage women and minorities to apply as a violation of the American Library Association Office of Library Personnel Resources policy on discrimination.

Letter:

Pelzer, Adolf. "More on 'Biased' Job Listings." *American Libraries* 18 (July/August 1987):565.

1987-19 Bender, David R. "Results of the 1986 Membership Survey." *Special Libraries* 78 (Summer 1987):221-232.
    Indicates that 84.7% of the membership is female.

1987-20 Berry, John. "The New Public Library Directors." *Library Journal* 112 (September 1, 1987):102.
    Writes about important new library directors including several women.

1987-21 Berry, John. "Nothing Ever Changes in Library Schools." *Library Journal* 112 (November 15, 1987):6.
    Refutes the old complaint, noting, for example, the increase in women deans and directors since 1983.

1987-22 Berry, John. "Protecting Our Turf." *Library Journal* 112 (March 15,1987):43-46.
    Reports on the 1987 Association for Library and Information Science Education Conference and Ellen Gay Detlefsen's paper comparing the careers, salaries, and lifestyles of MLS and MBA graduates. Notes that gender issues may "also be factors in the status problems of the library schools."

1987-23 Berry, John. "Standards for Library Salaries and Support." *Library Journal* 112 (October 15, 1987):4.
    Advocates minimum national standards for salaries and per capita library support noting inadequate beginning-level salaries, salary inequities at high levels, and variations in per capita support in libraries based on the sex of the director.

1987-24 Bowron, Albert. "Statistics Tell the Tale: Men Still Getting Top Jobs." *Canadian Library Journal* 44 (August 1987): 211-212.
    Examines statistical information about gender breakdowns

among Canadian librarians including an analysis of heads of Canadian universities listed in the 1948 and 1986 *American Library Directory*. Finds that in 1948 27.5% of chief librarians were men, while in 1986, 57.7% were men. Also, men have dominated the presidency of the Canadian Library Association and library board positions.

Letter:

Moon, Jeffrey. "Gender Bias." *Canadian Library Journal* 45 (February 1988):7.

1987-25 Buckland, Michael. "Library Education: A Centenary." In *The Bowker Annual*, 279-281. New York: Bowker, 1987.

Makes brief reference to discussions in *Library Journal* from 1886 on "comparable pay for women" as one example of the contemporary nature of last century's professional literature.

1987-26 Burrington, Gillian. *Equal Opportunities in Librarianship? Gender and Career Aspirations*. London: The Library Association, 1987.

A comprehensive study on the role of women in librarianship based on research conducted in the United Kingdom. Major themes are that (1) women are less interested in career development than men and see success as the acquisition of a husband and children and (2) women are subordinate to men through an institutionalized status system. (See also **1988-123**)

Reviews:

Blake, Fay M. *Library Journal* 112 (October 1, 1987):70.
Ivy, Barbara A. *Information Processing and Management* 24 (1988):505-506.
Jayawardene, Marion. *Library Association Record* 89 (August 1987):408.
Tilley, Christine. "Gender Equality in Librarianship: A Review Article." *Journal of Librarianship* 20 (January 1988):54-59.

1987-27 Calzonetti, Jo Ann. "Editorial." *Journal of Academic Librarianship* 13 (September 1987):226.
    Reflects on the correlation between the "crisis" in quality of reference service and the reality of status and compensation problems in academic libraries.

1987-28 Carpenter, Judi. *Trends in Bachelors and Higher Degrees, 1975-1985.* Washington, DC: U.S. Department of Education, Office of Educational Research and Improvement, Center for Education Statistics, [1987].
    Presents data by sex of recipient and field of study from 1974-75 through 1984-85 including library and information science.

1987-29 Cassell, Kay Ann. "The Women's Rights Struggle in Librarianship: the Task Force on Women." In *Activism in American Librarianship, 1962-1973*, edited by Mary Lee Bundy and Frederick J. Stielow, 21-29. Westport, CT: Greenwood, 1987.
    Discusses the evolution of the women's movement in librarianship including factors that contributed to the movement's rise: studies documenting inequities in the profession; the first organized meetings of women librarians; the profession's acceptance of discrimination as a fact of life; and tactics used to sensitize ALA members and the profession to women's issues. (See also **1987-03**)

1987-30 Cheatham, Bertha M. "SLJ News Report, 1986." In *The Bowker Annual*, 26-39. New York: Bowker, 1987.
    Mentions sex bias complaint filed by Linda R. Silver with the Equal Employment Opportunities Commission against Cuyahoga County Public Library (Ohio).

1987-31 "Child Care Reimbursement." *Library Hotline* 16 (February 2, 1987):3.
    Reports on the provision of reimbursement funds for parents with child care expenses from attending ALA Midwinter meetings.

1987-32 "COSWL Study Cites Increase in Male Council Nominees;

No School Representation." *American Libraries* 18 (March 1987):226.

    Reports that the Committee on the Status of Women in Librarianship's annual analysis of American Library Association Council found that in 1987 56% of the nominees were women and 44% were men.

1987-33 Cottam, Keith M. "Affirmative Action: Attitude Makes a Difference." *Library Journal* 112 (May 15, 1987):47-50.

    Reviews equal employment opportunity cases from 1964 to 1986 and urges acceptance and compliance with the law.

1987-34 Coughlin, Caroline. "Child Care: A Workplace Issue." *Library Personnel News* 1 (Spring 1987):12.

    Summarizes trends in child care and discusses ways libraries as employers can help.

1987-35 Curwood, Steve. "State College Women Employees Awarded $1.4 Million in Bias Suit." *Boston Globe Saturday*, 18 July 1987, 21.

    Reports that more than 400 women librarians and faculty on nine campuses of the Massachusetts state college system were awarded with back pay and salary increases to settle a class action suit alleging sexual discrimination.

1987-35a Dannreuther, Kathleen. "The Dress." *Library Journal* 112 (August 1987):39.

    Relates the story of a woman selecting her clothes and cosmetics for an American Library Association President's Dance.

Letters:

Alward, Emily. "The Woman of the Eighties." *Library Journal* 113 (March 15, 1988):6.
Lawton, Bethany. "'Sexist and Demeaning.'" *Library Journal* 113 (February 1, 1988):6.

1987-36 Donath, Ursula. "Libraries without 'Feminine Virtues'?" [Bibliotheken ohne 'weibliche Tugenden'?"] *Buch und Bibliothek* 39 (January 1987):35-40.

Urges women in libraries to be more involved in promoting women's interests and discusses from a historical perspective the feminization of librarianship. Describes the Centre for Research, Education and Information on Women (Frauenforschungs-bildungs-und-informationszentrum).

1987-37 "Double Winner." *American Libraries* 18 (July-August 1987):552.

Announces Kathleen Heim as winner of the American Library Association Equality Award for "promoting equality between men and women in the profession."

1987-38 Dudley, Edward. "Walking on Eggs." *New Library World* 88 (July 1987):

Tongue-in-cheek review of the role of women in librarianship.

1987-39 *Education of Library and Information Professionals: Present and Future Prospects*, edited by Richard K. Gardner. Englewood, CO: Libraries Unlimited, 1987.

Written in honor of Dr. Martha Boaz and contains a section on her life and accomplishments. (See also **1987-150**)

Reviews:

Burns, N. *Libraries & Culture* 24 (Summer 1989):388.
Catholic Library World 59 (May 1988):246.
Childers, Thomas. *Information Processing and Management* 25 (1989):216-218.
Editor. *Journal of Academic Librarianship* 13 (January 1988):370.
Patterson, Charles D. *Journal of the American Society for Information Science* 41 (March 1990):148.
Patterson, Charles D. *Library Journal* 113 (January 1988):62.
Reference & Research Book News 3 (February 1988):24.
Robbins, Jane B. *RQ* 27 (Summer 1988):584.

Rothstein, Samuel. *Canadian Library Journal* 45 (June 1988):190.
Stevens, Norman. *Wilson Library Bulletin* 62 (December 1987):79.
Theron, J.C. *South African Journal of Library and Information Science* 57 (March 1989):91-92.
White, Herbert S. *Journal of the American Society for Information Science* 40 (November 1989):437-438.
Wiegand, Wayne A. *Journal of Academic Librarianship* 14 (July 1988):168.

1987-40 "Edward Holley, Herbert White, and Lillian Morrison Win 1987 ALA Awards." *American Libraries* 18 (June 1987):509.
    Announces Kathleen Heim as winner of the ALA Equality Award.

1987-40a "Equal Opportunities." *Library Association Record* 89 (June 1987):268.
    Calls for input to the Manpower and Conditions of Service Committee on a proposed equal opportunity policy for the Library Association.

1987-41 "Equal Opportunities Monitoring." *Library Association Record* 89 (November 1987):554.
    Announces adoption of an equal opportunities policy for the Library Association.

1987-42 "Equal Opportunities: Request for Comments." *Library Association Record* 89 (April 1987):166.
    Calls for input from Library Association membership on proposed equal opportunities policy.

1987-43 Euster, Joanne R. *The Academic Library Director: Management Activities and Effectiveness.* Westport, CT: Greenwood, 1987.
    Examines the role of the director and the traits of effective directors. Reports results of a questionnaire sent to directors, middle managers, and deans from the same institutions and compares results. Includes gender data. Discusses four

dominant types of library managers.

Reviews:

Brophy, P. *Journal of Documentation* 45 (March 1989):73-75.
Caruso, R.M. *Library and Information Science Research* 10 (July 1988):364.
Dougherty, Richard M. *Library Quarterly* 59 (April 1989):171-172.
Editor. *Journal of Academic Librarianship* 14 (May 1988):116-117.
Morein, P.G. *Collection Management* 12 (1990):175-177.
Rochester, M.K. *Riverina Library Review* 6 (May 1989):151.
Savage, D.A. *Canadian Library Journal* 46 (April 1989):123.
Stevens, Norman. *Wilson Library Bulletin* 62 (May 1988):91.
Swan, John. *Library Journal* 113 (June 15, 1988):44.
Vasi, John J. *Journal of Library Administration* 12 (Winter 1990):125-128.

1987-44 Feinberg, Renee. "Job Satisfaction." *Library Personnel News* 1 (Summer 1987):21.
Reviews selected articles on job satisfaction and the library workforce. Many studies note gender and pay among the factors affecting job satisfaction.

1987-45 Fenske, Ruth Elizabeth. "Professional Socialization of Beginning Librarians as Measured by Involvement in Professional Activities." Ph.D. diss., University of Michigan, 1987.
Studies effect of the organization, supervisor, and supervisor's level on professional socialization of new librarians by surveying library school graduates from the University of Illinois and the University of Michigan. Findings show that men tend to be socialized more than women and that having children did not have a significant impact on level of socialization.

Review:

Moen, William E. *Library and Information Science Research* 10 (1988):357-360.

1987-46 Fisher, Edith Maureen. "Ethel Hall Norton and the Allensworth Colony." *American Libraries* 18 (February 1987):140-141.

Documents the work of Norton, a black public librarian in early 20th century California, who provided services to a settlement colony of blacks.

1987-47 "Flextime Fight Still Alive in Maryland." *Library Hotline* 16 (February 9, 1987):5.

Reports on battle for reinstatement of flextime at Prince George's County Memorial Library.

1987-48 Friedland, Claire. "Progress Report on 70th Anniversary Plans." *The Bookwoman* 50 (Winter 1987):1,3.

Discusses the Women's National Book Association awards program and the selection process for award recipients.

1987-49 Gaddis, Dale W. "The Female Public Library Director and Her Governing Board." *North Carolina Libraries* 45 (Spring 1987):21-26.

Notes salary inequities between male and female directors, discusses "presumed disadvantages" of female directors, and suggests ways to develop personal and professional power.

1987-50 Gerhardt, Lillian. "LC--That Sacred Cow." *School Library Journal* 33 (April 1987):4.

Urges that a credentialed woman be named Librarian of Congress.

1987-51 Gothberg, Helen M. "Time Management and the Woman Library Manager." *Library Journal* 112 (May 1, 1987):37-40.

Discusses effective time management techniques for both work and home.

1987-52 Goudy, Frank William. "Librarians and Teachers: Thoughts on Salary Equity." *Library Personnel News* 1 (Spring 1987):13.

Compares compensation between the two professions, citing 1986 Lynch/Myers survey.

1987-53 Hannaker, Carmen. "The Individual Member and the Future." *Australian Library Journal* 36 (November 1987):282-284.

Calls for the Library Association of Australia to address needs of women librarians, who comprise 80% of the Association's membership. Encourages particular focus on women in management and overall career opportunities for women.

Letters:

Borchardt, Max W. "Women's Issues--a Central Issue?" *InCite* 19 (October 1987):11, 15.
Emerton, Charles. "Pompous Ratbaggery." *InCite* 20 (November 1987):6-7.
Hannaker, Carmen. "Carmen's Comments." *InCite* 20 (November 1987):7.
Lodewycks, Axel. "Women's Issues." *InCite* 20 (November 1987):6.
Pivec, Cathleen S. "Are Most 'Good People' Male?" *InCite* 20 (November 1987):7.

1987-54 Heim, Kathleen M. "Men Work Their Way Up. Reasons for Status Differences Between Men and Women Librarians [Maenner machen Karriere. Gruende fuer die Statusunterschiede zwischen maennlichen und weiblichen Bibliothekaren]." *Buch und Bibliothek* 39 (January 1987):41-45.

Discusses the status of librarianship as a female intensive occupation in the United States and the disparity between women in the profession and women in management positions in libraries. Describes differences between men and women in achieving management positions and advancing their careers.

1987-55 Herring, Mark Youngblood. *Controversial Issues in Librarianship: An Annotated Bibliography.* New York: Garland, 1987.

Includes section "Librarians and ERA."

Reviews:

Anderson, A. J. *Library Journal* 112 (June 1, 1987):88.
Parker, Jean. *American Reference Books Annual* 19 (1988):236.
Reference & Research Book News 2 (Summer 1987):38.

1987-56 Hornaday, Ann. "Executive Assistants: Is There Power Behind the Throne?" *Ms.* 16 (October 1987):28, 32-35.
Discusses pros and cons of a career as an executive assistant.

Letter:

Chapman, Ellen. "The Power Behind the Tomes." *Ms.* 16 (January 1988):4.
Notes similarities to librarianship.

1987-57 Howden, Norman. "Catalogers and Competition." *Catholic Library World* 59 (July-August 1987):34-37.
Reports results of a survey of catalogers to study the decline in quantity and quality of applications for entry-level cataloging positions. Factors studied include the women's movement.

1987-58 "Image Overhaul Tips from SLA." *Library Hotline* 16 (January 12, 1987):4.
Reports on pamphlet issued by the Special Libraries Association with advice to librarians on improving their personal image.

1987-59 "International Forum on Women in Libraries." *Library Hotline* 16 (January 12, 1987):4.
Announces IFLA pre-conference seminar, "To Give or Not to Give: Women and the Power of Managing Information."

1987-60 Ivy, Barbara A. "COSWL and the Future of Women in Librarianship." *Library Journal* 112 (October 15, 1987):42-44.
Reflects on women and the library profession past, present, and future and discusses the impact of the American

The Bibliography

Library Association Committee on the Status of Women in Librarianship.

1987-61 Jick, Todd and Linda Mitz. "Sex Differences in Work Stress." *Journal of Library Administration* 7 (Spring 1986): 135-152.
   Reviews the empirical evidence of sex differences in handling stress and proposes a framework for examining the sources of those differences. Survey finds that stress has less to do with gender than with age and relative position of authority within an organization.

Letter:

Rorvig, Mark E. "Sex, Work, and Stress." *Library Journal* 112 (September 15, 1987):60-61.

1987-62 Johnson, Nancy P. "Comparable Worth in Libraries: A Legal Analysis." *Law Library Journal* 79 (Summer 1987):367-386.
   Discusses issues of undervaluation of the library profession and focuses on intraoccupational intentional wage discrimination. Also examines legislation and relevant cases.

1987-63 Jones, Kay F. "Sex, Salaries and Library Support." *Library Journal* 112 (October 15, 1987):35-41.
   Discusses growth in per capita support of U.S. libraries, gender distribution changes in library directorships, directors' salaries, beginning salaries, and the impact the gender of a library director has on wage rates.

1987-64 Jones, Kay F. "Women in Librarianship." In *ALA Yearbook of Library and Information Services*, v. 12, 308-311. Chicago: American Library Association, 1987.
   Reviews the activities of the Committee on the Status of Women in Librarianship, salary surveys, key articles and dissertations about women in librarianship, statistics, career concerns, and women in library history.

1987-65 Josephine, Helen. "The Fiscal Impact of Pay Equity." *Bottom Line* 1 (1987):18-21.

Discusses the costs of implementing comparable worth in libraries and the three typical approaches to achieving comparable worth--litigation, legislation, and negotiation--using case studies from Minnesota, Washington State, and Los Angeles.

1987-66 Karrenbrock, Marilyn H. "A History and Analysis of *Top of the News*, 1942-1987." *Journal of Youth Services in Libraries* 1 (Fall 1987):29-43.

Includes data for authorship of articles by sex, occupation, and location. Shows that 80.8% of authors were women, with women-authored articles peaking in 1951 through 1956 at 92.3%.

1987-67 Katz, Ruth M. "New Opportunities, New Choices: Some Observations About Libraries in North Carolina." *North Carolina Libraries* 45 (Spring 1987):21-26.

Discusses the status of minority and women librarians in the state including their representation across type of library and activities at the state library. Notes the resistance to change in the North Carolina Library Association and recent recommendations to open opportunities for broader participation.

1987-68 Kendra, William E. "Pay Equity and Librarians: A Selective Bibliography 1982-1986." *National Librarian* 12 (May 1987):1.

Cites articles dealing with this issue that are specific to librarians.

1987-69 King, Elizabeth J. "Libraries of Two Women's Colleges in Saudi Arabia." *International Library Review* 19 (July 1987):243-248.

Describes a visit to two colleges and includes a discussion of the availability of information and standards of education for librarians.

1987-70 Krompart, Janet and Clara D. Felice. "A Review of Faculty Status Surveys, 1971-1984." *Journal of Academic Librarianship* 13 (March 1987):14-18.

Reviews a study of 36 faculty status surveys and discusses

the need for equity in male/female salaries.

1987-71 Laynor, Barbara. "Librarianship and Motherhood: A Part-Time Solution." *Medical Reference Services Quarterly* 6 (Winter 1987):15-25.
    Recommends part-time work as a means for working mothers to balance career and family. Discusses advantages and disadvantages of part-time employment for both employee and employer and uses a case study to illustrate the work of a part-time reference librarian.

1987-72 Learmont, Carol L. and Stephen Van Houten. "Placements and Salaries, 1985: No Surprises." In *The Bowker Annual*, 311-327. New York: Bowker, 1987.
    Provides salary and placement data by type of position and sex.

1987-73 Learmont, Carol L. and Stephen Van Houten. "Placements and Salaries, 1986: An Upswing." *Library Journal* 112 (October 15, 1987):27-34.
    Provides job placement and salary information by sex.

1987-74 Levering, Mary Berghaus. "The Night We Celebrated Seventy Years of Making the Difference." *The Bookwoman* 52 (Fall/Winter 1987-88): 1, 3-5.
    Describes anniversary celebration of the Women's National Book Association including a salute to seventy notable women.

1987-75 "Library and Hospital to Offer Child-Care Program This Fall." *Library of Congress Information Bulletin* 46 (September 28, 1987):421.
    Announces availability of child care to Library of Congress employees.

1987-76 "Library of Congress Moving on Capitol Hill Hospital Child Care Option." *Library of Congress Information Bulletin* 46 (June 22, 1987):289.
    Reports on results of staff survey on child care support

and recommends collaboration between the library and the Capitol Hill Hospital Child Care Center.

1987-77 Little, Jane. "Women in Libraries." *New Library World* 88 (March 1987):
 Points out that men choose red ties to express their individuality in the corporate setting but questions the equivalent choice for women.

1987-78 deleted

1987-79 Luedtke, Helga. "Well-Read, Sympathetic, Poorly Paid: Librarians. On the Beginnings of a Women's Profession [Belesen, einfuehlsam, gering entichnt: Bibliothekarrinnen. Von den Anfaengen eines Frauenberufes]." *Buch und Bibliothek* 39 (January 1987):18-35.
 Reviews the history of women in German librarianship and the work of the Vereinigung Bibliothekarischarbeitender Frauen (Association of Women Working in Libraries) to improve working conditions, education, and salaries. Notes that the stereotype of the woman librarian persists today.

1987-80 Lynch, Beverly P. and Jo Ann Verdin. "Job Satisfaction in Libraries: A Replication." *Library Quarterly* 57 (1987):190-202.
 Repeats a 1971-72 study and corroborates earlier finding that there is no significant difference between men and women library employees on job satisfaction.

1987-81 deleted

1987-82 Malone, Cheryl Knott. *Gender, Unpaid Labor, and the Promotion of Literacy: A Selected, Annotated Bibliography.* New York: Garland, 1987.
 Contains dozens of citations to sources on women volunteers in libraries published from 1946 through 1986. Introduction raises questions about women's unpaid labor.

Reviews:

Buttlar, Lois. *American Reference Books Annual* 20 (1989):134.
Hermann, G.M. *Choice* 25 (June 1988):1538.
Journal of Economic Literature 26 (September 1988):1315.
Reference & Research Book News 3 (June 1988):16.
Signs 13 (Summer 1988):905.

1987-83 Manley, Will. "Facing the Public." *Wilson Library Bulletin* 61 (June 1987):42-43.

Focuses on librarian stereotypes and suggests that women break them by conducting wet T-shirt contests.

Letter:

Duncan, Ann. "A More Even Scale." *Wilson Library Bulletin* 62 (September 1987):8.

1987-84 Manley, Will. "Facing the Public." *Wilson Library Bulletin* 62 (December 1987):50-51.

Discusses the dichotomy between a profession of "women's libbers" and their fight for the right of clientele to have access to pornography.

Letters:

Burns, Grant. "Slanderous and Absurd." *Wilson Library Bulletin* 62 (February 1988):6.
Mark, Rosalyn. "The Last Straw." *Wilson Library Bulletin* 61 (March 1987):6.

1987-85 Martin, Clare. "A Woman's Place Is on the Platform." *Assistant Librarian* 80 (July 1987):100-101.

Describes a course in public speaking for women librarians held at the Pepperell Unit of the Industrial Society.

1987-86 Mellor, Earl F. "Weekly Earnings in 1986: A Look at More Than 200 Occupations." *Monthly Labor Review* 110 (June 1987):41-46.

Provides data by sex on median weekly earnings for 230 occupations including librarians, archivists, and curators.

1987-87 Michell, Gillian and Roma M. Harris. "Evaluating the Reference Interview: Some Factors Influencing Patrons and Professionals." *RQ* 27 (Fall 1987):95-105.

Explains differences between public library patrons and librarians in their assessments of competence of librarians in reference interviews. One finding was that female librarians gave lower competence ratings than male counterparts or patrons of either sex.

1987-88 Milbrath, Lester and Victor Doyno. "A Study of the Quality of University Life: SUNY at Buffalo." *Social Indicators Research* 19 (May 1987):173-190.

Reports results of study of faculty on level of satisfaction and importance of campus life. Reveals that librarians had especially low morale and quality of life on campus but that gender differences were not significant in overall assessment.

1987-89 Minudri, Regina U. "American Library Association." In *The Bowker Annual*, 68. New York: Bowker, 1987.

Includes reference to the Office for Library Personnel Resources publication *Academic and Public Librarians: Data by Race, Ethnicity and Sex* and the "Topics in Personnel" kit *Pay Equity: Issues and Strategies*. (See **1987-06** and **1987-117**)

1987-90 "Montgomery County's New Affirmative Action Plan." *Library Hotline* 16 (September 7, 1987):4.

Reports on plan and goals set for minorities and handicappers. No goals are established for women since they make up 81% of the staff.

1987-91 Moore, Nick. "The Employment Market for Librarians and Information Specialists in the United Kingdom." *Journal of Information Science* 13 (1987):327-333.

Suggests that changing career patterns for women have been a factor in the job market because there is no longer any real difference between the length of worklife for women and men.

1987-92 Moran, Barbara B. and Peter A. Neenan. "The Public

Library's Invisible Managers." *Library Journal* 112 (June 14, 1987):27-29.

Reports data indicating that females hold 41% of 74 administrative specialists positions concerned with general management, automation, budget, development, personnel, planning, public relations, and systems analysis. Data were analyzed regarding professional self-identification, educational background, civic and professional activity, career patterns, job satisfaction, and future plans.

1987-93 Morris, Beryl. "Keep Your Eyes on the Hills... and Your Feet on the Ground, or the Work of the Pepperell Unit in Helping Women in General and in Libraries in Particular!" *Training and Education* 4 (1987):28-32.

Discusses history and objectives of the unit in the areas of career development, employment issues, and education. Outlines future plans.

1987-94 Mudge, Charlotte R. "Benefits and Salaries Compared." *Canadian Library Journal* 44 (December 1987):405-411.

Analyzes contract clauses in Canadian library collective agreements in academic, public, and municipal libraries as of October 1986. Includes adoption leave and maternity leave benefits.

1987-95 Murgai, Sarla R. "Managerial Motivation and Career Aspirations of Library/Information Science Students." Ed.D. diss., University of Tennessee, Knoxville, 1987.

Reports results of questionnaire given to students in 11 masters' degree programs in the southeast. Finds no difference between the sexes on six of ten motivation criteria, while females scored higher on future orientation, perseverance, and social need and males scored higher on competitiveness. Males also rated females higher as managers than females rated themselves. Concludes that the low numbers of women in library management is not attributable to low motivation.

1987-96 Myers, Margaret. "Comparable Worth." *WLW Journal* 11 (December 1987):2-5.

1987-97 Myllykoski, Tuula. "Tietotekniikka ja Kirjastonaisten Tyo (Information Science and the Work of Female Library Employees)." *Kirjastolehti* 80 (1987):67-68.

1987-98 "New Members Named to Women's Program Advisory Committee." *Library of Congress Information Bulletin* 46 (July 27, 1987):339.

Announces new members and describes activities of committee including child care, information sharing, program planning, and development of a women's resource center.

1987-99 "New Members Sought for Women's Program Advisory Committee." *Library of Congress Information Bulletin* 46 (February 9, 1987):61.

Announces solicitation of members to fill committee vacancies.

1987-100 "Ninth Administrative Detail Program is Under Way." *Library of Congress Information Bulletin* 46 (June 8, 1987):248.

Describes affirmative action program which provides selected staff members an opportunity during a 90-day detail to test interest in and potential for administrative pursuits.

1987-101 Noel, Tod A. "BIALL Salaries Survey 1986." *The Law Librarian* 18 (April 1987):27-28.

1987-102 Nyren, Karl. "LJ News Report, 1986." In *The Bowker Annual*, 3-26. New York: Bowker, 1987.

Reports on progress in discrimination and pay equity cases and on salaries of librarians "as workers in a female-dominated occupation."

1987-103 Nyren, Karl. "News in Review, 1986." *Library Journal* 112 (January 1987):37-52.

Includes report on progress in various discrimination suits, professional salaries, and an upcoming study on video display terminal hazards, a "nagging fear especially to women of childbearing age."

1987-104 "Ohio Library Boards Seen as Discrimination Source." *Library Hotline* 16 (May 11, 1987):6.
Announces release of Ohio Women Librarians report by Jeanne M. Patterson and Linda R. Silver, *Sex of Director, Salary, and Size of Library*, which charges boards and trustees with discrimination against women public librarians. (See **1987-114**)

1987-105 "Ohio Women Librarians Issue Second Research Report." *Library Hotline* 16 (September 14, 1987):13.
Announces release of Ohio Women Librarians report, *Deference to Authority in the Feminized Professions* by Linda R. Silver, which explores the relationship among authority, patriarchy and professionalism in librarianship, nursing, social work, and teaching. (See **1987-140**)

1987-106 Oleen, Sandra. "The Image of Librarians in Modern Fiction." *Mousaion* 5 (1987):48-57.
Examines novels for their portrayal of the stereotypical librarian. Found negative and positive images of both sexes and representation from all types of libraries.

1987-107 "Open House Planned at Capitol Hill Hospital Child Care Center." *Library of Congress Information Bulletin* 46 (January 19, 1987):39.
Reports on open house for Library of Congress employees interested in child care.

1987-108 Pacifico, Michele F. "Founding Matters: Women in the Society of American Archivists, 1936-1972." *American Archivist* 50 (Summer 1987):370-389.
Discusses the status and role of women in the Society of American Archivists and provides statistics by sex in a number of categories: officers and council members; local arrangements committees; program participants; and authorship of articles and book reviews in *American Archivist*. Highlights individual women and their contributions. Includes photographs.

1987-109 deleted

1987-110 Parrish, Nancy B. "Pay Equity--An Issue for Librarians: A Summary and Selected Bibliography." *North Carolina Libraries* 45 (Spring 1987):10-16.

Reviews the literature on pay equity and summarizes the activities of the American Library Association. Notes both state and federal legislative action followed by a lengthy annotated bibliography.

1987-111 "Patriarchy in the Professions." *American Libraries* 18 (November 1987):874.

Announces Ohio Women Librarians' publication of Linda R. Silver's *Deference to Authority in the Feminized Professions* which looks at the role of "patriarchal notions of authority" in librarianship, nursing, and teaching. (See **1987-140**)

1987-112 Patterson, Jeanne M. and Linda R. Silver. "Sex, Salary and Size--A Report on Directors in Ohio Libraries." *National Librarian* 12 (November 1987):7.

Affirms and documents inequities among Ohio male and female public library directors.

1987-113 Patterson, Jeanne M. and Linda R. Silver. "Sex, Salary and Size--A Report on Directors in Ohio Libraries." *Ohio Library Association Bulletin* 57 (April 1987):36-38.

Reports on a comparison study of 1985 data from the American Library Association and the State Library of Ohio on public library directorships cross-tabulated by sex and salary. Finds that 80% of Ohio public libraries are directed by men and that a salary differential of $11,500 exists between male and female directors.

1987-114 Patterson, Jeanne M. and Linda R. Silver. *Sex of Director, Salary, and Size of Library.* [s.l.: s.n., 1987?].

Reports on a study conducted under the sponsorship of Ohio Women Librarians (OWL) on the relationship among these three elements. Provides a summary of sex-based characteristics of public libraries in the United States. Documents inequities and calls for action. (See also **1987-14**, **1987-104**, and **1987-175**)

1987-115 "Pay Equity." *Women in Libraries* 17 (November 1987):1.
Lists names and associations to contact for information and assistance.

1987-116 "Pay Equity 'Fair' at ALA San Francisco." *Library Hotline* 16 (June 29, 1987):4.
Reports on gathering of several pay equity groups including the American Library Association Committee on Pay Equity to exchange information.

1987-117 *Pay Equity: Issues and Strategies*, edited by Jeniece Guy. T.I.P. Kit #9. Chicago: American Library Association, Office for Library Personnel Resources, 1987.
Reprints articles and describes library pay equity cases. Includes fact sheets, brochures, and bibliographies. (See also **1987-89**)

1987-118 Pearson, Lois R. "Silver Sues Cuyahoga Board on Sex Discrimination Charge." *American Libraries* 18 (February 1987):103-104.
Reports Linda R. Silver's sex discrimination suit against the Cuyahoga County Public Library (Ohio).

1987-119 Phenix, Katharine. "The Status of Women Librarians." *Frontiers* 9 (1987):36-40.
Summarizes research, highlighting statistics and salary data. Topics include career experiences, job satisfaction, educational attainment, and other factors affecting status.

1987-120 Price, Cheryl A. et al. "What Professional Librarians Expect from Administrators: One Librarian's View; Another Librarian's View; and an Administrator's Response." *College and Research Libraries* 48 (September 1987):408-421.
Mentions the salary issue in a female intensive profession.

1987-121 Ptacek, Bill. "WANTED: Children's Services Librarians." *Library Personnel News* 1 (Winter 1987):2-3.
Reports on program at 1986 Public Library Association conference addressing the lack of children's librarians. Notes

recurring theme of the relationship between the lack of status of what has traditionally been a women's specialty and the current crisis in recruitment.

1987-122 Randall, Ann Knight. "Library Services to Minorities." In *The Bowker Annual*, 86-93. New York: Bowker, 1987.
    Mentions the American Library Association Office for Library Personnel Resources' annual list of Minority and Women's Organizations in Librarianship as well as the Committee on the Status of Women in Librarianship's conference program on racism.

1987-123 Ray, Jean Meyer and Angela Battaglia Rubin. "Pay Equity for Women in Academic Libraries: An Analysis of the ARL Salary Survey, 1976/77-1983/84." *College and Research Libraries* 48 (January 1987):36-49.
    Study reveals that while the number of women administrators has risen from 26.7% to 45% and women make up nearly one-third of middle management positions, the majority of women university librarians are still at lower levels of pay and status. Concludes that at the present pace, "pay equity will not even be achieved by the year 2000."

1987-124 "Recent Legal Trends in Personnel." *Library Personnel News* 1 (Spring 1987):9-11.
    Reports on legal developments pertaining to affirmative action, pregnancy leave, and sexual harassment.

1987-125 Reinitzer, Sigrid. "Women in Library, Documentation and Information Services" ["Die Frau im Bibliotheks-, Dokumentations- und Informationsdienst"]. *Mitteilungen der Vereinigung Oesterreichischer Bibliothekare* 40 (June 1987):70-76.
    Discusses increased numbers in library training programs in Austria since 1978 but continued underrepresentation of women in management positions. Urges women to take responsibility for preparing for management positions.

1987-126 Ricklefs, Dale L. "Pay Equity." *Texas Library Journal* 63 (Spring 1987):6-8.
    Reviews pay equity with specific applications to Texas

librarians.

1987-127 Ritchie, Sheila. "Women in Libraries--Ten Years On." *Information and Library Manager* 7 (September 1987):39-49.
   Summarizes research conducted from 1977 through 1987 on women in the library profession in English public libraries.

1987-128 Roy, Loriene. "A Survey of Children's Librarians in Illinois Public Libraries." *Library and Information Science Research* 9 (July-September 1987):187-211.
   Reports data from 111 librarians regarding education, job histories, present positions, and career choices. Almost all respondents were female.

1987-129 Rubin, Richard Evan. "A Study of Employee Turnover of Full Time Public Librarians in Moderately-Large and Large Size Public Libraries in Seven Midwestern States." Ph.D. diss., University of Illinois at Urbana-Champaign, 1987.
   Analyzes survey data from 421 library job turnovers between 1980 and 1984. Finds no statistical difference in turnover rates between men and women. Over half the women who leave do so in order to take other positions.

1987-129a Ruse, David. "Equal Opportunities 1988." *Library Association Record* 89 (August 1987):33-34.
   Presents results of a survey sent to renewing members of the Library Association (UK) to gather information on the characteristics of the membership. Includes profiles by age, gender, ethnic origin, employment sector, salary, and disability.

1987-130 Russell, Thyra Kaye. "Job Sharing in Illinois Libraries." Ph.D. diss., Southern Illinois University at Carbondale, 1987.
   Reports on survey of 42 job-sharers. Finds that the majority are married women with children, over half earned less than $5000/year, and only 38% receive fringe benefits. Both sharers and directors were positive about the effectiveness of job sharing. Recommends that steps be taken to increase the number of libraries using job sharing, that the lack of benefits be studied, that libraries establish written policies, and that future state and

national job sharing studies be conducted.

1987-131 Sapp, Gregg. "The Librarian as Main Character: A Professional Sampler." *Wilson Library Bulletin* 61 (January 1987):29-33.

Annotated bibliography of 35 short stories about librarians published between 1907 and 1983. Notes that the stereotype of the schoolmarmish librarian is alive and well.

1987-132 Savard, Rejean, Carole Matte, Francis Lacasse, and Mohammed Boubou. "Enquete sur les Diplomes de l'EBSI [Survey of University of Montreal Library School Graduates]." *Argus* 16 (September 1987):81-89.

Reports data on trends in graduate employment and notes that responses analyzed show that librarianship is still a female intensive profession.

1987-133 Schmall, Lorraine. "Illegal Discrimination Against Library Employees." *Public Libraries* 26 (Winter 1987):180-181.

Reviews laws governing employment discrimination including race, gender, religion, age, and handicap.

1987-134 Searing, Susan E. "Institutions of Memory: Libraries and Women's Work(s)." *Michigan Quarterly Review* 26 (Winter 1987):228-241.

Examines what librarians do as agents of memory-making and discusses that, although libraries were not designed with feminist goals in mind, libraries can nonetheless meet women's needs.

1987-135 "Semiannual Report on Developments at the Library of Congress April 1 Through September 30, 1986." *Library of Congress Information Bulletin* 46 (January 5, 1987):3-11.

Includes section on equal employment opportunity programs which discusses activities of the Women's Program Office: day care, women in management, and information sources.

1987-136 "Semiannual Report on Developments at the Library of Congress October 1, 1986 Through March 31, 1987." *Library of*

Congress Information Bulletin 46 (June 15, 1987):255-278.
Reports activities of the Women's Program Office on child care, personnel data analysis, women in management, staff programs and publications, and the selection of new members of the Women's Program Advisory Committee. Data on percent of female supervisors were collected and findings show that among 501 supervisors, 37% are female.

1987-137 "Semiannual Report on Developments at the Library of Congress April 1, 1987 Through September 30, 1987." *Library of Congress Information Bulletin* 46 (December 28, 1987):571-594.
Reports that the Women's Program Office is forming a parent advisory committee to work on a child care program and announces preparation of a brochure honoring 15 Asian American/Pacific Islander women for Asian/Pacific Heritage Week.

1987-138 "Seminar on Women and Info." *Library Journal* 112 (March 1, 1987):22.
Spotlights a preconference seminar on "Women and the Power of Managing Information" at the Library Association of Australia/International Federation of Library Associations and Institutions conference. Topics include women as information providers and the power of information and librarians to bring about social change.

1987-139 "Seventy WNBA Book Women Award Winners." *The Bookwoman* 51 (Spring/Summer 1987):9-10.
Announces recipients, including librarians, of this award honoring women in the book world.

1987-140 Silver, Linda R. *Deference to Authority in the Feminized Professions*. OWL Research Report #2. Northfield, OH: Ohio Women Librarians, 1987.
Explores authority, patriarchy, and professionalization in teaching, nursing, librarianship, and social work. (See also **1987-105**, **1987-111**, and **1988-108**)

1987-141 "Silver Claims Sex Discrimination, Sues Cuyahoga Library Board." *Library Journal* 112 (March 1, 1987):15.

Reports on Linda Silver's filing of a sex discrimination case against the Cuyahoga (Ohio) library board.

1987-142 "Silver Sues Library Board, Claims Sex Discrimination." *School Library Journal* 33 (February 1987):10.

Reports on Linda Silver's filing of a sex discrimination case against the Cuyahoga (Ohio) library board.

1987-143 Simeone, Angela. *Academic Women: Working Towards Equality*. South Hadley, MA: Bergin & Garvey, 1987.

Makes reference to library science as one of several stereotypically feminine fields into which women are clustered. Includes table of "Percentage of Women Among Doctoral Degree Recipients and Percentage of Women Doctoral Recipients by Discipline" which includes library science.

Reviews:

Butcher, Patricia Smith. *Library Journal* 112 (February 1, 1987):87.
Chafetz, Janet Saltzman. *American Journal of Sociology* 93 (September 1987):510-512.
Clark, Shirley M. *Journal of Higher Education* 60 (November-December 1989):718-720.
Editor. *Journal of Academic Librarianship* 13 (January 1988): 394-395.
Heim, Kathleen M. *Journal of Academic Librarianship* 14 (May 1988):107-108.
Klingberg, Susan. *College and Research Libraries* 50 (September 1989):587.
Margolis, Anne. *Women's Review of Books* 5 (November 1987): 11-13.
Park, Rosemary. *Change* 19 (May/June 1987):61.
Reference & Research Book News 2 (Spring 1987):19.
Scollay, Susan. *Educational Studies* 21 (Summer 1990):133-139.
Tidball, M. Elizabeth. *Journal of Higher Education* 59 (January-February 1988):101-104.

1987-144 Slater, Margaret. "Careers and the Occupational Image." *Journal of Information Science* 13 (1987):335-342.
Cites stereotypical images of librarians as one contributor to "corporate invisibility" as demonstrated in a survey of 448 industrial and commercial respondents to a non-user study.

1987-145 Somerville, Mary and Carolyn Markuson. "Facing the Shortage of Children's Librarians . . . and in Schools: Short Supply, Tall Order." *American Libraries* 18 (June 1987):418-428.
Points to the perception of children's librarianship as "women's work" as a contributing factor to the shortage and low status and pay of children's librarians. Perception also discourages men from pursuing children's librarianship and creates reverse sexism.

Letters:

Arrivee, Sally D. "Lack of $, Burnout Outweigh Dedication." *American Libraries* 18 (September 1987):642.
Nielsen, Laura. "Part-time Jobs May Solve Shortage." *American Libraries* 18 (September 1987):642.
Rees, Douglas. "What Shortage of Children's Librarians?" *American Libraries* 18 (September 1987):642.
Wemett, Lisa C. "YA Librarians in Short Supply, Too." *American Libraries* 18 (September 1987):642.

1987-146 Spaulding, Frank H. "Special Libraries Association." In *The Bowker Annual*, 173-178. New York: Bowker, 1987.
Includes findings of a 1986 association membership survey which found that 85 percent of the membership is female.

1987-147 Stafford, Audrey A. "Certification Can't Replace MLS." [letter] *Library Journal* 112 (January 1987):10.
Reflects on the irony of a letter on education for the profession by Del Cain (*Library Journal*, September 1, 1986, p. 120) which appeared in the same issue as Kay Jones' "Sex, Salaries and Library Support" and questions how librarians can expect top salaries if they do not have high expectations of the profession. (See **1987-63**)

1987-148 Sturm, Rebecca. "Emma Guy Cromwell: In Search of a Forgotten Trailblazer." *The Southeastern Librarian* 37 (Spring 1987):8-10.
   Historical study of pioneer woman of Kentucky who was appointed State Librarian and Director of Archives. Notes the difficulty in finding information about Cromwell and suggests that librarians research other successful but unacknowledged women in order to make them better known.

1987-149 Sullivan, Peggy. "Back to the Future, Circa 1907." *American Libraries* 18 (January 1987):32-36.
   Celebrates the American Library Association's 80th anniversary and notes the impact of women in the association's development and history.

1987-150 Sullivan, Peggy. "The Space She Occupied: Martha Boaz and Librarianship." In *Education of Library and Information Professionals: Present and Future Prospects*, edited by Richard K. Gardner, 1-16. Englewood, CO: Libraries Unlimited, 1987.
   Reviews Boaz's career and impact on library education, focusing on her contributions to the University of Southern California. (See also **1987-39**)

1987-151 Sussex, Gay. "Brooching the Subject." [letter] *Library Association Record* 89 (March 1987):118.
   Remarks on the "President's Lady's Brooch" worn by the wife of the Library Association president and the implications for a future female president's mate--"Is he expected to wear the President's Lady's Brooch?"

1987-152 deleted

1987-153 "They're Singing Our Tune-Up." *Women in Libraries* 17 (November 1987):3.
   Commends the Chilton Book Company for its use of a positive image on a poster distributed at the American Library Association 1988 Annual Conference.

1987-154 deleted

1987-155 "'To Give or Not to Give': An International Women in Libraries Forum." *RQ* 26 (Summer 1987):362.
  Announces the 1988 Library Association of Australia/International Federation of Library Associations and Institutions Preconference Seminar, "Women and the Power of Managing Information."

1987-156 Treiman, Donald J. "Recognition of Merit: Its Effect on Pay Equity." *Library Administration and Management* 1 (January 1987):23-30.
  Text of speech presented at the Library Administration and Management Association, Personnel Administrators Section, Economic Status and Staff Welfare Committee program at the 1986 American Library Association Annual Conference in New York. Discusses differences between concepts of comparable worth and pay equity in major job evaluation studies and in terms of librarians' salaries relative to other jobs with similar qualifications. Provides statistical data on number of female librarians and their earnings relative to male librarians.

Response:

Neal, James G., Jean M. Ray and Jane E. Marshall. "Responses to 'Recognition of Merit: Its Effect on Pay Equity.'" *Library Administration and Management* 1 (September 1987):144-147.

1987-157 U.S. Center for Education Statistics. *Bachelors and Higher Degrees Awarded in 1984-1985.* Washington, DC: U.S. Department of Education. Office of Educational Research and Improvement. Center for Education Statistics, 1987.
  Includes data on bachelors, masters, and doctoral degrees conferred in library and archival sciences by sex for 1983-4 and 1984-5.

1987-158 U.S. Center for Education Statistics. *Bachelors and Higher Degrees Conferred in 1985-1986.* Washington, DC: U.S. Department of Education, Office of Educational Research and Improvement, Center for Education Statistics, 1987.
  Includes data on bachelors, masters, and doctoral degrees

conferred in library and archival sciences by sex for 1984-5 and 1985-6.

1987-159 U.S. Center for Education Statistics. *College Faculty Salaries, 1976-1986*. Washington, DC: U.S. Department of Education, Office of Educational Research and Improvement, Center for Education Statistics, 1987.
   Tables show data by sex of recipient of instructional and noninstructional faculty including library science.

1987-160 U.S. Center for Education Statistics. *The Condition of Education: Statistical Report, 1986 Edition*, edited by Joyce D. Stern; associate editor Marjorie O. Chandler. Washington, DC: U.S. Department of Education. Office of Educational Research and Improvement. Center for Education Statistics, 1987.
   Includes data on degrees conferred and student enrollment by sex including library science.

1987-161 U.S. Center for Education Statistics. *Digest of Education Statistics 1987*, Thomas D. Snyder, Project Director. Washington, DC: U.S. Department of Education. Office of Educational Research and Improvement. Center for Education Statistics, 1987.
   Includes data for total enrollment in library science in institutions of higher learning by level, sex, and attendance status.

1987-162 U.S. Center for Education Statistics. *Higher Education Act, Title II-B, FY87 Abstracts, Library Career Training Program*. Washington, DC: U.S. Department of Education. Office of Educational Research and Improvement. Center for Education Statistics, 1987.
   Annual directory of FY87 on library education grants to assist minority, women, and economically disadvantaged students.

1987-163 U.S. Center for Education Statistics. *Instructional Faculty Salaries for Academic Year 1985-86*, by Elaine P. Kroe. Washington, DC: U.S. Department of Education. Office of Educational Research and Improvement. Center for Education Statistics, 1987.
   Provides salary data by rank, sex, and level of institution.

1987-164 U.S. Congress. House. Committee on Education and Labor. Subcommittee on Employment Opportunities. 100th Congress. *A Prospectus of Working Women's Concerns: Hearings... July 21 and 22, 1987.* Washington, DC: U.S. Government Printing Office, 1987.

Table entitled "Sex-composition and mean annual earnings of selected occupations: 1980" includes librarians.

1987-165 deleted

1987-166 U.S. Congress. Senate. Committee on Governmental Affairs. Subcommittee on Federal Services, Post Office, and Civil Service. 100th Congress. *Federal Employee Compensation Equity Act of 1987: Hearing . . . April 22, 1987.* Washington, DC: U.S. Government Printing Office, 1987.

Witnesses from National Federation of Federal Employees and U.S. Chamber of Commerce mention libraries in their testimony.

1987-167 U.S. Library of Congress. *Annual Report of the Librarian of Congress, 1986.* Washington, DC: U.S. Government Printing Office, 1987.

Discusses equal employment opportunity programs including activities of the Affirmative Action Office, Women's Program Office, and the Equal Employment Opportunity Complaints Office. Includes tabular data on employment by department, differentiated by sex.

1987-168 U.S. Office of Personnel Management. *Comparable Worth for Federal Jobs: A Wrong Turn off the Road Toward Pay Equity and Women's Career Advancement.* Washington, DC: U.S. Office of Personnel Management, [1987].

Weighs the case for using "comparable worth" in the federal government's personnel system and provides data on federal employees by field or professional degree, including library science, and college graduates by age and sex for 1986.

1987-169 Van Beresteijn, E. A. "Public libraries and Women [De openbare leeszaal en de vrouw]." *Bibliotheek en Samenleving* 15

(April 1987):116-122.
Reprint of text originally published in 1914 describing the growth of public libraries in the Netherlands and the suitability of women for employment in libraries. Attributes low status and salary to the large number of women employed in public libraries and encourages the improvement of salaries and conditions and the introduction of professional training.

1987-170 Van House, Nancy A. "Labor Market Segmentation and Librarian Salaries." *Library Quarterly* 57 (1987):171-189.
Uses labor market theory to explain how the structure of the library labor market may determine salary difference by type of library. Discusses difference in earnings functions across library types and by sex.

1987-171 "The 'We Are Not Pleased' Manifesto." *Library Journal* 112 (August 1987):33.
Discusses a manifesto presented to the American Library Association Social Responsibilities Round Table Committee on Problems Within the Profession which includes criticism of the American Library Association for the absence of women in administrative positions in the association.

1987-172 Weldon, Jean. "Introduction." [Special Issue on the Status of Women and Minorities in Librarianship] *North Carolina Libraries* 45 (Spring 1987):5-6.
Provides an overview of the special issue's contents and offers a historical perspective on the status of women and sex stereotyping.

1987-173 White, Herbert S. "Library Managers--Female and Male." *Library Journal* 11 (February 1, 1987):58-59.
Reflects on management, ranging from the defense of good management as a sex-neutral process to a discussion of the role of the family as a supporting or detracting influence in the development of managers.

Letters:

Kellen, Erin. "Gaining Praise & Little Else." *Library Journal* 112 (June 1, 1987):10.
Schuman, Patricia Glass. "Women & White." *Library Journal* 112 (April 15, 1987):6.

Response:

White, Herbert S. "Managing Libraries and the Societal Moral Good." *Library Journal* 113 (April 15, 1988):60-61.
Comments on letters received about the column and addresses issues such as child care, family responsibility, and the impact of sex on management and managerial commitment.

1987-174 "WNBA Honors 70 Book Women." *Publishers Weekly* 232 (November 27, 1987):10.
Announces winners of awards given by the Women's National Book Association. Recipients included women librarians.

1987-175 "Women Librarians Document 'Inequities' in Ohio." *American Libraries* 18 (June 1987):412.
Announces publication of a study by Jeanne M. Patterson and Linda R. Silver entitled *Sex of Director, Salary, and Size of Library* which looks at the ratios of male to female library directors and the gender of directors to the size of library. Also examines the difference between average salaries for male and female library directors. (See **1987-114**)

1987-176 "Women's Book Awards." *AB Bookman's Weekly* 80 (December 7, 1987):2242-2244.
Announces winners of the Women's National Book Association awards given to "women in the book world who have made a difference in bringing authors and their readers together." Winners include librarians.

1987-177 "Women's Committee Sponsors Brown Bag Luncheon on Career Mobility." *Library of Congress Information Bulletin* 46 (February 23, 1987):82.
Announces luncheon program on "strategies for moving up in the federal system."

1987-178 "Women's Committee Sponsors Brown Bag Lunch on Contributions of Black Women." *Library of Congress Information Bulletin* 46 (January 26, 1987):45.

Announces luncheon program on "Black women in the work force."

1987-179 Wood, Frances, Diana Richardson, and Herbert Schur. "Scientists and Information Work: The Careers of the 1979-1985 MSc Graduates from the Department of Information Studies, University of Sheffield." *Journal of Information Science* 13 (1987):297-306.

Reports results of a survey including factors such as job mobility, job satisfaction, professional involvement, and evaluation of the Information Studies program. Employment data indicate that several female respondents are "geographically restricted for domestic reasons" and that all respondents not working at the time of the survey were women.

1988 BIBLIOGRAPHY

1988-01 Abbott, Andrew. *The System of Professions: An Essay on the Division of Expert Labor*. Chicago: University of Chicago Press, 1988.
   Makes several references to the feminization of the library profession throughout the text.

Reviews:

Contemporary Psychology 34 (May 1989):520.
DiMaggio, Paul. *American Journal of Sociology* 95 (September 1989):534-535.
Krone, Robert. *Society* 26 (September-October 1989):95.
Perkins, Kenneth B. *Sociological Inquiry* 61 (Winter 1991):124-126.
Roberts, Norman. *Journal of Academic Librarianship* 15 (January 1990):389.
Roberts, Norman. *Journal of Librarianship* 15 (July 1989):212-214.
Scull, Andrew. *Isis* 81 (March 1990):148-149.
Stinchcombe, Arthur L. *Contemporary Sociology: An International Journal of Reviews* 19 (January 1990):48-50.
Tolbert, Pamela S. *Administrative Science Quarterly* 35 (June 1990):410-413.
Turner, Bryan S. *Sociology* 23 (August 1989):472.
University Press Book News 1 (March 1989):15.
Wiegand, Wayne A. *Journal of Academic Librarianship* 17 (March 1991):51.
Wiegand, Wayne A. *Library Quarterly* 60 (October 1990):362-364.

1988-02 "ACRL Programs in New Orleans." *College and Research Libraries News* 49 (May 1988):298-301.
    Notes activities of the Association of College and Research Libraries Women's Studies Section.

1988-03 "ALA Employee Minority Profile." *American Libraries* 19 (March 1988):226-227.
    Shows American Library Association employee profile broken down by sex and race.

1988-04 "ALA Highlights--Conference '88 Notes." *Women in Libraries* 18 (September 1988):1.
    Summarizes conference programming on women's issues from the American Library Association Annual Conference including thorough coverage of the Feminist Task Force's program on strategies for combating racial, ethnic and gender discrimination in libraries.

1988-04a "ALA Officers & Awards." *Library Journal* 113 (August 1988):36.
    Announces Kathleen Weibel as the winner of the ALA Equality Award.

1988-05 Allanach, David. "Them and Us." *New Library World* 89 (September 1988):168.
    Quotes comments said about librarians in the media.

1988-06 Altman & Weil, Inc. *Private Law Libraries: A Survey of Compensation, Operations and Collections: 1988 Edition.* Conducted for the American Association of Law Libraries, Private Law Libraries Special Interest Section. Ardmore, PA: The Association, 1988.
    Provides statistics on 524 law libraries including data on maternity leave, distribution and compensation by position and sex, and hourly billing rates by position and sex.

1988-07 "Annual ARL Salary Survey." *The Innocent Bystander* (A Weekly Newsletter of the University of Connecticut Libraries) 18 March 1988, 1.

Notes survey highlights including the average salaries of male and female directors.

1988-08 "Are Librarians 'Out' at Work?" *GLTF Newsletter* 1 (Fall 1988):1-2.

Summarizes and discusses results of a survey distributed to attendees at the 1988 American Library Association annual conference program sponsored by the Gay and Lesbian Task Force.

1988-08a *ARL Annual Salary Survey, 1988.* Washington, DC: Association of Research Libraries, 1988.

Provides data on staff of ARL libraries by sex and position and includes salary statistics.

1988-09 "ARL Reports on Serials, Salaries." *Library Journal* 113 (July 1988):22.

Provides summary data from the *ARL Annual Salary Survey*, including data by gender.

1988-10 "Association News and Views." *Journal of Education for Library and Information Science* 28 (Spring 1988):302.

Notes presentation of 1988 Research Grant Award to John V. Richardson and Donald O. Case for a proposed study of variables, including gender, which can be used to predict success of applicants to graduate school in library science. (See **1988-84**)

1988-11 Association of College and Research Libraries. New England Chapter. *1987/88 Salary Survey of New England College Libraries*. Worchester, MA: [The Association], 1988.

Results of survey of four-year undergraduate institutions in six New England states including data on number, average salaries, and average years of experience by sex.

1988-12 Association of Theological Schools in the United States and Canada. *Fact Book on Theological Education for the Academic Year 1987-1988*, edited by William L. Baumgaertner. Vandalia, Ohio: [The Association], 1988.

Includes sex distribution of faculty and administrative

personnel including librarians, changes in employment of women and blacks by position held, and trends in salaries for administrators, faculty, and librarians.

1988-12a "Avram, Goldhor, and Thomas Win 1988 ALA Awards." *American Libraries* 19 (June 1988):532.
    Announces Kathleen Weibel as the winner of the ALA Equality Award.

1988-13 Bennett, George E. *Librarians in Search of Science and Identity: The Elusive Profession.* Metuchen, NJ: Scarecrow Press, 1988.
    Makes several references throughout the text to the feminization of librarianship as a factor in the status of librarianship as a profession.

Reviews:

Chasen, Larry. *Special Libraries* 81 (Spring 1990):163-164.
Cutcher, Dan. *National Librarian* 14 (August 1989):2-3.
Foster, Stephen Paul. *Information Technology and Libraries* 8 (September 1989):332-333.
Goldhor, Herbert. *Library Journal* 113 (November 1, 1989):58.
Hayes, Robert M. *Library Quarterly* 60 (January 1990):69-72.
Stevens, Norman. *Wilson Library Bulletin* 63 (January 1989):106-107.
Wall, Tom. *American Libraries* 20 (February 1989):152.
Wiegand, Wayne A. *Library and Information Science Research* 11 (January/March 1989):80-81.

1988-14 Bering-Jensen, Helle. "Plenty of Jobs, Too Few Librarians." *Insight* (June 13, 1988):58-59.
    Attributes the shortage of librarians to changes in female employment patterns and cites statistics verifying that librarianship is a female intensive profession.

1988-15 Berman, Sanford. *Worth Noting.* Jefferson, NC: McFarland, 1988.
    Subtitled "Editorials, Letters, Essays, An Interview, and

Bibliography." Includes brief references to the American Library Association Committee on the Status of Women in Librarianship, the Social Responsibilities Round Table, *Women in Libraries*, and *WLW Journal*.

1988-16 Berry, John, GraceAnne DeCandido and Nora Rawlinson. "Leadership, Access and Internal Politics." *Library Journal* 113 (August 1988):33-42.
Includes report on the program "The Creation of Patriarchy: Its Implications for Leadership" and on pay equity.

1988-17 Bierbaum, Esther Green. "Museum, Arts and Humanities Librarians: Careers, Professional Development, and Continuing Education." *Journal of Education for Library and Information Science* 29 (Fall 1988):127-134.
Discusses career tracks and continuing education needs of museum, arts, and humanities librarians and notes that 90% of librarians in that group are female while 80% of corporate library managers are female. Concludes that "the not-for-profit library setting may be more feminized than the corporate special library setting."

1988-18 "Blue Ribbon Panel on Librarians' Salaries." *Connecticut Libraries* 30 (February 1988):2-4.
Includes comment on relationship between the number of women in the profession and salary level.

1988-18a Bobay, Julie. "Job Sharing: A Survey of the Literature and a Plan for Academic Libraries." *Journal of Library Administration* 9 (1988):59-69.
Profiles job-sharers, primarily women, and discusses advantages and disadvantages of job-sharing. Outlines issues which affect job-sharing for librarians and suggests ways to deal with these issues.

1988-19 "British Library Association Issues Statements on Recruitment of Black Librarians and on Equal Opportunities in Employment." *Journal of Multicultural Librarianship* 2 (March 1988):42, 44.

1988-20 Bryant, Sue Lacey. "Women Not in Libraries." *New Library World* 89 (October 1988):187.
    Laments the trials and tribulations of a librarian confronted with motherhood.

1988-21 Bustman, Mary Jane and Barbara J. Via. "Employment and Status of Part-time Librarians in U.S. Academic Libraries." *Journal of Academic Librarianship* 14 (May 1988):87-91.
    Discusses results of survey to determine the employment, status, utilization, and compensation of part-time librarians in U.S. academic libraries. Includes gender data.

1988-22 Cain, Mark E. "Academic and Research Librarians: Who Are We?" *Journal of Academic Librarianship* 14 (November 1988):292-296.
    Uses data provided by 1,771 individuals from the U.S. and Canada to examine demographics of academic and research librarianship. Finds that academic librarianship cannot be characterized by the label "woman's profession" since respondents to the survey were 48.5 percent male and 51.5 percent female.

1988-23 Caldwell, John. "Data Collected from the Private Academic Libraries in Illinois for Academic Year July 1985-June 1986." *Illinois Libraries* 70 (November 1988):597-602.
    Includes statistics on library staffing broken down by sex.

1988-24 Carmichael, James Vinson, Jr. "Dora Barker and Southern Librarianship." Ph.D. diss., University of North Carolina at Chapel Hill, 1988.
    History of pioneer of southern librarianship who opened the first Black branch library in Atlanta in 1921 and raised awareness of the poor conditions in southern libraries. Became dean of the Emory University library school where she upgraded faculty and curriculum.

1988-25 Chepesiuk, Ron. "Librarianship: Opportunities for the Minority Graduate." *Equal Opportunity* 22 (Fall 1988):32-33.
    Encourages minorities to consider librarianship as a career and notes that activities to achieve pay equity in the "women's

profession" is having some success.

1988-26 Choi, Jin M. and Nancy Washington. *Learning Styles of Academic Librarians and Implications for Professional Development*. Washington, DC: Council on Library Resources, 1988. ERIC, ED 307 892

Examines characteristics of learning styles based on Kolb's Learning Style Inventory. Gender is reviewed as a factor in learning style distributions.

1988-27 Clifford, Geraldine Jonich. "Women's Liberation and Women's Professions: Reconsidering the Past, Present, and Future." In *Women and Higher Education in American History: Essays from the Mount Holyoke College Sesquicentennial Symposia*, edited by John Mack Faragher and Florence Howe, 165-182. New York: W.W. Norton and Co., 1988.

Indicates the numbers of women in traditionally "women's occupations" and points out that many, including librarianship, were male careers before becoming women's work. (See also **1988-137**)

1988-28 *Collective Bargaining Agreement Between Montgomery County Community College and Montgomery County Community College Faculty, Pennsylvania Federation of Teachers, AFT/AFL-CIO, 1988-1991*. Washington, DC: American Federation of Teachers; Conshohocken, PA: Montgomery County Community College, 1988. ERIC, ED 301 291

Outlines terms of employment, including article forbidding sex discrimination. Librarians are included in the bargaining agreement.

1988-29 Conkling, Dee. "Never Done: FTF Meetings at Midwinter '88." *Women in Libraries* 17 (April 1988):3.

Includes announcements and future programming notes for the American Library Association Social Responsibilities Round Table Feminist Task Force.

1988-30 Conlin, Elizabeth A. "25 Hottest Careers: 1988." *Working Woman* 13 (July 1988):55-64ff.

Lists librarianship in corporations and law firms. Mentions librarians' expertise in storage and retrieval of information.

Letter:

Bender, David. "Salary Survey Addendum." *Working Woman* 14 (March 1989):27.
Calls attention to the 1988 mean salary of $34,110 for members of the Special Libraries Association, an increase of 14.9% over 1987 median salary.

1988-31 Dagg, Anne Innis and Patricia J. Thompson. *MisEducation: Women & Canadian Universities*. Toronto: Ontario Institute for Studies in Education, 1988.
Discusses the status of women in librarianship in the chapter "Traditional 'Feminine' Disciplines." Notes that "although library schools are willing to teach women to be librarians, universities are less willing to hire and promote them as professional librarians." Includes statistics on the percentage of library school students and academic librarians who are women.

Reviews:

Geller, Gloria. *Canadian Review of Sociology and Anthropology* 27 (November 1990):582-583.
Grant, Agnes. *Canadian Dimension* 22 (October 1988):39-40.
Jackel, Susan. *Resources for Feminist Research/Documentation sur la Recherche Feministe* 18 (March 1989):32-33.
Klingberg, Susan. *College and Research Libraries* 50 (September 1989):587.
Quill & Quire 54 (August 1988):108.

1988-32 DeCandido, GraceAnne A. "High Energy & Social Concern." *Library Journal* 113 (August 1988):43-50.
Reports on the Special Libraries Association's annual conference including a program, "While You're Minding the Library, Who's Minding the Children?"

1988-33 DeCandido, GraceAnne A. "Library Directions in 1987." *Library Journal* 113 (January 1988):47-52.
　　Includes story on "Women Librarians and Money" indicating that male directors still make more money and receive more money per capita than libraries with women directors. Also notes that beginning librarians working for a woman director make a higher starting salary.

1988-34 DeCandido, GraceAnne A. "LJ News Report, 1987." In *The Bowker Annual*, 3-10. New York: Bowker, 1988.
　　Includes section on "Women Librarians and Money" which reports data from the *Library Journal* salary survey.

1988-35 DeCandido, GraceAnne A. "World's First Library School Celebrates Centennial." *Library Journal* 113 (January 1988):16.
　　Notes the 100th anniversary of the Columbia University School of Library Service including the controversy over the admission of women in the 1880s.

1988-36 DeLoach, Lynda. "Meeting Report of the Committee on the Status of Women." *Women's Caucus Newsletter* (Society of American Archivists) 10 (September 1988):5,6.
　　Notes statistics on program panelists by gender, a proposal to devise a salary survey, and proposed sessions for the 1988 annual conference.

1988-37 Devore-Chew, Marynelle, Brian Roberts, and Nathan M. Smith. "The Effects of Reference Librarians' Nonverbal Communications on the Patrons' Perceptions of the Library, Librarians, and Themselves." *Library and Information Science Research* 10 (October-December 1988):389-400.
　　Examines combination of gender and nonverbal communication to determine its effect on patrons' perceptions of the library, librarians, and themselves. Concludes that in general patrons notice nonverbal communication more if the librarian is female.

1988-38 *Directory of Library and Information Professions Women's Groups*, edited by Katharine Phenix. 4th ed. Chicago: American

Library Association, 1988.
Lists associations and groups of interest to women librarians. (See also **1989-53** and **1989-81**)

Announcement:

Library Journal 114 (May 1, 1989):60.

Review:

Mahmoud, Donna Sayed. *Canadian Library Journal* 47 (October 1990):367.

1988-39 Dowell, David R. "Sex and Salary in a Female Dominated Profession." *Journal of Academic Librarianship* 14 (May 1988): 92-98.
Examines the relationship of gender to salaries paid to librarians when variables such as longevity, supervisory responsibility, peer ratings, education and professional activities are held constant. Uses Association of Research Libraries members in the South Atlantic Census Region for the study.

1988-39a "Ella Yates Cleared of Criminal Charges." *American Libraries* 19 (June 1988):422.
Reports that Yates, Virginia State Librarian, was cleared of charges of bribery and embezzlement but did find "technical violations" and errors in judgment.

1988-40 Eng, Sidney and Joanna Bevacqua. "Profile of Success: Interviews with Female Chief Librarians in the City University of New York." *Urban Academic Librarian* 6 (Spring 1988):50-65.
Reports results of a questionnaire designed to study the career paths of CUNY female chief librarians.

1988-41 Everett, Susan Hope. "Sue Rugge: Blueprint for Success." *Wilson Library Bulletin* 63 (November 1988):74-75.
Tells the story of the woman who started Information on Demand. Notes that Rugge, to support other women, employed 57 full- and part-time women workers.

1988-42 Fisher, David P. "Is the Librarian a Distinct Personality Type?" *Journal of Librarianship* 20 (January 1988):36-47.
   Assesses psychological investigations of the personality of librarians conducted over 30 years. Gender stereotypes are discussed.

1988-43 Fisher, David P. "The Mysterious Case of the Archetypal Librarian." *New Library World* 89 (June 1988):105.
   Describes the fictional image of a librarian as "a woman of indeterminate age, who wears spectacles; a person with either a timorous...or an austere disposition" and points out that the classic librarian images have little to do with reality.

Letters:

Denny, Mavis. *New Library World* 89 (September 1988):168.
Humphreys, Garry. *New Library World* 89 (August 1988):149.

1988-44 Foggin, Carol M. "Reentry: A Viable Option for Professionals." *Library Administration and Management* 2 (June 1988):137-140.
   Discusses reentry as it affects women across careers and looks at the issue as it relates to librarians and library administrators.

1988-45 Gartanganis, Arthur. "Trends in Bachelor's and Higher Degrees." *Occupational Outlook Quarterly* 32 (Summer 1988):9-15.
   Provides data on number of degrees earned by field and percentage earned by women by field.

1988-46 Gaughan, Tom. "ARL Salaries Surveyed; AL Writer Stymied." *American Libraries* 19 (May 1988):416.
   Comments on the 1987 salary survey conducted by the Association of Research Libraries.

1988-46a Gaughan, Tom. "Tail Gunners on Bread Trucks." *American Libraries* 19 (July/August 1988):632.
   Notes recent problems and changes in library administration including Ella Gaines Yates, Virginia State

Librarian who was investigated and cleared of charges of bribery, and Anne Woodsworth, Director of Libraries at University of Pittsburgh who was appointed to Associate Provost then later asked to resign for a post in the library school. In both cases, gender is mentioned as a factor.

Letters:

Kenney, W. Robert. "Vexed in Virginia." *American Libraries* 19 (November 1988):856.
Rowland, Anne E. "Trivializing 'The Troubles.'" *American Libraries* 19 (December 1988):938.

1988-47 Gerhardt, Lillian N. "Home Is Where the Heart Is." [editorial] *School Library Journal* 34 (January 1988):7.

Affirms statement by Margaret Bush at the Midwest Federation of Library Association's meeting, November 1987, that women contribute to the problems of recruiting youth librarians by their refusal to move for better working conditions and salaries.

1988-48 Goetsch, Lori A. "Yesterday and Today: The Status of Women in Librarianship." *WLW Journal* 12 (Fall 1988):2-4.

Discusses findings from annual reviews of the literature by the American Library Association Committee on the Status of Women in Librarianship's Bibliography Task Force.

1988-48a Goudy, Frank William. "Viewpoint: Comparing Librarian and Teacher Salaries Is Valid." *The Bottom Line* 2 (1988): 17-19.

1988-49 Greiner, Joy M. "A Comparative Study of the Management Styles and Career Progression Patterns of Recently Appointed Male and Female Public Library Administrators (1983-1987)." *Advances in Library Administration and Organization* 7 (1988):1-27.

Studies public library directors serving populations of 100,000 or more who assumed their positions between 1983 and 1987. Leadership styles, professional association activities, and publishing records were principal areas of investigation.

1988-50 Gualtieri, Bob. "Pay Equity for Library Workers." *Connecticut Libraries* 30 (November 1988):6.
    Reports on progress on pay equity at the national, state, and regional level.

1988-50a Hamshari, Amr-Ahmad and Muhammad M. al-Dhunaybat. "Employee Motivation in University Libraries in Jordan." *Dirasat* 15 (February 1988):212-240.
    Reports results of study of 73 male and 29 female library employees regarding motivation and assessing the applicability of Maslow's need hierarchy their to university environments. Determined differences based on gender.

1988-51 Harris, Roma M. and Christina-Sue Chan. "Cataloging and Reference, Circulation and Shelving: Public Library Users and University Students' Perceptions of Librarianship." *Library and Information Science Research* 10 (January-March 1988):95-107.
    Notes that a possible reason offered for lack of prestige associated with librarianship has been the feminization of the profession. Reports results of survey indicating that users perceive librarians as likely to engage in lower status or women's tasks and overestimated the number of men in librarianship. Suggests a correlation between the number of males thought to be working as librarians and respondents' rating of the prestige of the profession and shows that estimates of average annual starting salaries were lower for female librarians.

1988-52 Harris, Roma M. and Gillian Michell. "Home Insulating and Home Births: Do Patrons' Sex-Typed Questions Influence Judgments About the Competence of Reference Librarians?" *RQ* 28 (Winter 1988):179-184.
    Evaluates perceptions of reference librarians' competence when responding to "male" or "female" questions. Results revealed that students judged librarians to be most effective when answering questions consistent with their sex roles.

1988-52a Harris, Roma M. and Joanne K. Reid. "Career Opportunities in Library and Information Science: An Analysis of Canadian Job Advertisements in the 1980's." *Canadian Journal of*

Information Science 13 (September 1988):17-29.
Reports results of a study of job postings for librarian positions including type of position, job setting, location, and salary as well as experience, skill, and language requirements. Correlates results with student enrollment by gender in elective courses at the University of Western Ontario. Concludes that an increasing number of available positions seek computing experience and education. Finds that male students are taking courses to better prepare themselves for changes in the job market while females continue to take traditional service courses.

1988-53 Hollaway, Pat et al. "Blue Ribbon Panel on Librarians' Salaries." *Connecticut Libraries* 30 (February 1988):2-4.
Summarizes a report for the Connecticut Library Association which includes salary data.

1988-54 Hudson, Phyllis. "Recruitment for Academic Librarianship." In *Librarians for the New Millennium*, edited by William E. Moen and Kathleen M. Heim, 72-82. Chicago: American Library Association, Office for Library Personnel Resources, 1988.
Examines key issues such as salaries, the wage gap, and librarianship as a female intensive profession as factors impacting recruitment. (See also **1988-73**)

1988-55 Hulme, Amanda J. and Thomas D. Wilson. "Professional Education and Subsequent Careers in Library-Information Work: A Follow-up Study of Former Students in the MA-MSc Information Studies (Social Sciences) Courses at the University of Sheffield." *Journal of Information Science* 14 (March-April 1988):109-117.
Includes comment noting decreasing tendency for women to leave the workforce at marriage.

1988-56 Immroth, Barbara. "Recruiting Children's Librarians." In *Librarians for the New Millennium*, edited by William E. Moen and Kathleen M. Heim, 37-46. Chicago: American Library Association, Office for Library Personnel Resources, 1988.
Includes discussion of gender as a factor affecting

recruitment efforts. Notes findings by the American Library Association Committee on the Status of Women in Librarianship on occupational segregation in librarianship. (See also **1988-73**)

1988-57 "Iron(wo)man Librarian." *American Libraries* 19 (December 1988):927.
 Profiles Rochester, Michigan, school librarian Laura Sophiea's third place triathalon finish.

1988-58 Jennings, Kriza A. "Applauds ALA's Focus on Racism." [letter] *American Libraries* 19 (March 1988):166.
 Commends the focus on racism by the American Library Association Social Responsibilities Round Table Feminist Task Force.

1988-59 deleted

1988-60 Jones, Kay F. "Sex, Salaries, and Library Support." In *The Bowker Annual*, 305-316. New York: Bowker, 1988.
 Discusses growth in per capita support of U.S. libraries, gender distribution changes in library directorships, directors' salaries, beginning salaries, who pays better (male or female library administrators), and general trends.

1988-61 Jones, Kay F. "Women in Librarianship." In *The ALA Yearbook of Library and Information Services*, v. 13, 329-331. Chicago: American Library Association, 1988.
 Provides a brief literature review of items published in 1987 on the status of women in librarianship, summarizes salary surveys, and discusses pay equity issues.

1988-62 Korytnyk, Christine A. "Comparison of the Publishing Patterns Between Men and Women Ph.D.s in Librarianship." *Library Quarterly* 58 (1988):52-65.
 Studies publishing patterns of men and women who received library science Ph.D.s between 1969 and 1979. Shows a significant difference between mean number of citations per person among male and female educators.

1988-63 Krantz, Les. *The Jobs Rated Almanac.* New York: World Almanac, 1988.
   Includes table of occupations broken down by percentages of male and female employees, including "Librarians, Archivists & Curators."

Reviews:

Spillman, Nancy Z. *Library Journal* 113 (November 1, 1988):41.

1988-64 Land, Mary. "Librarians' Image and Users Attitudes Towards Reference Interviews." *Canadian Library Journal* 45 (February 1988):15-20.
   Discusses image of librarians in popular culture including gender stereotypes.

1988-65 Lauer, Jonathan D. et al. *Faculty Status, Longevity, and Salaries Among Librarians in LIBRAS.* 1988. ERIC, ED 329 253
   Reports results of survey of librarians employed by a Chicago-area consortium of liberal arts colleges to compare salary levels of librarians with and without faculty status and to test whether length of professional experience correlates to salary level. Concludes that areas for further study include analysis by gender.

1988-66 Lazare, Arthur. "Gay Librarians on the Job." *New York Native*, 23 May 1988, 29-30.
   Examines national networks of gay and lesbian librarians and discusses gays and lesbians in a women's profession.

1988-67 Learmont, Carol and Stephen Van Houten. "Placements and Salaries 1987: The Upswing Continues." *Library Journal* 113 (October 15, 1988):29-36.
   Provides salary and placement information by sex for United States and Canadian library school graduates.

1988-68 Learmont, Carol and Stephen Van Houten. "Placements and Salaries, 1986: An Upswing." In *The Bowker Annual*, 289-305. New York: Bowker, 1988.
   Provides salary and placement information by sex for

United States and Canadian library school graduates.

1988-69 Leather, Deborah J. "Comparable Worth: The Limitations of Federal Legislation and Litigation." *Library Administration and Management* 2 (September 1988):181-187.
Defines comparable worth and looks at documentation that library professionals and support staff can use to convince employers to upgrade their pay.

1988-70 *The Librarian*. Scottsdale, AZ: Preservation Comics, 1988-.
The inaugural issue of this comic, July 1988, features the female superhero going up against a patron who has torn a page out of a book.

1988-71 "Librarian Superhero Debuts in Preservation Comics." *Library Journal* 113 (October 1, 1988):21.
Announces first issue of "The Librarian," a comic featuring a female superhero who "fights the never-ending battle against acidic paper, book vandalism, and the destruction of books."

1988-72 "Librarians Cross Racial Lines to Empower Minorities." *American Libraries* 19 (September 1988):708.
Notes program by the Social Responsibilities Round Table Feminist Task Force to bring together a multiracial group of librarians to discuss strategies to empower minority librarians.

1988-73 *Librarians for the New Millennium*, edited by William E. Moen and Kathleen M. Heim. Chicago: American Library Association, Office for Library Personnel Resources, 1988.
Provides background information on personnel strategies and needs faced by the profession including recruitment of minorities and specialists. (See also **1988-54, 1988-56, 1988-81, 1988-92, 1988-98,** and **1988-124**)

Reviews:

Kirkland, Janice. *Library Journal* 114 (May 1, 1989):103.
Knowles, Em Claire. *Journal of Academic Librarianship* 15

(January 1990):371.
Wilson Library Bulletin 63 (February 1989):121.

1988-73a *Library and Information Science Education Statistical Report 1988*, edited by Timothy W. Sineath. State College, PA: Association for Library and Information Science Education, 1988.

Provides data from 60 ALA-accredited schools on faculty salaries and related data pertaining to library education as of January 1, 1988.

1988-74 Lott, Barbara F. "A Cross Cultural Exchange: China." *Connecticut Libraries* 30 (November 1988):1-2.

Comments on number of women employed in academic libraries in China.

1988-75 Marquis, Kathy. "Committee on the Status of Women." *Women's Caucus Newsletter* (Society of American Archivists) 10 (September 1988):1,2.

1988-76 McCombs, Gillian M. "Is There a Nancy Drew in You? An Attempt to Resolve Some Problems of Communication and Leadership with the Help of 'Popular' Culture." Paper presented at the Library Administration and Management Association President's Program, Annual Conference of the American Library Association, 10 July 1988, New Orleans, LA. ERIC, ED 304 142

Argues that role models from children's literature can be used to resolve current difficulties that women in the profession have with leadership and communication.

1988-77 McFarland, Anne S. et al. *Selecting a Director: Professional and Managerial Characteristics Preferred by Ohio Public Library Boards*. OWL Research Report #3. Northfield, OH: Ohio Women Librarians, 1988.

Reports results of a questionnaire sent to public library board presidents in Ohio to identify characteristics and skills needed by library administrators in order to provide career guidance and development data for women seeking administrative positions.

1988-78 McNeer, Elizabeth J. "The Mentoring Influence in the Careers of Women ARL Directors." *Journal of Library Administration* 9 (1988):23-33.

Explores similarities in the careers and the opportunities for mentoring of women directors of Association of Research Libraries institutions.

1988-79 McReynolds, Rosalee. "A Heritage Dismissed." *Women's Caucus Newsletter* (Society of American Archivists) 10 (September 1988):8-12.

Examines image of librarians and archivists and efforts to establish professional identities and eliminate stereotypes.

1988-80 Mika, Joseph J. and Bruce A. Shuman. "Legal Issues Affecting Libraries and Librarians." *American Libraries* 18 (January 1988):26-28, 30-31.

Offers management tutorials on the legal components of affirmative action, discrimination and sexual harassment.

Letter:

Whisner, Mary. "Harassment Discussion Misleading." *American Libraries* 19 (May 1988):346.

1988-81 Moen, William E. "Library and Information Science Students' Attitudes, Demographics, and Aspirations Survey: Who We Are and Why We Are Here." In *Librarians for the New Millennium*, edited by William E. Moen and Kathleen M. Heim, 93-109. Chicago: American Library Association, Office for Library Personnel Resources, 1988.

Reviews previous surveys and presents preliminary findings of a new survey including enrollment, age, family status and work experience. Includes statistics by gender. (See also **1988-73**)

1988-82 Moen, William E. and Kathleen M. Heim. "The Class of 1988: Librarians for the New Millennium." *American Libraries* 19 (November 1988):858-860, 885.

Reports results of a survey of 3,484 students enrolled in accredited U.S. master's programs in library science in spring,

1988, to determine who will be librarians in the year 2000. Notes that there are more full-time employed men than women in libraries which may advantage males in terms of professional socialization and career advancement. Also, men enroll in library school at an earlier age than women except for the very youngest categories.

1988-83 deleted

1988-84 Morrisey, Locke J. and Donald O. Case. "There Goes My Image: The Perception of Male Librarians by Colleague, Student and Self." *College and Research Libraries* 49 (September 1988): 453-464.

Analyzes survey responses of undergraduate students, MLS students, and academic librarians to twenty semantic differential word-pair scales to show perceptions of male librarians. Concludes that male librarians consider their image as worse than other respondents. (See also **1988-10**)

1988-85 Nelson, Mary Ann. "Emerging Legal Issues for Library Administrators. Preparing for the 1990s--A Bibliographic Essay." *Library Administration and Management* 2 (September 1988):188-190.

Includes legal theories, precedents and laws related to sex discrimination.

1988-86 "New Members Are Sought for Women's Program Advisory Committee." *Library of Congress Information Bulletin* 47 (January 18, 1988):22.

Announcement to solicit members to fill vacancies.

1988-87 "News." *Women in Libraries* 17 (April 1988):8.

April Fool's Day news that reflects stereotypes and image problems facing women library workers.

1988-88 "OWL." *National Librarian* 13 (February 1988):1.

Notes that Ohio Women Librarians was officially formed in October 1986 to educate women candidates for administrative positions, to advocate promotion of qualified female candidates, and to provide support for women administrators.

1988-89 "OWL Reports." *National Librarian* 13 (May 1988):6.
Describes research report that states that within the framework of the male management model, women either become substitute men or they learn to accept a subordinate role. (See also **1988-109**)

1988-90 "Panel--The Creation of Patriarchy." *Women in Libraries* 18 (September 1988):6-7.
Details a panel sponsored by the American Library Association Library History Round Table on the growth of the patriarchal system, gender conditioning in school librarianship, and the history of the absence of women in academic libraries.

1988-91 Panigaburra, Anchalee. "Racism in the Feminist Movement in ALA." Madison, WI: University of Wisconsin School of Library and Information Science. Spring 1988.
Examines activities of the Social Responsibilities Round Table Feminist Task Force as an organization for white women and women of color and the outcomes of those activities. Discusses racism at the association level and as it appears in the Feminist Task Force.

1988-92 Paskoff, Beth M. "Recruitment for Special Librarianship." In *Librarians for the New Millennium*, edited by William E. Moen and Kathleen M. Heim, 57-64. Chicago: American Library Association, Office for Library Personnel Resources, 1988.
Includes sections on recruitment, student support and scholarships, and types of special libraries. Notes that the majority of special librarians--84.7%--are women. (See also **1988-73**)

1988-93 Passet, Joanne E. "Quest for a Profession: The Origins of Library Education in Indiana." Ph.D. diss., Indiana University, 1988.
Presents a feminist interpretation of librarianship by using a case study of the history of the Indiana University Library School through 1912. Discusses the marginalization and feminization of librarianship from 1890 to 1910 as a microcosm for the sexual

division of labor in America.

Reviews:

Harris, Michael H. *Journal of Academic Librarianship* 17 (March 1991):51.
Harris, Michael H. *Library and Information Science Research* (July-September 1990):315-316.

1988-94 "Pay Equity: A National View and Action Steps for Library Workers." *Library Personnel News* 2 (Fall 1988):54.
Summarizes speakers' comments at a program sponsored by the ALA Committee on Pay Equity held at the 1988 Annual Conference addressing wage gaps and local efforts.

1988-95 "Pay Equity Committee Readies Action Manual." *American Libraries* 19 (March 1988):179.
Reports on ALA-funded plan to produce a manual of strategies for documenting inequities and getting salary adjustments.

1988-96 Payne, Judith. *Public Libraries Face California's Ethnic and Racial Diversity*. Santa Monica, CA: Rand Corp., [1988].
Makes no specific reference to gender issues in librarianship or to the status of women, but prompted the responses below.

Response:

Tarin, Patricia A. "RAND Misses the Point: A 'Minority' Report." *Library Journal* 113 (November 1, 1988):31-34.
Critiques report as a "weakly drawn impression of library services to ethnic minorities." Also criticizes the description of typical library users as "white, female, affluent, well-educated" and that description's relationship to the "typical librarian."

Letter:

Carlson, Pam. *Library Journal* 114 (March 16, 1989):8.

The Bibliography

1988-97 Pearson, Lois R. "Sex Discrimination Case Settled in Ohio." *American Libraries* 19 (September 1988):637.
  Reports on out-of-court settlement of Linda Silver's sex discrimination case against the Cuyahoga County (Ohio) Public Library Board of Trustees.

1988-97a Pearson, Lois R. "Va. State Librarian Yates Faces Two Investigations." *American Libraries* 19 (March 1988):245-246.
  Reports grievances against Ella Gaines Yates, described by the state's governor as "a strong-willed woman who would provide leadership." Quotes a public library director that "the resentment against Yates stemmed from the fact she is the first black and the first woman to hold the state library post."

1988-98 Randall, Ann Knight. "Minority Recruitment in Librarianship." In *Librarians for the New Millennium*, edited by William E. Moen and Kathleen M. Heim, 11-25. Chicago: American Library Association, Office for Library Personnel Resources, 1988.
  Includes data in table entitled "Distribution of Total Work Force by Racial/Ethnic/Sexual Group for Librarians in Academic and Public Libraries." (See also **1988-73**)

1988-99 "Recruitment Preconference." *Library Personnel News* 2 (Fall 1988):54.
  Highlights include reference to preliminary recruitment data by sex gathered by Moen and Heim. (See also **1988-81**)

1988-100 deleted

1988-101 Richards, Diane and Paula Elliot. "How Others See Us." *College and Research Libraries News* 49 (July/August 1988):422-424.
  Reports on the Washington state chapter of ACRL's meeting on the librarian's image.

1988-102 Riggs, Donald E. and Gordon A. Sabine. *Libraries in the '90s: What the Leaders Expect*. Phoenix: Oryx Press, 1988.

Interviews with library leaders including 13 women. Comments on the impact of feminization of librarianship on salaries (Anne Heidbreder Eastman, pp. 64-65) and the profession's service philosophy (Margaret Chisholm, pp. 127-128).

Reviews:

Alloway, Catherine Suyak. *Special Libraries* 80 (Spring 1989):153.
Editor. *Journal of Academic Librarianship* 14 (November 1988):312.
Jasper, Richard P. *Journal of Academic Librarianship* 15 (July 1989):157.
King, David E. *Library Quarterly* 59 (July 1989):267-268.
Library Hi Tech News (January 1989):107.
Osburn, Charles B. *LRTS* 33 (April 1989):203-204.
Reference & Research Book News 3 (December 1988):32.
SciTech Book News 12 (November 1988):35.
Stevens, Norman. *Wilson Library Bulletin* 63 (January 1989):107.
Wilson Library Bulletin 63 (October 1988):116.

1988-103 Rooks, Dana C. *Motivating Today's Library Staff.* Phoenix, AZ: Oryx Press, 1988.

Includes discussion of research which explores the relationship between job satisfaction and gender.

Reviews:

Black, Sophie K. *Booklist* 84 (April 1988):1310.
Burckel, Nicholas C. *American Archivist* 51 (Fall 1988):512.
Carpenter, Kathryn Hammell. *Library Journal* 113 (June 1, 1988):88.
Editor. *Journal of Academic Librarianship* 14 (May 1988):135.
Flagg, Gordon. *American Libraries* 19 (October 1988):829.
Goetsch, Lori A. *Journal of Academic Librarianship* 14 (January 1989):373-374.
Montanelli, Dale. *Journal of Library Administration* 12 (Winter 1990):129-130.
Stevens, Norman. *Wilson Library Bulletin* 62 (May 1988):90.

1988-104 Ross, B. "Rebellious Librarians Occupy Hart House." *Rites* 4 (February 1988):4.

1988-104a Sanchez, James Joseph. "Comparable Worthlessness." [letter] *American Libraries* 19 (September 1988):650.

    Accompanies an advertisement sent in by Sanchez for an unsalaried library position advertised in the *Seattle Times*. Calls it "far more serious than the usual stereotype of the withdrawn, pallid, and grey-bunned librarian."

Letter:

Weinberg, Belle. "Comparable Worthlessness II." *American Libraries* 19 (November 1988):855.

1988-105 Scarborough, Katie and Constance W. Nyhan. "Meeting the Need for Librarians: The California Library School Recruitment Project." *Library Journal* 113 (October 15, 1988):44-49.

    Discusses a California recruitment campaign to attract students to library schools in anticipation of a projected shortage of librarians.

1988-106 "Semiannual Report on Developments at the Library of Congress, October 1, 1987, Through March 31, 1988." *Library of Congress Information Bulletin* 47 (June 27, 1988):267-269.

    Includes data on the number of women and minorities in management-level positions, progress on a child care facility and the activities of the Women's Program Advisory Committee.

1988-107 Sicherman, Barbara. "College and Careers: Historical Perspectives on the Lives and Work Patterns of Women College Graduates." In *Women and Higher Education in American History: Essays from the Mount Holyoke College Sesquicentennial Symposia*, edited by John Mack Faragher and Florence Howe, 130-164. New York: W.W. Norton and Co., 1988.

    Draws on alumnae surveys and recent scholarship on women's higher education to explore work patterns of three generations of women college graduates in terms of employment.

Indicates statistics for women in library science in the late 19th and into the 20th centuries as compared with other occupations. (See also **1988-137**)

1988-108 Silver, Linda R. "Deference to Authority in the Feminized Professions." *School Library Journal* 34 (January 1988):21-27.

Explores concepts of authority, patriarchy, and professionalization as they relate to professions in which women predominate, including librarianship. Based on Ohio Women Librarians, OWL Research Report #2 (see **1987-140**).

1988-109 Silver, Linda R. *The Outsider's Eye: A Critique of the Male Management Model and Its Impact on Women in Organizations.* OWL Research Report #4. Northfield, OH: Ohio Women Librarians, 1988.

Refutes the myth that complex organizations and their management principles are neutral and value free by revealing them to be carriers of an ideology that idealizes the rational male. Cites Rosabeth Moss Kanter's research showing that structure, not sex differences, determines the organizational behavior of men and women. (See also **1988-89**)

1988-110 Slinger, Michael J. "The Career Paths and Education of Current Academic Law Library Directors." *Law Library Journal* 80 (Spring 1988):217-239.

Provides profile of current academic law library directors, highlighting their educational attainment, work experience, academic ranks, and publications. Comparative data by gender.

1988-111 Smayda, Susan. "Taking Responsibility for Equitable Salaries." *Connecticut Libraries* 30 (May 1988):11.

Reports discussion of salary inequities between men and women and current status in the state.

1988-112 Smith, Elizabeth Martinez. "Racism: It Is Always There." *Library Journal* 113 (November 1, 1988):35-39.

Discusses racial differences, confusion about racism, manifestations of racism, and statistics reflecting racism in the

United States. Includes personal experiences with racism and sexism and ways in which the library she directs has "instituted policies to ensure fairness."

Letter:

Wood, Linda M. "Don't Forget Sexism." *Library Journal* 114 (March 15, 1989):6.

1988-112a Smith, Nathan M., Howard C. Bybee, and Martin J. Raish. "Burnout and the Library Administrator: Carrier or Cure." *Journal of Library Administration* 9 (1988):13-21.
    Discusses indicators of burnout and suggests practices of administrators which contribute to burnout of librarians. Suggests ways administrators can alleviate burnout among staff. Notes that one contributing factor beyond a manager's control is the conflict between increased demand for technical skills and the image of librarians as "dowdy, middle-aged women with little education."

1988-113 Somerville, Mary. "Facing the Shortage of Children's Librarians." *The Education Digest* 53 (January 1988):44-47.
    Condensed from article in *American Libraries* 18 (June 1987): 418-428.

1988-114 Special Libraries Association. *SLA Triennial Salary Survey 1989*. Washington, DC: Special Libraries Association, 1988.
    Provides salary date for U.S. and Canadian special librarians.

1988-115 Starr, Carol. "White Women Working Together on Personal and Institutional Racism." *American Libraries* 19 (March 1988):184.
    Discusses a workshop on racism held as a follow-up to the Social Responsibilities Round Table Feminist Task Force 1987 Preconference on Racism.

1988-116 "Statement of James H. Billington, the Librarian of Congress, Before the Joint Committee on the Library, October 4." *Library of Congress Information Bulletin* 47 (October 24,

1988):423-427.
Includes reference to equal employment and affirmative action programs at the Library of Congress.

1988-117 Stevens, Norman. "Our Image in the 1980s." *Library Trends* (Spring 1988):825-851.
Reviews the history and literature of images of librarians many of which relate sex stereotypes growing out of librarianship being a female intensive profession.

1988-118 Tague, Jean and Roma Harris. "Evolutionaries and Revolutionaries: Careers of Canadian Library Directors." *Canadian Library Journal* 45 (August 1988):236-243.
Interviews with 26 Canadian public, academic, and government librarians about their careers and achievements. Gender differences are noted.

1988-119 "Talkin' 'bout Tenure." *American Libraries* 19 (July/August 1988):624,626.
Announces publication of *Women and Tenure at Albany: A Guide for Faculty* (Albany: SUNY, 1987).

1988-120 Thistlethwaite, Polly. "The NYU Strike: Librarians and Pay Equity for Library Staff." *Women in Libraries* 18 (November/December 1988):6.
Chronicles the strike and discusses the issues.

1988-121 Thistlethwaite, Polly. "The Ways of White Folks." *Women in Libraries* 17 (April 1988):1-2.
Highlights the 1987 preconference on racism sponsored by the American Library Association Social Responsibilities Round Table Feminist Task Force including participants' reactions.

1988-122 Tilley, Christine. "Female Librarianship in Australia." *International Library Review* 20 (October 1, 1988):425-433.
Reports on results of a questionnaire to 42 students to determine career aspirations as a means of studying the reasons for the few women in senior library posts in Australia. Results suggest that a majority of students seek their first promotion within

three years. Suggests implications for library education.

1988-123 Tilley, Christine. "Gender Equality in Librarianship: A Review Article." *Journal of Librarianship* 20 (January 1988):54-59.
Discusses strengths of Gillian Burrington's research (see **1987-26**) as an extension of previous studies and suggests areas for further research.

1988-124 Turner, Philip M. "Recruiting School Library Media Specialists." In *Librarians for the New Millennium*, edited by William E. Moen and Kathleen M. Heim, 47-56. Chicago: American Library Association, Office for Library Personnel Resources, 1988.
Reports results of a national study of supply and demand for these librarian specialists. Notes that the vast majority are female and, the author assumes, married and therefore less mobile. As a result, fewer new positions are available. (See also **1988-73**)

1988-125 deleted

1988-126 U.S. Bureau of Labor Statistics. *Occupational Projections and Training Data: A Statistical and Research Supplement to the 1988-1989 Occupational Outlook Handbook, 1988 edition*, prepared by Alan Eck with the assistance of Sandra Gamliel. Washington, DC: Bureau of Labor Statistics, 1988.
Table A-1 provides data for occupational employment for 1986 and projected for 2000 and selected employee characteristics including sex and part-time status.

1988-127 U.S. Center for Education Statistics. *Digest for Education Statistics 1988*, Thomas D. Snyder, Project Director. Washington, DC: U.S. Department of Education, Office of Educational Research and Improvement, Center for Education Statistics, 1988.
Data for library science degrees conferred by sex, 1984-85.

1988-127a U.S. Center for Education Statistics. *Higher Education Act, Title II-B, FY88 Abstracts, Library Career Training Program*. Washington, DC: U.S. Department of Education, Office of Educational Research and Improvement, Center for Education

Statistics, 1988.

Lists library education grants to assist women, minorities, and the economically disadvantaged.

1988-128 U.S. Center for Education Statistics. *Racial/Ethnic Data for 1984 Fall Enrollment and Earned Degree Recipients for Academic Year 1984-85*. Washington, DC: U.S. Department of Education, Office of Educational Research and Improvement, Center for Education Statistics, 1988.

Tables on degrees conferred includes data by sex.

1988-129 U.S. Library of Congress. *Annual Report of the Librarian of Congress for the Fiscal Year Ending September 30, 1987*. Washington, DC: Government Printing Office, 1988.

Discusses equal employment opportunity programs including activities of the Affirmative Action Office, Women's Program Office, and Equal Employment Opportunity Complaints Office.

1988-130 Van House, Nancy A. "MLS Students' Choice of a Library Career." *Library and Information Science Research* 10 (1988):157-176.

Reports study of library school students' decisions to enter librarianship. Includes possible differences between male and female students that may relate to differences in employment outcomes and satisfaction.

1988-131 Vatanen, Pirjo. "Naiset Kirjastossa [Women in Librarianship]." *Kirjastotiede ja Informatiikka* 7 (1988):56-60.

1988-132 Vlasova, A. "Pomniu, Is Eshche Moloduskoi Byla... [I Remember, I Was Still a Young Woman...]" *Bibliotekar* no. 1 (1988):35.

Relates the story of a woman librarian who established grandmothers' clubs in remote Soviet villages to bring women together for educational and cultural activities and discussions.

1988-133 Walker, Luise E., ed. *Library Statistics of Colleges and Universities in the Pacific Northwest, 1986-1987*. Baker, OR:

Pacific Northwest Library Association, 1988.
   Presents data by institutional categories and includes personnel as a variable, noting the percentage of female/male library directors.

1988-134 Walsh, W. Bruce and Robert E. Huston. "Traditional Female Occupations and Holland's Theory for Employed Men and Women." *Journal of Vocational Behavior* 32 (June 1988):358-365.
   Reports results of the administration of Holland's Vocational Preference Inventory to 75 males and 76 females in three professions: nursing, teaching, and librarianship. Findings suggest that women in the same occupations as men reported similar scores on the social scale as well as the investigative, conventional, enterprising, and artistic scales.

1988-135 White, Herbert S. "Basic Competencies and the Pursuit of Equal Opportunity, Part 2." *Library Journal* 113 (September 15, 1988):62-63.
   Continues his article from *Library Journal*, July 1988. Discusses recruitment of minorities into library science, paralleling it to that of the recruitment of women in doctoral programs.

1988-136 Winter, Michael F. *The Culture and Control of Expertise: Toward a Sociological Understanding of Librarianship.* Contributions in Librarianship and Information Science Series no. 61. New York: Greenwood Press, 1988.
   Notes that feminist historians have suggested that the low social recognition accorded librarians is a result of the entry of large numbers of women into the field but concludes that social recognition develops from an interdependence of traits, not from feminization alone.

Reviews:

Asheim, Lester. *Library Quarterly* 59 (July 1989):264-265.
Awe, Susan. *Special Libraries* 80 (Winter 1989):80.
Carpenter, Raymond L. *Contemporary Sociology* 19 (March 1990): 234-235.
Eaton, E. Gale. *Public Libraries* 28 (March-April 1989):127-128.

Editor. *Journal of Academic Librarianship* 14 (November 1988):109.
Information Retrieval and Library Automation 25 (August 1989):9.
Shiflett, Lee. *RQ* 28 (Summer 1989):584-585.
Stevens, Norman. *Wilson Library Bulletin* 63 (November 1988):109.
Wiegand, Wayne A. *Journal of Academic Librarianship* 15 (July 1989):160-161.

1988-137 *Women and Higher Education in American History: Essays from the Mount Holyoke College Sesquicentennial Symposia*, edited by John Mack Faragher and Florence Howe. New York: W.W. Norton and Co., 1988.

Presents essays from the Mount Holyoke College Sesquicentennial Symposia. (See also **1988-27** and **1988-107**)

Reviews:

Gordon, Lynn D. *American Quarterly* 41 (June 1989):385-390.
History: Reviews of New Books 16 (Summer 1988):156.
McNew, Janet. *Virginia Quarterly Review* 65 (Autumn 1989):742-749.
New Directions for Women 17 (September 1988):19.
Reference & Research Book News 3 (August 1988):20.
Schwager, Sally. *Journal of American History* 76 (March 1990):1280-1281.
Stuttaford, Genevieve. *Publishers Weekly* 233 (April 15, 1988):68.

1988-137a "WLB Conference Summary Award Highlights." *Wilson Library Bulletin* 63 (September 1988):22.

Announces Kathleen Weibel as winner of the ALA Equality Award.

1988-137b *Women in Academe: Progress and Prospects*, edited by Mariam K. Chamberlain. New York: Russell Sage Foundation, 1988.

Discusses library science as a female intensive occupation and the status of employment in the field, degrees awarded, and salaries. Includes statistics on women faculty in library schools, degrees awarded by sex and level of degree, and the percentage of women heading libraries and library schools.

Reviews:

Antler, Joyce. *Journal of American History* 77 (June 1990):371.
Baker, Therese L. *Gender & Society* 4 (June 1990):277-281.
Burgan, Mary. *Change* 22 (April 1990):74-76.
Huber, Bettina J. *Contemporary Sociology* 19 (May 1990):394-395.
Russ, A.J. *Choice* 27 (October 1989):364.

1988-138 "Women's Program Resource Center Opens in the Madison Building." *Library of Congress Information Bulletin* 47 (January 11, 1988):15.
Reports opening of the Center in the Library of Congress.

1988-139 Yoo, Jakyung. "An Exploratory Study of Academic Librarians' Attitudes Toward Computer Technology and Their Relationship to Library Science Education." Ph.D. diss., University of Pittsburgh, 1988.
Results of survey of 190 academic librarians, mostly female and over 40, find they have positive attitudes toward computers. No significant relationship to gender, age, or length of experience was found.

1989 BIBLIOGRAPHY

1989-01 "The 25 Hottest Careers." *Working Woman* 14 (July 1989):67-79.
   Lists special librarianship and describes the special librarian. Notes that fewer students are enrolling in librarianship while retirements increase. Gives salary information.

1989-02 "1988 ARL Annual Salary Survey Issued." *Library Hotline* 18 (March 20, 1989):2.
   Highlights Association of Research Libraries survey, including salary differences between male and female librarians.

1989-03 *1988 Association of Research Libraries Annual Salary Survey: Preliminary Report*, compiled by Gordon Fretwell. Washington, DC: Association of Research Libraries, 1989.
   Includes table on number and average salary by position for men and women.

1989-04 *1988 Salary Survey of Pennsylvania Academic Libraries*, compiled by Gordon Fretwell. Harrisburg, PA: Pennsylvania Library Association, College and Research Libraries Division, 1989.
   Data provided by 93 out of 147 academic libraries include number and average salaries by years of experience, by position, and by sex.

1989-05 "ALA Elections/Endorsements." *Women in Libraries* 18 (February 1989):3.
   Notes candidates for American Library Association offices that have been endorsed by the Feminist Task Force. Also notes search underway for an Executive Director and that an earlier

attempt to find a woman for the position failed.

1989-06 "ALA Midwinter: LAMA Women Administrators Discussion Group." *Women in Libraries* 18 (February 1989):4.
Reports on a meeting of the American Library Association Library Administration and Management Association Women Administrators Discussion Group on the role of mentors. Includes advice to ambitious librarians and to mentors.

1989-06a "ALA Officers & Awards." *Library Journal* 114 (August 1989):54.
Announces Sanford Berman as winner of the ALA Equality Award.

1989-07 "ALA to Sponsor Delegation to Women's Equality March." *Library Journal* 114 (March 1, 1989):11.
Announces sponsorship of a delegation to the March for Women's Equality/Women's Lives by the American Library Association.

Letter:

Perry, Rebecca. "The Right to March?" *Library Journal* 114 (May 15, 1989):6.

Responses:

Abrams, Ann. "Response to Reproductive Rights." *Library Journal* 114 (September 15, 1989):10.
Conkling, Diedre. "ALA and the NOW March." *Library Journal* 114 (October 15, 1989) 6.
Watstein, Sarah Barbara. "The Real Issues for ALA Women." *Library Journal* 114 (October 1, 1989):6.

1989-08 American Library Association. Office for Library Personnel Resources. *Minorities and Women: A List of Major Organizations in Librarianship, 1989-1990*. Chicago: The Office, 1989.
Contains contact persons for women and minority

librarians groups.

1989-09 Anderson, A. J., Joseph Green and Marde Ojala. "What Do I Tell Them?" *Library Journal* 114 (September 15,1989):66-68.
    Case study from the "How Do I Manage?" series concerns a pregnant woman seeking her first library position. Issues discussed include single parenting, financial problems, lack of support systems, and disclosure of pregnancy in a job interview.

Letter:

Cothroll, Victoria. *Library Journal* 115 (February 1, 1990):8.

1989-10 Anderson, Rachael K. "Reinventing the Medical Librarian." *Bulletin of the Medical Library Association* 77 (October 1989):323-331
    Explores factors which have influenced who does or does not become a medical librarian and discusses ways in which the profession should be restructured. Includes a historical discussion of the issue of gender in medical librarianship and its continuing effect.

1989-11 *ARL Annual Salary Survey, 1989*, compiled by Gordon Fretwell. Washington, DC: Association of Research Libraries, 1989.
    Provides distribution of professional staff in ARL libraries by sex and position. Reveals that men's salaries averaged 10.4% higher than their female counterparts except in directorships, where women were paid an average of $1530 more per year.

1989-12 Association of College and Research Libraries. New England Chapter. *1988-89 Salary Survey of New England College Libraries*. Worchester, MA: [The Association], 1989.
    Reports results of annual salary survey of library professionals in four-year undergraduate academic institutions excluding members of the Association of Research Libraries. Provides statistics by sex for salary, position, experience, and minority employment.

1989-13 Auld, Lawrence W.S. "GRE General Test Scores and Grade Point Averages as Predictors of Professional Salaries for Librarians." *Library and Information Science Research* 11 (October-December 1989):369-382.

Examines two sets of data for University of Illinois MLS graduates and found that several high values were found for males and for persons employed in some type of library. Data are analyzed by gender.

1989-13a "Award Highlights." *Wilson Library Bulletin* 64 (September 1989):30.

Announces Sanford Berman as winner of the ALA Equality Award.

1989-14 "Awareness/Content Analysis." *Women in Libraries* 18 (February 1989):2.

Reports on a detailed study to be done of overt and covert sexism and racism in five professional journals. Notes informal monitoring of sexism in library journals by the American Library Association Social Responsibilities Round Table Feminist Task Force.

1989-15 "Bad Tempered Old Lady gets Great Bookshelves at Midwinter." *Library Journal* 114 (March 1, 1989):24.

Notes stereotypical language in an ad that appeared in the *Washington Post* during the ALA Midwinter Conference (1989).

1989-16 Bailey, Brenda. "Reflections on the Profession." *Colorado Libraries* 15 (March 1989):8.

Introductory essay to special issue on professionalism. Comments on librarianship as a predominantly female profession and notes emerging stereotypes.

1989-17 Barroso, Maria Alice. "Librarianship: What Is Happening in Brazil?" *Library Times International* 6 (July 1989):3-4.

Makes reference to librarianship in Brazil as a feminized profession with 96% of librarians being female.

1989-18 Berry, John. "Dear Linda." *Library Journal* 114 (June 15,

1989):4.
Open letter to the three female candidates for the directorship of the American Library Association questioning how being a woman will affect their priorities for the association.

Letter:

Brown, Charles M. *Library Journal* 114 (October 1, 1989):9.

1989-19 Berry, John. "Old Questions for the New Year." *Library Journal* 114 (January 1989): 4.
Highlights the stories *Library Journal* will be watching in 1989 including women, an "issue" that commands editorial attention, particularly in relation to the open position of American Library Association Executive Director.

1989-20 Berry, John, GraceAnne A. DeCandido, and Nora Rawlinson. "The Midwinter of Our Discontent." *Library Journal* 114 (March 1, 1989): 31-38.
Summarizes the 1989 American Library Association Midwinter Meeting including council actions relating to AIDS testing in the workplace, child care, and support for the 1989 March for Women's Equality.

1989-21 Bolton, Sandra Lee. "Librarians and Liberation: A Feminist View." In *Social Responsibility in Librarianship: Essays on Equality*, edited by Donnarae MacCann, 13-30. Jefferson, NC: McFarland, 1989.
Discusses redefining equality to include both sexes; recovering literature by and about women; and revising "traditional, sexist paradigms" in scholarship and communications. Encourages librarians to work to end the silencing of women's voices. (See also **1989-130**)

1989-22 Bryant, Sue Lacey. "A Woman Not in Libraries." *New Library World* 90 (July 1989):126-128.
Bemoans the low pay for librarians and notes the correlation between salaries and the number of women in the profession.

1989-23 Bunge, Charles A. "Stress in the Library Workplace." *Library Trends* 38 (Summer 1989):92-102.
  Notes job stresses that particularly affect women: discrimination, sex-typing of jobs, and child and home care. Suggests that special attention be given to women, particularly in library management, to minimize stress and encourage their use of support systems.

1989-24 Burrington, Gillian A. "Libraries, Employment, and Equal Opportunities." *New Library World* 90 (November 1989):205-208.
  Describes improvements available to women including increased salaries, management responsibilities, and reentry opportunities. Discusses need for devising work patterns to keep women active in librarianship during the child-bearing years.

1989-25 Caldwell, John. "Data Collected from the Private Academic Libraries in Illinois for Academic Year July 1986-June 1987 and Academic Year July 1987-June 1988." *Illinois Libraries* 71 (September 1989):324-333.
  Data from about 50 libraries include statistics on library staffing with breakdown according to gender.

1989-26 Campbell, Saundra. "Children's Services in Public Libraries: Some Areas for Improvement." *Kentucky Libraries* 33 (Summer 1989):8-13.
  Focuses on areas in need of improvement in children's services and comments on women's issues involved in children's services including low status of women and children in society, low pay for those who work with children, and the feminization of the library profession.

1989-27 *Characteristics and Trends of Illinois Public Community College Faculty and Staff, Fall Terms 1986-1988.* Springfield, IL: Illinois Community College Board, 1989. ERIC, ED 307 004
  Tables include statistics on gender by education and length of employment for academic support staff including librarians.

1989-28 Cheatham, Bertha M. "*SLJ* News Report, 1988." In *The Bowker Annual*, 13-23. New York: Bowker, 1989.

Notes the sex discrimination case of Linda R. Silver and Silver's election as president of Ohio Women Librarians.

1989-28a Choi, Jin M. "Learning Styles of Academic Librarians." *College and Research Libraries* 50 (November 1989):691-699.

Reports results of a study of public and technical services librarians using Kolb's Learning Style Inventory. Findings indicate significant differences between the two groups of librarians. Discusses relationship between styles and other variables including sex.

1989-29 Clack, Mary Elizabeth and John Riddick. "The Balance Point: Focus on Women in Serials." *Serials Review* 15 (Winter 1989):53-58.

Comments on the status of women in serials librarianship including views on comparable pay, promotions, men's sensitivity to women's issues, and the "Mommy Track." Assesses progress that has occurred and what remains to be done.

1989-30 Clinefelter, Ruth W. and Jack E. Hibbs. "The Neglected Information Specialist." *Academe* 75 (July-August 1989):26-30.

Discusses the continuing problem of lower pay and status for academic librarians in comparison with teaching faculty due to lack of recognition of librarians' contributions to the educational and research mission of colleges and universities. Explores historical roots for this practice.

1989-31 Coats, Patricia Boyne and Steven Overman. *Childhood Antecedents of Achievements in Professional Women.* Paper presented at the Annual Meeting of the Mid-South Educational Research Association, Little Rock, AR, 9-10 November 1989. ERIC, ED 312 588

Examines childhood preferences for play activities of women in traditional and nontraditional professions to assess its impact on career choice. Names librarianship as a traditional women's profession.

1989-32 Cravey, Pamela Jean Bristow. "The Occupational Role Identity and Occupational Role Image of Female Librarians in

Four Traditional Subspecialties of Librarianship." Ph.D. diss., Georgia State University, 1989.

Reports results of survey of 826 female librarians representing equally the subspecialties of academic, public, school, and special librarianship. Finds that librarians were satisfied with their careers, except for the pay, and had excellent occupational self-images. Professional associations are criticized for not showing more librarians in their publications and not showing an image reflecting the occupational role identity of practitioners.

1989-33 "Dallas '89 Report on FTF Meetings." *Women in Libraries* 19 (November 1989):2.

Reports progress on *SHARE Directory*; programming at Midwinter and Annual conferences; changes in *Women in Libraries*; the status of sexism in library journals; the task force's position on Margaret Randall; election results; and the retirement of Feminist Task Force member Betty-Carol Sellen.

1989-34 Davis, Donald G. and John Mark Tucker. "Women in Librarianship." In *American Library History: A Comprehensive Guide to the Literature*, 275-280. Santa Barbara, CA: ABC-CLIO, 1989.

Contains bibliographic essay and bibliography of key sources for researching the history of women librarians.

1989-35 DeCandido, GraceAnne A. "Academic Librarians Do-Have-Try It All: ACRL in Cincinnati." *Library Journal* 114 (May 15, 1989):17.

Notes presentation by Ellen Broidy on women's studies and feminist approaches to bibliographic instruction.

1989-36 DeCandido, GraceAnne A. "ACRL Conference Tackles Digital Info, Education, Power and Post-Feminism." *Library Journal* 114 (May 1, 1989):16.

Includes summary of Mary Anne Dolan's argument that feminism has failed in the workplace and notes reactors' comments. Sarah Pritchard is characterized as the "most impressive" reactor.

1989-37 DeCandido, GraceAnne A. "Alarums and Diversions." *Library Journal* 114 (February 15, 1989):114.

Bemoans scheduling conflicts at American Library Association conferences, particularly of women's groups.

1989-38 DeCandido, GraceAnne A. "Alarums and Diversions." *Library Journal* 114 (November 15, 1989):25.

Briefly notes that some female librarians from a midwestern academic library have formed a social group which goes out on Tuesday evenings as an antidote to "midweek blahs."

1989-39 DeCandido, GraceAnne A. "Library Directions in 1988." *Library Journal* 114 (January 1989):49-55.

Highlights key issues in 1988, noting that women's issues "remain of deep, pressing, and personal concern." Questions if openings at the New York Public Library, the American Library Association, and the Library of Congress will be filled by women.

1989-40 DeCandido, GraceAnne A. "*LJ* News Report, 1988." In *The Bowker Annual*, 3-13. New York: Bowker, 1989.

Notes author's concern for women's issues and the current vacancies for chief executives--will they be filled by women?

1989-41 DeCandido, GraceAnne A. "Nancy Evans on Mentoring: Permission to Be Yourself." *Conference Daily* (June 26, 1989):1.

Summarizes a program sponsored by Visionary Leaders for 2020 and the American Library Association Junior Members Round Table. Evans comments that family concerns are not, nor should they be, only a problem for women.

1989-42 DeCandido, GraceAnne A. and Michael Rogers. "Change in the City." *Library Journal* 114 (August 1989):57-62.

Reports on the Special Libraries Association Conference, June 1989, including coverage of the Women's Issues Caucus discussion on child care and the results of a survey on the image of the librarian.

1989-43 DeCandido, GraceAnne A. and Michael Rogers. "The First Woman: Linda Crismond Named Executive Director, ALA."

Library Journal 114 (July 1989):14,17.
   Feature on Crismond discusses her position in terms of feminism and the advocacy of a feminist agenda.

1989-44 "Directory of Gay and Lesbian Library Workers." *GLTF Newsletter* 2 (Fall/Winter 1989):3-4.
   Announces decision by the American Library Association Gay and Lesbian Task Force to compile and publish a directory. Includes discussion of the need and potential uses for the directory.

1989-45 Donovan, Mary. *Sex Discrimination in Higher Education and the Professions: An Annotated Bibliography*. New York: National Center for the Study of Collective Bargaining in Higher Education and the Professions, Baruch College, the City College of New York, 1989. ERIC, ED 310 693
   Includes a few citations concerning librarianship.

1989-46 Duda, Frederick. "Compensation Management." In *Personnel Administration in Libraries*, edited by Sheila Creth and Frederick Duda, 2nd ed., 221-246. New York: Neal-Schuman, 1989.
   Discusses equal pay and comparable worth in the context of developing compensation systems. (See also **1989-112**)

1989-47 Duda, Frederick. "Developing Compensation Systems in Academic Libraries." *Library Trends* 38 (Summer 1989):103-126.
   Provides an introduction to the personnel specialty of compensation and discusses external factors which influence compensation. Notes that the American Library Association, representing a female intensive profession, supports equal pay and comparable worth.

1989-48 DuMont, Paul F. and Rosemary Ruhig DuMont. "The Information Professional and the New Technology: An Investigation of Possible Differential Responses by Gender." *Library Trends* 37 (Spring 1989):510-520.
   Results of a pilot study suggest that attitude toward technology is not a factor in the gender imbalance in library management positions.

1989-49 Eisenberg, Michael. "Trends in Library and Information Science, 1989." *ERIC Digest*. Syracuse, NY: ERIC Clearinghouse on Information Resources, 1989. ERIC, ED 308 884

Content analysis of library literature discusses trends including status and image of librarians as a major concern for the profession.

1989-50 "Facts About Libraries and Librarians." *Library Hotline* 18 (July 10, 1989): 6.

Highlights facts prepared by the American Library Association Public Information Office including percentage of the profession that is female.

1989-51 Feye-Stukas, Janice. "Pay Equity in Minnesota." In *The ALA Yearbook of Library and Information Services*, v. 14, 250-252. Chicago: American Library Association, 1989.

Reviews pay equity cases for public employees, including library personnel.

1989-52 Fimian, Michael J., Sandra A. Benedict, and Stacie Johnson. "The Measure of Occupational Stress and Burnout Among Library Media Specialists." *Library and Information Science Research* 11 (January-March 1989):3-19.

Presents the development of the Media Specialist Stress Inventory and results of one survey which received 97% of the usable replies from women. None of the factors are analyzed by gender.

1989-53 "For Women Librarians." *Library Journal* 114 (May 1, 1989): 60.

Announces publication edited by Katharine Phenix of *Directory of Library and Information Professions Women's Groups*. (See **1988-38**)

1989-54 Freedman, Janet. *Information for Transformation: The Perspective of a Library Director*. Paper presented at the National Women's Studies Association Conference, June 1989. ERIC, ED 315 100

Explores current and future roles of feminist librarians

and urges librarians to make the "study of information" part of the discourse in their libraries and in their work with women's studies programs on their campuses. (See also **1991-34**)

1989-55 "FTF Cosponsors ALA Programming in 1989." *Women in Libraries* 18 (June 1989):2-3.
   Lists programs, events, and meetings of the American Library Association Social Responsibilities Round Table Feminist Task Force.

1989-56 Gasaway, Laura N. and Barbara B. Moran. "The Legal Environment." In *Personnel Administration in Libraries* edited by Sheila Creth and Frederick Duda, 2nd ed., 13-39. New York: Neal-Schuman, 1989.
   Reviews law and legislation regarding equal employment opportunity, affirmative action, sexual harassment, and pregnancy/maternity. (See also **1989-112**)

1989-57 "Gender Issues (and More) in Dallas." *Library Journal* 114 (August 1989):52-53.
   Reviews American Library Association programs and actions taken relating to women during the 1989 Annual Conference.

1989-58 Granger, Dorothy. "The Presidency." *Women in Libraries* 19 (November 1989):1-2.
   Excerpts from interviews with ALA presidential candidates Richard Dougherty and Rebecca Bingham. Observes that while "both are highly qualified, in this organization of women it is interesting to continue to watch the positions of power and authority go to men."

1989-59 Gregory, Pamela. "Women in Libraries--A Bibliography About Gender and Salaries." *Law Library Lights* 35 (May/June 1989):5-6.
   Lists survey articles containing statistics on the differences in salaries, mobility, and career advancement of men and women in librarianship from 1976 to date. (See also **1989-60**)

1989-60 Gregory, Pamela. "Women in Libraries--A Bibliography About Gender and Salaries." *Women in Libraries* 19 (December 1989):3-4.
    Lists survey articles containing statistics on the differences in salaries, mobility, and career advancement of men and women in librarianship. Reprint of **1989-59**.

1989-61 Gunn, Arthur C. "A Black Woman Wants to Be a Professional..." *American Libraries* 20 (February 1989):154-157.
    History of first African-American woman to complete a professional education program in librarianship.

1989-62 Harragan, Betty Lehan. "Dear Betty Harragan." *Working Woman* 14 (April 1989):49-50.
    Response to woman librarian trapped on a career plateau. Notes that while librarianship is a women-dominated profession, plateauing itself is not discriminatory. Suggests cooperating with others in the workplace to improve structure.

1989-63 deleted

1989-64 Harris, Roma M. and Jean M. Tague. "Reaching the Top in Canadian Librarianship: A Biographical Study of Sex Differences in Career Development." *Library Quarterly* 59 (April 1989):116-130.
    Study conducted by intensive biographical interviews with male and female directors of academic, government, and large public library systems across Canada about their careers. Results reveal number of differences in career paths followed by men and women prior to their appointments as directors.

1989-65 Hegvik, Robin L. "Study Reports Librarians are Victims of Sex Bias." *National Law Journal* 11 (June 19, 1989):17.
    Reports results of study by the American Association of Law Librarians to determine personnel policies, library collections, and salaries of private law libraries. Indicates disparities between men and women in compensation with the greatest differences appearing at the highest ranges of salary, particularly at the director's level. Provides information about maternity leave

policies at law firms.

1989-65a Heim, Kathleen M. and William E. Moen. *Occupational Entry: Library and Information Science Students' Attitudes, Demographics, and Aspirations Survey*. Chicago: American Library Association, Office of Library Personnel Resources, 1989.

Includes data by gender for enrollment, ethnicity, age, family status, majors, degrees, and work attitudes.

Reviews:

Brown, Lorene B. *RQ* 29 (Spring 1990):471-472.
Carpenter, Kathryn Hammell. *Library Journal* 115 (February 15, 1990):217.
DeScossa, C. *Canadian Library Journal* 47 (June 1990):216.

1989-66 "Her Own Name." *Women in Libraries* 18 (February 1989):5.

Reports that a Japanese professor of library science is suing the government to allow her to use her maiden name professionally.

1989-67 Higginbothan, Barbara. "Why Children's Jobs Go Begging." [letter] *American Libraries* 20 (January 1989): 27.

Response to J.C. Bennett's contention that there is not a shortage of librarians (*American Libraries*, September 1988, 724-725). Highlights limitations which school and children's library positions place on women interested in career advancement.

1989-67a Higley, Georgia Metos. "The Land Grant College Movement and Western Libraries: Women Librarians at Selected Land Grant Institutions." M.S.L.S. thesis, University of North Carolina, 1989.

Reviews activities and contributions of women librarians at the University of Arizona, Colorado Agricultural College, Agricultural College of New Mexico, and Agricultural College of Utah. Focuses particularly on the work of Ida Kidder, Charlotte Baker, and Estelle Lutrell.

1989-68 Hildenbrand, Suzanne. "The Crisis in Cataloging: A Feminist Hypothesis." In *Recruiting, Educating, and Training Cataloging Librarians*, edited by Sheila Intner, 207-225. Westport, CT: Greenwood Press, 1989.

Discusses the relationship between recruitment of librarians into cataloging and the low status and earnings of librarians as members of a female intensive occupation. Reviews the literature and calls for data collection and analysis to document the status of catalogers. (See also **1989-119**)

1989-69 Hildenbrand, Suzanne. "'Women's Work' Within Librarianship: Time to Expand the Feminist Agenda." *Library Journal* 114 (September 1, 1989):153-155.

Discusses the status of women in children's librarianship and cataloging as examples of areas in which great inequities still exist in the profession.

Letter:

Kirkland, Janice. "End Female-Intensive Specialities." *Library Journal* 114 (November 15, 1989):8.

Summary:

"Feminism in Libraries." *Library Currents* 7 (January 1990):1.

1989-70 Holley, Edward G. "ACRL's Fiftieth Anniversary: For Reflection, for Celebration, and for Anticipation." *College and Research Libraries* 50 (January 1989):11-24.

Includes review of leadership positions which women and minorities have held in the 50 years of the association.

1989-71 Imroth [sic], Barbara. "Empowering Women as Information Seekers and Information Providers in the United States: Actions Taken." In *Women and the Power of Managing Information*, 15-19. Melbourne, Victoria, Australia: Status of Women in Librarianship, 1989.

Highlights achievements of the American Library Association's Committee on the Status of Women in Librarianship.

(See also **1989-156**)

1989-72 "Incoming SLA President Sets Agenda." *Library Hotline* 18 (June 19 1989):2
   Includes Special Libraries Association President-elect Muriel M. Regan's comments that "the public perception of a librarian's work and our collective self-image" are areas of concern as are empowerment and leadership.

1989-73 Klingberg, Susan. "Book Review Essay: Against All Odds--The Status of Women in Higher Education," *College and Research Libraries* 50 (September 1989):587-594.
   Notes that women academic librarians have relatively low status in comparison to male colleagues and that in academe women have been tracked into traditionally female areas such as libraries.

1989-74 Kniffel, Leonard. "First Woman to Serve as ALA Executive Director--Linda Crismond Envisions 'The Association of the World.'" *American Libraries* 20 (July-August 1989):622-623.
   Highlights statements made by Crismond concerning her management style, her plans and vision for the organization, and her thoughts on the profession itself.

1989-75 Latham, Joyce M. "What Are We Coming To?" [letter] *Library Journal* 114 (October 1, 1989):9.
   Pokes fun at the current diversity in the profession and pleads, "Gimme a pinchy-nosed, tight-bunned, tight- (ahem...), lip-shusher anyday...."

1989-76 *Leadership in the Library/Information Profession*, edited by Alice Gertzog. Jefferson, NC: McFarland, 1989.
   Presents proceedings of the 26th Annual Symposium of the Graduate Alumni and Faculty of The Rutgers School of Communication, Information and Library Studies, 8 April 1988. (See also **1989-96**)

Reviews:

Editors. *Journal of Academic Librarianship* 15 (November 1989):303.
Magnuson, Nancy. *Library Journal* 114 (October 1, 1989):123.
Reference & Research Book News 4 (October 1989):38.
Rogerson, Holly. *American Libraries* 20 (November 1989):995.
Stevens, Norman. *Wilson Library Bulletin* 64 (October 1989):120-121.
Williams, Robert V. *Special Libraries* 81 (Spring 1990):164.

1989-77 Learmont, Carol L. and Stephen Van Houten. "Placements and Salaries 1988: The Demand Increases." *Library Journal* 114 (October 15, 1989):37-44.

Includes data by sex on employment status, placements, and salary.

Letter:

Cowling, Charles V. *Library Journal* 115 (January 1990):14.

1989-78 Learmont, Carol and Stephen Van Houten. "Placements and Salaries, 1987: The Upswing Continues." In *The Bowker Annual*, 310-327. New York: Bowker, 1989.

Provides data on salaries, cross-tabulated by type of library, and placements by type of position by sex.

1989-78a Lee, Frank. "Lillian Moore Bradshaw and the Dallas Public Library: 'From the Innocent Voyage to the Razor's Edge.'" Ph.D. diss., Texas Woman's University, 1989.

Traces the career of Bradshaw and her impact on public libraries based on interviews with her. (See also **1991-64**)

1989-79 Levy, Claudia. "Montgomery Grants 5% Raises in Move Against Race, Sex Bias." *The Washington Post*, 15 February 1989, sec. 1, p. 1.

Concerns increase to 2900 county workers including librarians. Librarians are granted raises, in part, because they have to deal with "deinstitutionalized" people and "latchkey children" in additional to regular responsibilities.

1989-80 *Library and Information Science Education Statistical Report 1989*, edited by Timothy W. Sineath. Sarasota, FL: Association for Library and Information Science Education, 1989.

Survey of faculty at ALA-accredited library schools includes data by sex on rank, new appointments, and salaries.

1989-81 "Library Women's Groups." *Women in Libraries* 18 (February 1989):6.

Announces the publication of *Directory of Library and Information Professions Women's Groups,* edited by Katharine Phenix. (See **1988-38**)

1989-82 Looker, E. Dianne and Karen L. McNutt. "The Effect of Occupational Expectations on the Educational Attainments of Males and Females." *Canadian Journal of Education* 14 (1989):352-367.

Notes that traditionally female occupations such as library science are requiring more education which encourages more women to enroll in universities.

1989-83 Louw, Anna. "Women in Managerial Positions in the Library and Information Services of South Africa." *South African Journal of Library and Information Science* 57 (September 1989):305-309.

Reviews the status of women in management in South African libraries. Includes statistics on numbers of men and women holding administrative posts in all types of libraries; earned degrees; and publishing output.

1989-84 "Managing Diversity." *Library Personnel News* 3 (Fall 1989):60-61.

Summarizes an address to the Human Resources Management Association of Chicago, January 1989, by Dr. R. Roosevelt Thompson, Jr., regarding the status of females and minorities in the workforce.

1989-85 Marquis, Kathy. "Fifteenth Anniversary Party: Committee on the Status of Women--Smashing Success." *SAA Newsletter* 11 (September 1989):2,3.

Summarizes activities and describes program "Women in Archives: Three Generations Speak Out."

1989-86 Marquis, Kathy. "SOWC SAA Session: Gender Dynamics in the Workplace." *SAA Newsletter* 11 (September 1989):3.

Highlights workshop which outlined traditional areas of tension between men and women in the workplace and discussed extent to which these problems are present in the archival profession.

1989-87 McCombs, Gillian. "Library Leadership: Some Lessons from Nancy Drew." *Wilson Library Bulletin* 63 (January 1989):60-63.

Relates how the positive attitudes portrayed in the Nancy Drew series can be applied to improving the self-image of female librarians and of the library profession itself.

1989-88 McCulloch, Deborah. "Women, Librarians and the Power of Information." In *Women and the Power of Managing Information*, 5-14. Melbourne, Victoria, Australia: Status of Women in Librarianship, 1989.

Discusses the status of women in Australian society including a summary of conditions of women librarians. (See also **1989-156**)

1989-89 McGrath, Lynnley. "Women, Information and Bureaucracy." In *Women and the Power of Managing Information*, 20-25. Melbourne, Victoria, Australia: Status of Women in Librarianship, 1989.

Discusses the establishment of the Women's Information and Referral Exchange in Australia and the pros and cons of a women's service agency within a government service bureaucracy. Notes the value of women providing services to and for women. (See also **1989-156**)

1989-90 Mech, Terrence. "Public Library Directors: A Career and Managerial Profile." *Public Libraries* 28 (July-August 1989):228-235.

Reports results of survey of 217 public library directors in medium-sized libraries in the northeast. Confirms that gender-based career patterns exist, with women tending to head smaller libraries, to be internally appointed, and to receive their first directorships later than men. Notes an increase in the number of female directors.

1989-91 "Meeting Report of the Committee on the Status of Women." *SAA Newsletter* 11 (September 1989):1,2.
Discusses poor attendance at 1988 workshop "Image and Self-Projection: Women in Management" and attributes low turnout to scheduling and narrow scope.

1989-92 "Men Still Rule in City Government." *U.S. News and World Report* 107 (October 8, 1989):81.
Chart of 15 jobs in city government shows that the librarian is female in 79.2% of cases studied. Premise of the report is that although 24% of top city officials are female, their ranks have increased only 2% since 1986. Reprinted in: *Library Hotline* 18:45 (November 13, 1989): 3.

1989-93 Metz, Paul. "A Statistical Profile of *College and Research Libraries*." *College and Research Libraries* 50 (January 1989): 42-47.
Provides data on sex of authors published in the journal.

1989-94 Miccioli, Gloria. "Reflections of a . . . Librarian." *Law Library Lights* 35 (May/June 1989):1,3.
Explores the stereotypical image of librarians and image problems in the profession. Notes that the fact that the profession is female intensive "seems to be the kiss of death as far as professional respect is concerned." Suggestions are made for convincing others that librarianship is a profession.

1989-95 "Midwinter Council Resolutions." *Women in Libraries* 18 (February 1989):3.
Notes resolutions passed that are of concern to feminist librarians.

1989-96 Mobley, Emily R. "Women and Minorities as Leaders." In *Leadership in the Library/Information Profession*, edited by Alice

Gertzog, 43-50. Jefferson, NC: McFarland, 1989.
Discusses absence of women and minorities in literature on leadership personality traits and statistics on leadership positions. Stresses the importance of mentoring and risk-taking. (See also **1989-76**)

1989-97 "Monitor Your Opportunities." *New Library World* 90 (June 1989):103-105.
Reports male/female ratio of Library Association Council members, councillors, and chairs and invites readers to draw conclusions.

1989-98 Moran, Barbara B. "Getting Ahead in Academic Library Administration." *Library Personnel News* 3 (Fall 1989):54-55.
Reviews research on career patterns of academic library administrators and reports on a recent study that replicates research from 1981. Study attempts to determine whether career progression patterns of men and women would be more similar now than in the past. Results indicate that major changes have occurred which benefit women.

1989-99 Moran, Barbara B. "A Reexamination of the Career Patterns of Academic Library Administrators." In *Building on the First Century: Proceedings of the Fifth National Conference of the Association of College and Research Libraries*, 276-280. Chicago: Association of College and Research Libraries, 1989.
Reports on replication of 1981 study of the personal and professional characteristics of administrators to assess their success in attaining directorships. Significant changes in results include a finding that many variables which were associated with success for men in the first study were found to contribute to the success of both sexes in the second study (e.g., educational level, professional activities). Also concludes that women's career paths have changed from promotion from within to reaching directorships as an external candidate.

1989-100 Moran, Barbara B. "The Unintended Revolution in Academic Libraries: 1939 to 1989 and Beyond." *College and Research Libraries* 50 (January 1989):25-41.

Traces the development of academic libraries including statistics on the numbers of female librarians and female library administrators.

1989-101 Morgan, Paul. "Frances Wolfreston and 'Hor Bouks': A Seventeenth-Century Woman Book-Collector." *The Library* Sixth Series 11 (September 1989):197-219.

Chronicles the life and collections of Wolfreston. Notes that few records of bookwomen survive.

1989-102 Newcomer, Audrey Powderly and Robert A. Pisciotta. "Career Progression of Academic Medical Library Directors." *Bulletin of the Medical Library Association* 7 (April 1989):185-195.

Looks at how career progression, based on the criteria of record of publishing, professional activity, acquisition of credentials, and geographic mobility, was influenced by gender. Results address specific issues of proportions of male and female medical librarians, career paths of male and female directors, and differences between male and female medical library directors in respect to other professional characteristics.

1989-103 Nicolle, Ray. "Boys and the Five-Year Void." *School Library Journal* 35 (March 1989):130.

Expresses the viewpoint that libraries have no suitable literature for boys ages seven to twelve because most librarians are female or gay, incompetent, and censorious. This commentary prompted over 40 letters to the editor which appear in the May to December 1989 issues of *School Library Journal*. (See also **1990-56a**)

Responses:

"Backtalk." *Emergency Librarian* 17 (September-October 1989):78.
Gerhardt, Lillian N. "Opinion Publishing." *School Library Journal* 35 (May 1989):4
Robbins, Robert J. "Hens' Teeth and Other Nonsense." *School Library Journal* 35 (June 1989):57.

1989-104 Norman, Nita Vegamora. "Women: Information Providers to the Non-Library User." In *Women and the Power of Managing Information*, 25-31. Melbourne, Victoria, Australia: Status of Women in Librarianship, 1989.

Discusses contributions of women who have provided information to U.S. inner city residents, providing some demographic and biographical data of public librarians involved. (See also **1989-156**)

1989-105 *On Account of Sex: An Annotated Bibliography on the Status of Women in Librarianship, 1982-1986*, edited by Katharine Phenix et al. for the Committee on the Status of Women in Librarianship. Chicago: American Library Association, 1989.

Reviews:

Abbott, L.M.C. *Choice* 28 (December 1990):613.
Carpenter, Kathryn Hammell. *Journal of Academic Librarianship* 16 (September 1990):258.
Carpenter, Kathryn Hammell. *Library Journal* 115 (June 15, 1990):142.
Coughlin, Caroline M. *Journal of Academic Librarianship* 17 (March 1991):33.
Coughlin, Caroline M. *Journal of Academic Librarianship* 17 (May 1991):121. [A digest of the March review]
Harmon, Charles. *Booklist* 86 (July 1990):2068.
Mahmoud, Donna Seyed. *Canadian Library Journal* 47 (October 1990):365.
Mahmoud, Donna Seyed. *Journal of Academic Librarianship* 16 (January 1991):387.
Pastine, Maureen. *American Reference Books Annual* (1991):365-366.

1989-106 Para, A. "Thanks for the Invitation." *Colorado Libraries* 15 (March 1989):12-13.

Written by a paraprofessional cataloger on the paraprofessional's place in librarianship. Notes that the profession is dominated by women who are generally low paid and low status.

Comments that paraprofessionals are often overeducated and underpaid and that university libraries take advantage of faculty spouses, especially wives, to fill paraprofessional jobs.

1989-107 Parker, Sandra. "Equal Opportunities and the LA." [letter] *New Library World* 90 (March 1989):45-46.

Notes failure of the Library Association Council to budget for the implementation of the Equal Opportunities Policy passed in 1987 and urges readers to write her.

Response:

Barnes, Melvyn. "Equal Opportunities and the LA." *New Library World* 90 (May 1989):92-93.

1989-108 Pasca, T. M. "The Woman in the Reserved Seat." *Wilson Library Bulletin* 63 (January 1989): 10.

Protests the censorship of the author's recent article (*Wilson Library Bulletin*, November 1988, 72-73) because of what the editor decided was "sexism."

1989-109 *Pay Equity: An Action Manual for Library Workers*, Carolyn Kenady, Project Director. Chicago: American Library Association, 1989.

Covers organizing for pay equity, identifying sex-based wage discrimination, and job evaluation and illustrates how libraries have achieved pay equity.

Reviews:

Foster, Connie. *Journal of Academic Librarianship* 16 (May 1990):106.
Moscatt, Angeline. *Library Journal* 114 (October 1, 1989):123.
Rogerson, Holly. *American Libraries* 20 (October 1989):905.

1989-110 Peattie, Noel. *A Passage for Dissent: The Best of Sipapu, 1970-1988.* Jefferson, NC: McFarland, 1989.

Reprints several articles of interest from *Sipapu*, an

alternative library newsletter, including interviews with several women: Jackie Eubanks, Carole Leita, and Nancy Osborne.

Reviews:

Bate, J. *Library Review* 39 (1990):67.
Editors. *Journal of Academic Librarianship* 15 (September 1989):245.
JQ: Journalism Quarterly 66 (Winter 1989):1014.
Pendergrast, Mark. *Library Journal* 114 (July 1989):114.
Rogerson, Holly. *American Libraries* 20 (December 1989):1099.
Stevens, Norman D. *Wilson Library Bulletin* 64 (September 1989):118-119.

1989-111 "Pennsylvania LA Publishes 88-89 Academic Librarian Salary Poll." *Library Journal* 114 (September 15, 1989):22.
    Highlights Pennsylvania academic library survey, including salary differences between women and men.

1989-112 *Personnel Administration in Libraries*, edited by Sheila Creth and Frederick Duda. 2nd ed. New York: Neal-Schuman, 1989.
    Provides overview of various issues and practices in personnel management for libraries. (See also **1989-46** and **1989-56**)

Reviews:

Dewey, Patrick. *Booklist* 86 (January 1, 1990):888.
Jaffe, Martin Elliot. *RQ* 29 (Summer 1990):613.
Painter, Frances O. *Journal of Academic Librarianship* 16 (May 1990):107.

1989-113 Peterson, Sandra K. "Women in Librarianship." In *The ALA Yearbook of Library and Information Services '89*, 249, 252-254. Chicago: American Library Association, 1989.
    Summarizes salary surveys, reviews pay equity cases, and discusses the 1988 ALISE report on accredited graduate programs.

1989-114 "Placement of Graduates, 1988." *Library Hotline* 18 (July 30, 1989):4.

    Highlights survey of the 1988 graduates of Southern Connecticut State University School of Library Science and Instructional Technology, including average salaries for men and women.

1989-115 Pritchard, Sarah M. "The Impact of Feminism on Women in the Profession." *Library Journal* 114 (August 1989):76-77.

    Remarks delivered at the Association of College and Research Libraries National Conference, Cincinnati, Ohio, April 1989, responding to Mary Anne Dolan, syndicated columnist and broadcast commentator.

Letter:

Maller, Mark. "Too Much Feminism." *Library Journal* 114 (November 1, 1989):6-8.

1989-116 "Programming for Dallas 1989." *Women in Libraries* 18 (February 1989):4.

    Highlights programs of interest to feminist librarians at the American Library Association annual conference.

1989-117 Pyatt, Sherman E., Josephine B. Williamson and Edgar Williamson. "Faculty Status in South Carolina." *College and Research Libraries News* 50 (November 1989):927-933.

    Reports results of survey of academic librarians' attitudes toward faculty status in the state, including statistics on publishing patterns by sex.

1989-118 Rawlinson, Nora. "When Will They Ever Learn?" *Library Journal* 114 (August 1989):116.

    Bemoans an advertisement in the July 14, 1989 issue of *Publishers Weekly* which stereotypically presents a librarian.

1989-119 *Recruiting, Educating, and Training Cataloging Librarians*, edited by Sheila Intner. Westport, CT: Greenwood Press, 1989.

    Presents papers from the Simmons College Symposium on

Recruiting, Educating, and Training Cataloging Librarians. (See also **1989-68**)

Reviews:

Hastreiter, J. *Collection Management* 13 (1990):185-186.
Morris, A. *Library Association Record* 91 (October 1989):605.
Quoika-Stanka, W. *Canadian Library Journal* 46 (December 1989):407-408.
Reynolds, Sally Jo. *Library Quarterly* 60 (January 1990):79-81.
Seely, Edward. *Journal of Library and Information Science* 16 (April 1990):117-119.
Soper, Mary Ellen. *Libraries & Culture* 27 (Winter 1992):103-104.
Stevens, Norman D. *Wilson Library Bulletin* 63 (June 1989):112-113.
Tolson, Stephanie D. *Library Journal* 114 (June 15, 1989):85.
Whittick, M.H. *Journal of Documentation* 45 (December 1989):345-347.

1989-120 Rubin, Richard. "Employee Turnover Among Full-Time Public Librarians." *Library Quarterly* 59 (January 1989):27-45.

Study examines turnover in 31 public libraries in the Midwest and emphasizes the relationship of gender to turnover behavior.

1989-121 "Salary Update." *Library Personnel News* 3 (Spring 1989):29.

Cites salary information from recent issues of *College and Research Libraries News* and *American Libraries* and from the Association of Research Libraries.

1989-122 Schell, B. and L. Bonin. "Factors Affecting Censorship by Canadian Librarians." *Journal of Psychology* 123 (July 1989):357-367.

Study found no statistical difference between male and female librarians. Analyses of survey results indicate that librarians were "liberal in attitude but conservative in behavior with respect to censorship and book selection."

1989-123 Searing, Susan. "Quiet Revolution." *Women's Review of Books* 6 (February 1989):19-21.

Discusses the role of librarians in the advent of women's studies programs and the vested interest female librarians, as members of a female intensive profession, have to further women's studies research.

1989-124 Selsky, Deborah. "Increasing Educational Attainment Levels Good News for Librarians." *Library Journal* 114 (October 1, 1989):30.

Notes that recent surveys indicate that the most frequent readers, library users, and book buyers are college-educated women and discusses the impact of gender and educational attainment on book buying and readership.

1989-125 Selsky, Deborah. "Library Salaries: Substantial Gains Expected in 1989." *Library Journal* 114 (October 15, 1989):26,28.

Reports on 1989 Public Library Salary Survey conducted by *Library Journal*. Includes data by sex for salaries by job title, library size, and regional location.

1989-126 "Sexual Harassment Leaflet." *Women in Libraries* 18 (February 1989):6.

Mentions availability of the publication, "Sexual Harassment in the Workplace," which defines harassment, its effects, and action steps.

1989-127 Shah, Shaila. "Whatever Happened at the Lesbian Archive?" *Spare Rib* 119 (March 1989):17.

Reports internal management disputes over censorship and racism with the Archive's collective and the resulting negotiations and reorganization.

1989-128 "*SHARE Directory*." *Women in Libraries* 18 (February 1989):2.

Announces that a new edition of the *SHARE Directory*, a guide to feminist librarians, has reached the planning stages.

1989-129 Silver, Linda R. *Partial Answers to Persistent Problems: Economic Perspectives on Occupational Sex Segregation and the Wage Gap*. OWL Research Report #5. Northfield, OH: Ohio Women Librarians, 1989.
    Reviews the literature on economic perspectives and trends on occupational sex segregation and includes data on women in the labor force and on the wage gap. Discusses three economic theories (neoclassical, institutional, and radical) as they apply to occupational sex segregation.

1989-130 *Social Responsibility in Librarianship: Essays on Equality*, edited by Donnarae MacCann. Jefferson, NC: McFarland, 1989.
    Offers essays on the role of librarians in social action. (See also **1989-21**)

Reviews:

Barber, Gary D. *Journal of Academic Librarianship* 16 (September 1990):234.
Editors. *Journal of Academic Librarianship* 16 (March 1990):61.
Harmon, Charles. *American Libraries* 21 (February 1990):143.
Harmon, Charles. *Booklist* 86 (January 1, 1990):891.
Ney, Neal J. *Library Quarterly* 60 (October 1990):380-381.
Peattie, Noel. *Sipapu* 20 (Summer 1990):10-11.
Reference & Research Book News 5 (April 1990):39.
Sanders, Lou Helen Devine. *RQ* 30 (Fall 1990):152.

1989-131 Sokoloff, Natalie J. "Are Professions Becoming Desegregated? An Analysis of Detailed Professional Occupations by Race and Gender." Paper given at American Sociological Association, 1989.
    Notes that black women increased their numbers in librarianship as well as in other female professions.

1989-132 Special Libraries Association. *The Triennial Salary Survey*. Washington, DC: Special Libraries Association, 1989.
    Includes data by sex for special librarians and information specialists.

1989-133 Stevens, Norman. "Cats and Dogs in the American Public Library: A Hidden Aspect of the Feminization of the Profession." *Wilson Library Bulletin* 63 (June 1989):42-45.
   Discusses the relationship among cats, librarians, and libraries. Concludes that this relationship provides evidence that librarianship is essentially a feminine profession.

1989-134 Stevens, Norman. "Introduction." *Wilson Library Bulletin* 63 (June 1989):26-27.
   Discusses librarian's self-image and the female stereotype.

1989-135 Stone, Elizabeth W. and Jean L. Preer. "Empowerment for Libraries and Literacy: A General Federation of Women's Clubs Tradition." *Public Libraries* 28 (September-October 1989):296-299.
   Traces role of women's clubs in the development of public libraries and in the obtaining of federal monies.

1989-136 "SUNY Buffalo Calls for Papers on Women in American Libraries." *Library Journal* 114 (December 1989):34.
   Notes call for contributions on women of color, women library founders, women patrons, and library workers by Suzanne Hildenbrand of the State University of New York at Buffalo School of Information and Library Studies.

1989-137 Tainton, Madeleine. "March on Washington." *Women in Libraries* 18 (February 1989):1,2.
   Reports highlights of the April 9, 1989, march to support women's rights and reproductive choice and notes the American Library Association's participation.

1989-138 Tate, Thelma. "The Status of Women as Providers of Information: An International Perspective." In *Women and the Power of Managing Information*, 31-35. Melbourne, Victoria, Australia: Status of Women in Librarianship, 1989.
   Summarizes key ideas of the conference and outlines directions for action. (See also **1989-156**)

1989-139 Tilley, Christine M. "Achievement Motivation (Fear of Success Syndrome in Australian Women in Library School)." *International Library Review* 21 (July 1989):279-287.
    Provides a profile of achievement motivation in 42 graduating female library students at the Queensland Institute of Technology.

1989-140 "Tips: Trends and Issues for Library Planners." *California State Library Newsletter* 105 (September 1989):7.
    Refers to article in *Successful Meetings* (38:3, pp. 36-36D) on gender differences in communication patterns and their impact on meetings. Points out that in librarianship, where there are traditionally more women than men at meetings, it is important not to let the "female model" dominate because valuable input will be lost.

1989-141 U.S. Employment Standards Administration. *Opportunity 2000: Creative Affirmative Action Strategies for a Changing Workforce*. Washington, DC: Government Printing Office, 1989.
    Discusses the labor market challenges facing employers, including work and family issues, recruiting women, and benefits.

1989-142 U.S. Center for Education Statistics. *Completions in Institutions of Higher Education, 1986-87*. Washington, DC: U.S. Department of Education, Office of Educational Research and Improvement, Center for Education Statistics, 1989.
    Provides data on the number of bachelors, masters, and doctoral degrees conferred including computer and information sciences and library and archival sciences. Data cross-tabulated by sex and race.

1989-143 U.S. Center for Education Statistics. *Digest of Education Statistics 1989*. Washington, DC: U.S. Government Printing Office, 1989.
    Statistics include library degrees conferred, cross-tabulated by sex, 1986-87.

1989-144 U.S. Center for Education Statistics. *Higher Education Act, Title II-B, FY89 Abstracts, Library Career Training Program*.

Washington, DC: U.S. Department of Education, Office of Educational Research and Improvement, Center for Education Statistics, 1989.
　　　Lists FY89 library education grants to assist minorities, women, and economically disadvantaged students.

1989-145 "UC/Irvine to Investigate Bias Charges at Campus Library." *American Libraries* 20 (May 1989):392.
　　　Report on charges of unfair hiring and promotion practices toward minority and female library employees.

1989-146 Vogel, Sandra. "A Woman in Libraries." *New Library World* 90 (April 1989):67.
　　　Discusses typical reasons to explain why women cluster at lower levels of the profession.

1989-147 Vogel, Sandra. "Women in Libraries." *New Library World* 90 (July 1989):129-130.
　　　Inaugurates new column and outlines goals. Calls attention to monitoring of Library Association membership which shows that 75% are women.

1989-148 Vogel, Sandra. "Women in Libraries." *New Library World* 90 (October 1989):189-190.
　　　Describes a project to look at career trends of men and women completing library school in 1988.

1989-149 "Wad Some Power the Giftie Gie Us to See Oursels as Others See US!" *Library Hotline* 18 (June 26, 1989):2.
　　　Report of Special Libraries Association survey on the image of the information professional.

1989-150 Wallace, Linda. "The Image--and What You Can Do About It in the Year of the Librarian." *American Libraries* 20 (January 1989): 22-25.
　　　Discusses the librarian's image, including the female stereotypes.

1989-150a "Wedgeworth, McClarren, Campbell Win 1989 ALA

Awards." *American Libraries* 20 (June 1989):604.
   Announces Sanford Berman as winner of the ALA Equality Award.

1989-151 Welch, Jeanie M. and Linda Dugger. "Suggested Guidelines for Salary Determination in an Academic Library." *Journal of Academic Librarianship* 14 (January 1989):361-365.
   Discusses salary guidelines developed at Lamar University's Gray Library to assure pay equity. Includes the schedule of determinant fields used.

1989-152 White, Herbert S. "Cheapness Through 'Fairness': The Unholy Conspiracy." *Library Journal* 114 (May 15, 1989):52-53.
   States that some public libraries hire individuals without advanced degrees to fill professional positions for a variety of reasons including to provide "professional growth opportunities for women." Argues that such actions devalue librarians and do nothing for women's rights.

Letter:

Halliday, John. *Library Journal* 114 (September 14, 1989):6.

1989-153 Wiegand, Wayne A. "The Development of Librarianship in the United States." *Libraries and Culture* 24 (Winter 1989): 9-109.
   Includes discussion of a hypothesis to account for the gender composition of the American library profession.

1989-154 Williamson, Edgar. "Authorship Characteristics in Five Selected Regional Library Journals." *The Southeastern Librarian* 39 (Summer 1989):47-62.
   Presents study of five regional library journals for authorship characteristics including distribution by gender, library occupation and state. Compares results to national studies.

1989-155 Williamson, Edgar and Josephine B. Williamson. "Multiple Authorship in the Southeast." *The Southeastern Librarian* 39 (Spring 1989):13-15.

Studies author collaboration in periodical articles of five regional library journals. Compares results with national studies on amount of collaboration and gender differences in collaborative work.

1989-156 *Women and the Power of Managing Information.* Proceedings of an International Women in Libraries Seminar held in conjunction with the L.A.A./I.F.L.A. Conference, 27 August 1988, Basser College, University of New South Wales. Melbourne, Victoria, Australia: Status of Women in Librarianship, 1989.

Presents five conference papers plus summary of workshop discussions and list of conference participants. (See also **1989-71, 1989-88, 1989-89, 1989-104,** and **1989-138**)

Review:

Magnuson, Nancy. *Library Journal* 115 (September 1, 1990):264.

1989-157 "Women's March on Washington." *Women in Libraries* 18 (February 1989):1.

Notes that the American Library Association will sponsor a delegation to participate in the March for Equality/Women's Lives on April 9, 1989, in Washington, DC.

1989-158 Woodsworth, Anne. "Getting off the Library Merry-Go-Round: McAnally and Downs Revisited." *Library Journal* 114 (May 1, 1989):35-38.

Reviews the plight of directors of large libraries who either have considered or have made dramatic career changes. Many of the director changes noted are women.

1989-159 "Work and Family Issues in Libraries." *Library Personnel News* 3 (Winter 1989):11-12.

Follow-up of the Fall 1988 issue of *Library Personnel News* which reports results of a canvass of librarians to determine the nature of work and family conflicts experienced by librarians and the policies and benefits provided by libraries.

1989-160 Zimmerman, Judy. "Pink Flamingos and Other Image Problems." *Colorado Libraries* 15 (March 1989):14-15.

Written by a paralibrarian in a one-person library in a small community; comments on media stereotypes of women librarians.

1990 BIBLIOGRAPHY

1990-01 *1989 Salary Survey of Pennsylvania Academic Libraries.* Introduction by Salvatore Meringolo; data compiled by Gordon Fretwell. Harrisburg, PA: Pennsylvania Library Association, 1990.
Provides data including number and average salaries by years of experience, by position, and by sex.

1990-01a "ALA Awards & Officers." *Library Journal* 115 (August 1990):40.
Announces Betty-Carol Sellen as the winner of the ALA Equality Award.

1990-02 "ALA Council Gets 26 New Members." *Library Journal* 115 (July 1990):16.
Announces results of American Library Association Council elections for 1990 to 1994 term and includes statistics by sex.

1990-03 Albritton, Rosie L. and Thomas W. Shaughnessy. *Developing Leadership Skills: A Source Book for Librarians.* Englewood, CO: Libraries Unlimited, 1990.
Gives special attention to women in part 2 on self-awareness, part 3 on self-development, and part 4 on professional growth.

Reviews:

Austen, G. *Australian Library Journal* 40 (May 1991):174-175.
Brawner, Lee B. *Public Library Quarterly* 11 (1991):63-64.
Editors. *Journal of Academic Librarianship* 16 (May 1990):111-112.
Emergency Librarian 17 (May 1990):45.

Humphrey, E.G. *Canadian Library Journal* 47 (December 1990):442.

Markowitz, Lois. *Special Libraries* 81 (Fall 1990):368.

Munford, W.A. *Library Association Record* 92 (August 1990):591.

Reference & Research Book News 5 (June 1990):43.

Shank, Russell. *Journal of Academic Librarianship* 16 (November 1990):306-307.

Terblanche, F. *South African Journal of Library and Information Science* 58 (December 1990):394.

Varnet, Harvey. *Library Journal* 115 (June 15, 1990):142.

Whitehead, D. *Australian Library Review* 7 (August 1990):235-236.

1990-04 Alvarez, Robert S. "From the Editor's Desk: Gains for Women." *Library Administrator's Digest* 25 (October 1990):62-63.

Reports results of informal study of *American Library Directory* from 1982 to 1986 to check the gender of public library directors in all New Jersey cities with populations over 10,000. Found that men directed 75% of the libraries in cities over 100,000; women ran eleven of the sixteen libraries in cities 50,000-99,999. Notes that six male directors were replaced by women while three female directors were replaced by men.

1990-05 American Library Association. Committee on Minority Concerns. "Report to Council, Annual Conference 1990," 1989-90 Council Document #98. Chicago: American Library Association, 1990.

Summarizes the activities of the committee including an assessment of minority participation in the association which reports data by gender.

1990-06 *ARL Annual Salary Survey 1989*, compiled by Gordon Fretwell. Washington, DC: Association of Research Libraries, 1990.

Includes tables for number and average salaries of librarians by position and sex including a table for minority librarian data.

1990-06a Association of College and Research Libraries. New England Chapter. *1989-90 Salary Survey of New England College Libraries*. Worchester, MA: The Association, 1990.
   Reports results of annual salary survey of library professionals in four-year undergraduate academic institutions excluding members of the Association of Research Libraries. Provides statistics by sex for salary, position, experience, and minority employment.

1990-06b "Award Highlights." *Wilson Library Bulletin* 65 (September 1990):47.
   Announces Betty-Carol Sellen as winner of the ALA Equality Award.

1990-06c "Barbara Bush Is Among 1990 Award Winners." *American Libraries* 21 (June 1990):612.
   Announces Betty-Carol Sellen as winner of the ALA Equality Award.

1990-06d Berger, Patricia Wilson. "American Library Association." In *The Bowker Annual*, 166-171. New York: Bowker, 1990.
   Notes the appointment of Linda Crismond as the director of the American Library Association and other personnel changes, including many women.

1990-07 Berry, John. "Editorial: There's a Candidate on Our Cover." *Library Journal* 115 (March 1, 1990):4.
   Discusses the decision to put Patricia Glass Schuman, ALA presidential candidate, on the cover and how the "integrity" of the election was not jeopardized.

1990-07a Berry, John. "Martinez Smith Appointed LA City Librarian: First Hispanic Woman to Direct Library (Freedman Reports Offer)." *Library Journal* 115 (June 1, 1990):33-34.
   Announces appointment of Elizabeth Martinez Smith, the first Hispanic woman to head the Los Angeles Public Library.

1990-08 Berry, John. "Picks of the Programs." *Library Journal* 115

(June 1, 1990):62-72.
   Mentions five programs geared towards women in librarianship.

1990-09 Berry, John et al. "So Many Programs, So Little Time." *Library Journal* 115 (August 1990):34-43.
   Highlights 1990 ALA Annual Conference in Chicago with a section on Committee on the Status of Women in Librarianship's activities and mention of presentations by Catharine Stimpson and author Sara Paretsky.

1990-10 Blake, Virgil L. P. and Renee Tjoumas. "Research as a Factor in Faculty Evaluation: The Rules Are A-Changing." *Journal of Education for Library and Information Science* 31 (Summer 1990): 3-24.
   Reports findings of various authorship studies which conclude that a higher-than-expected number of males published articles in five major journals of library science and that female authors are underrepresented but are better represented than in academic library journals. Men consistently publish more frequently than women overall. Raises questions on work pattern differences of males and females.

1990-10a "Book on Library Services for Gays and Lesbians Scheduled for June Publication." *GLTF Newsletter* 2 (Spring 1990):5.
   Announces the "first comprehensive manual on how librarians can improve their collections and services for gay and lesbian library users" entitled *Gay and Lesbian Library Service*. (See **1990-40**)

1990-11 Bradley, Kate. "Nurses Neglected." [letter] *American Libraries* 21 (June 1990):496-497.
   Draws parallels between the status of nurses and the status of librarians, both female intensive occupations in response to an analogy of hospitals to libraries made by Herbert S. White (*LJ*, February 1990, 103-106).

1990-12 Brimsek, Tobi A. "SLA Biennial Salary Survey

Preliminary Report." *Special Libraries* 84 (Fall 1990):338-340.
   Reports results of a random sampling of 25% of the membership. Includes statistical profiles and tables showing mean and median salaries from April 1, 1989, to April 1, 1990, and mentions female and male academic library directors.

1990-13 Bruyns, R.A.C. "Who Holds the Rod of Office?: A Survey of Library Directors [Wie Voeren de Scepter? Directeuren van Bibliotheken Onderzocht]." *Open* 22 (July/August 1990):248-250.
   Reports results of survey done by library school students on the age, education, and experience of library administrators in the Netherlands. Notes that one-quarter of the respondents were women, most of whom were employed in public libraries, and that most women had professional training while men did not.

1990-14 Bryant, Sue Lacey. "A Woman Not in Libraries." *New Library World* 91 (January 1990):11-12.
   Discusses "Immobile Female Professionals" and their mid-career options in light of the fact that geographic moves are rarely made for the benefit of a wife's career.

1990-15 Burgin, Robert and Patsy Hansel. "Library Management: A Dialogue." *Wilson Library Bulletin* 64 (March 1990):81-82, 91.
   Reviews the literature on mentors and mentoring in libraries and cites studies which indicate that mentoring relationships differ by sex.

1990-16 Buttlar, Lois J. "Profiling Review Writers in the Library Periodical Literature." *RQ* 30 (Winter 1990):221-229.
   Provides unique information about the role of reviews as well as information related to the sex, occupation, affiliation, and geographic location of reviewers. Analyzes 1,305 reviews published in 14 basic periodicals for a two-and-a-half-year period from 1987 to 1989. More than half of the reviewers described are women.

1990-17 "Call for Speakers on Women's Concerns." *Library Journal* 115 (February 1, 1990):20.

Announces establishment of a speakers' bureau by the American Library Association Committee on the Status of Women in Librarianship.

1990-18 Case, Donald O. and John V. Richardson. "Predictors of Student Performance with Emphasis on Gender and Ethnic Determinants." *Journal of Education for Library and Information Science* 30 (Winter 1990):163-182.

Concludes that gender is predictive of graduate GPA and completion of program.

Erratum:

Journal of Education for Library and Information Science 30 (Spring 1990):344.

Discussion:

White, Herbert S. *Library Journal* 117 (February 15, 1992):138-139.
Journal of Education for Library and Information Science 32 (Winter 1992):84-86.

Letters:

Seavey, Charles A. "Ignorance Never Settles a Question." *Library and Information Science Research* 13 (July/September 1991):171-172.
Shiller, Dan et al. "From Our Readers." *Journal of Education for Library and Information Science* 31 (Fall 1991):173.

1990-19 Chadbourne, Robert. "Ireland's First Woman of Libraries Tours U.S." *Wilson Library Bulletin* 64 (February 1990):22.

Discusses a visit to the United States by Patricia Donlon, the first woman director of the National Library of Ireland.

1990-20 "Chalk One Up for Our Side." *Library Hotline* 19 (May 28, 1990):1-2.

Notes Kathleen Heim's selection as Dean of the Graduate

Schools at Louisiana State University as a breakthrough in administration for women with library and information science backgrounds.

1990-20a "Changing Occupational Stereotypes." *Library Issues* 10 (1990):n.p.
Discusses factors contributing to the stereotype of librarians including its status as a female intensive profession and offers questions for institutions who want to change this image to consider including power, wages, status, and roles of librarians.

1990-20b Cheatham, Bertha M. "*SLJ* News Report, 1989." In *The Bowker Annual*, 11-21. New York: Bowker, 1990.
Notes the appointment of Linda Crismond as the first woman director of the American Library Association.

1990-21 "CompuServe Apologizes." *Library Hotline* 19 (May 14, 1990):2.
Notes company's apology for reinforcing librarian stereotypes in an ad in the April 9, 1990, *InfoWorld*. Many complaints were received.

1990-22 "Conference Highlights." *Women in Libraries* 19 (June 1990):5.
Provides an overview of anniversaries celebrated by the Feminist Task Force, Social Responsibilities Round Table, and the Black Caucus and describes the FTF's program "The Feminist Librarian."

1990-23 "Conference Notes, Midwinter 1990." *Women in Libraries* 19 (March 1990):3.
Includes announcements, report on the status of the *SHARE Directory*, a program on library recruitment, and the formation of the Progressive Librarians Guild.

1990-24 Connors, Sue. "Librarians in Books." *Australian Library Journal* 39 (May 1990):134-137.
Reviews the treatment of librarians in literature beginning

with the governess in *Jane Eyre* as the precursor to librarianship as an acceptable occupation for women. Concludes that the recent obsession with image and stereotypes extends beyond librarianship.

1990-25 Cravey, Pamela J. "Focusing on the Librarian: Are Librarians Selling Themselves?" *The Georgia Librarian* 27 (Summer 1990):28-31.

Analyzes portrayal of librarians in 8,706 product/services advertisements in four library periodicals from 1968 to 1987 and concludes that, to some extent, librarians have internalized a negative professional image and need to promote positive images within the profession.

1990-26 DeCandido, GraceAnne A. "Alarums and Diversions." *Library Journal* 115 (March 15, 1990):20.

Draws attention to the cover story of the January 1990 *Library Journal* on women motorcyclists as debunking another stereotype about librarians.

1990-26a DeCandido, GraceAnne A. "*LJ* News Report, 1989." In *The Bowker Annual*, 3-10. New York: Bowker, 1990.

Discusses Linda Crismond's appointment as the first woman director of the American Library Association and notes a number of other personnel changes in libraries, including many women.

1990-26b DeCandido, GraceAnne A. "The Year End Review 1990." *School Library Journal* 36 (December 1990):34-38.

Refers to the Learmont/Van Houten salary survey (see **1990-59**) and notes the salary differentials between men and women.

1990-27 DeCandido, GraceAnne A. and Michael Rogers. "Gay/Lesbian Task Force Seeks Index Access." *Library Journal* 115 (September 15, 1990):16.

Notes efforts to get gay and lesbian periodicals indexed in standard sources such as *Readers' Guide to Periodical Literature*.

1990-28 DeCandido, GraceAnne A. and Michael Rogers. "UCI

Librarian Under Fire Over Affirmative Action Report." *Library Journal* 115 (April 1, 1990):20.
Reports on academic senate report regarding leadership and affirmative action record of University of California at Irvine Librarian Calvin Boyer.

1990-29 Detlefsen, Ellen Gay and Josephine E. Olson. "The Special Librarian: Results from a Survey of MLS and MBA Graduates." *Special Libraries* 81 (Fall 1990):294-304.
Presents survey results on demographics, career patterns, work histories, and attitudinal issues of special librarians as compared with other librarians and with a group of business professionals.

1990-30 Dryden, Sherre. "FTF Renews the Fight Against Racism." *Women in Libraries* 19 (March 1990):7.
Describes in detail the Feminist Task Force's pursuit of racial and cultural diversity in the workplace and its role in increasing understanding of other ethnic grounds, banishing stereotypes, and defeating racist practices.

1990-30a Duffy, Joan R. "Images of Librarians and Librarianship: A Study." *Journal of Youth Services in Libraries* 3 (Summer 1990):303-308.
Reports on interviews with 117 young people on their career aspirations, librarianship as a potential career, positive and negative characteristics of librarians, and their image of librarians as expressed through drawings. Responses showed a generally positive attitude based on personal experience, with most librarians being portrayed as females but few depicting the stereotypical librarian.

1990-30b Durrance, Joan C. "Librarians: The Invisible Professionals." In *The Bowker Annual*, 92-99. New York: Bowker, 1990.
Discusses image problems of librarians, librarians' role in creating those image problems, and solutions for overcoming them.

1990-31 Eaglen, Audrey. "Why God Invented Librarians." [column] *School Library Journal* 36 (March 1990):161.

    Reaction to research by psychologist Carol Gilligan which suggests a radical change in girls from the age of eleven to fifteen in terms of self-image and confidence. Notes that "what Dr. Gilligan ought to realize is that keeping these role models of strong and independent women for girls to discover has long been the function of librarians who work with young people."

1990-32 "Eighteen Women, Eight Men Elected to ALA Council." *Library Hotline* 19 (June 25, 1990):1.

    Reports election results from the American Library Association.

1990-33 Elder, Terry and Jeff Hadland. *The Gender Gap: A Comparison of Alaskan Female and Male Wage Income and Employment Patterns in 1988.* Juneau, AK: Alaska Department of Labor, 1990.

    Data by sex and occupation for local government sector, private sector, and state government sector includes percent of female employment, female average income, and ratio of male/female average income.

1990-34 "FTF Endorses Pat Schuman for ALA President." *Women in Libraries* 19 (March 1990):1.

    Profiles Schuman as an advocate for the rights of women and minorities, highlights her career, and lists other Feminist Task Force endorsements.

1990-35 Feye-Stukas, Janice and Janice Kirkland with Margaret Myers. "Do Libraries Pay Fair?" *Library Journal* 115 (July 1990):36-39.

    Defines pay equity and reports on activities in libraries and steps taken in Minnesota, California, and Vermont to achieve fair compensation for both sexes. Sidebar on criticisms of and obstacles to the methods of achieving equity.

1990-36 "A First?" *Library Hotline* 19 (February 26, 1990):8.

    Announces the selection of Louise Berry, Director, Darien

(CT) Public Library as vice-president/president-elect of the Darien Rotary Club, "probably making her the first female library director to preside over a Rotary Club in the U.S."

1990-37 Fitch, Donna K. "Job Satisfaction Among Library Support Staff in Alabama Academic Libraries." *College and Research Libraries* 51 (July 1990):313-320.
Study shows a significant difference in job satisfaction according to sex with women indicating higher levels of satisfaction. Suggests need for further comparative studies of men's and women's attitudes toward their jobs.

1990-38 Freedman, Janet. "Work That Is Real: Perspectives on Feminist Librarianship." *WLW Journal* 14 (Fall 1990):3-5.
Based on remarks given at the 20th Anniversary of the American Library Association Social Responsibilities Round Table Feminist Task Force, July 1990. Highlights the work of feminist librarians in providing and using information to help "transform lives."

1990-38a Frye, Michael A. "Career Patterns of Children's Services Librarians." M.S.L.S. thesis, University of North Carolina, 1990.
Reports results of survey of 37 children's services librarians serving populations of 100,000 or more in the southeastern United States. Respondents were 99% female and commented on career opportunities, career development, and mentoring. Refers to feminization of librarianship as a negative factor in the advancement of children's services librarians although respondents' remarks suggest otherwise.

1990-39 Garland, Kathleen. "Gender Differences in Scholarly Publication Among Faculty in ALA Accredited Library Schools." *Library and Information Science Research* 12 (April-June 1990):155-166.
Reports on a study analyzing recent productivity studies of faculty and investigates gender differences in publication among a sample of faculty over a five-year period. Notes implications for hiring and retention and concludes that no significant gender

differences were found.

1990-40 *Gay and Lesbian Library Service*, edited by Cal Gough and Ellen Greenblatt. Jefferson, NC: McFarland, 1990.
    Examines and discusses issues concerning gay and lesbian library users and reflects the work of the American Library Association Social Responsibilities Round Table Gay and Lesbian Task Force. (See also **1990-10a** and **1991-38**)

Reviews:

Azzolina, David S. *Small Press* 9 (February 1991):19.
Broidy, Ellen. *Choice* 28 (June 1991):1612.
Bryant, Eric. *Library Journal* 116 (April 15, 1991):131.
The Editors. *Journal of Academic Librarianship* 17 (March 1991):62-63.
Harmon, Charles. *American Libraries* 22 (May 1991):426.
Harmon, Charles T. *Booklist* 87 (January 1, 1991):906.
Labonte, Richard. *Advocate* (February 26, 1991):77.
Labonte, Richard. *Lambda Book Report* 2 (March 1991):16.
McIver, G. *Australian Library Review* 8 (November 1990):400-401.
McIver, G. *Australian Library Review* 9 (May 1992):31-32 supplement.
Reference & Research Book News 6 (June 1991):41.
SantaVicca, Edmund F. *Journal of Academic Librarianship* 17 (September 1991):239.
Stevens, Norman D. *Wilson Library Bulletin* 65 (February 1991):125.
Wavle, Elizabeth M. "A Gay and Lesbian Core Collection." [bibliographic essay] *Choice* 28 (July 1991):1743.

1990-41 Gertzog, Alice. "Library Leaders: Who and Why?" *Library Journal* 115 (July 1990):45-51.
    Reports on study which explored the relationship between leadership and the social structure of librarianship, lists 101 identified leaders and profiles 16 of them including four women.

1990-41a Gittings, Barbara. "Gays in Library Land: The Gay and

Lesbian Task Force of the American Library Association: The First Sixteen Years." [pamphlet] Philadelphia, PA: B. Gittings, 1990.

Includes history of the Gay Book Award, highlights of conference programs, and Task Force initiatives and accomplishments as well as disappointments and experiences with prejudice. (See also **1991-38** and **1992-08**)

1990-42 Glaviano, Cliff and R. Errol Lam. "Academic Libraries and Affirmative Action: Approaching Cultural Diversity in the 1990s." *College and Research Libraries* 51 (November 1990):513-523.

Statistics show that minorities are underrepresented and suggests alternative strategies for correcting unequal representation. Mentions that the *ALA Yearbooks* for 1982 through 1986 focus more on the status of women in librarianship and other social issues rather than concerns of people of color.

Letter:

Heim, Kathleen M. *College and Research Libraries* 52 (May 1991):296.

1990-43 Goetsch, Lori and Sandra K. Peterson. "Women in Librarianship." In *The ALA Yearbook of Library and Information Services: A Review of Library Events 1989*, Vol. 15, 252-253. Chicago: American Library Association, 1990.

Reviews the activities of the Committee on the Status of Women in Librarianship, salary surveys, and other research conducted on the status of women in librarianship.

1990-43a Gordon, Henry and Patricia Q. Brown. *Degrees Conferred in Institutions of Higher Education, by Race/Ethnicity and Sex: 1976-77 Through 1986-87.* Washington, DC: U.S. Department of Education, Office of Educational Research and Improvement, Center for Education Statistics, 1990.

Data for library science degrees conferred by sex for a 10-year period.

1990-44 Hale, Kaycee. "Image Enhancement." In *The Bowker Annual*, 72-91. New York: Bowker, 1990.

Reports on the progress of a project begun in 1989 by the Special Libraries Association on the image of librarians. Includes preliminary results of survey of executives and community leaders.

1990-45 Hart, Richard, Timothy Carsteens, Michael La Croix, and K. Randall May. "Funded and Non-funded Research: Characteristics of Authorship and Patterns of Collaboration in the 1986 Library and Information Science Literature." *Library and Information Science Research* 12 (January-March 1990):71-86.

Concludes that sex of the author relative to funded and non-funded publications was not a measure of the quality of the publication and suggests that women are capable of procuring funding and generating high-quality research on a par with their male counterparts.

1990-46 "Heim Named Grad School Dean at LSU." *Library Journal* 115 (June 1, 1990):25.

Announces appointment of Kathleen Heim, describing it as "a victory for librarians and feminists."

1990-47 Heim, Kathleen M. and William E. Moen. "Information Services Recruitment: The Challenge of Opportunity." *RQ* 29 (Summer 1990):562-566.

Presents results of the 1988 Library and Information Science Students' Attitudes, Demographics, and Aspirations Survey which show that reference and information service positions were most often selected by students enrolled in accredited programs. Data by sex included.

1990-48 Hole, Carol. "Click! The Feminization of the Public Library." *American Libraries* 21 (December 1990):1076-1079.

Suggests that since most librarians are female, public library collections reflect women's reading interests, thus creating a predominantly female user group. Also discusses how this feminization extends into book reviewing, collection development policies, and services. Encourages increased services and collections to encourage men to use libraries.

1990-49 Holsworth, Pat. "Liaisoning at Midwinter." *Ohio Women Librarians* 4 (April 1990):9.
Reports on discussion at the LAMA Women Administrators Discussion Group including gender-related issues in negotiating.

1990-50 "Improving Librarians' Salaries." *Library Personnel News* 4 (Spring 1990):20-21.
Discusses Minnesota state association recommendations for a minimum salary to combat predominantly female job salary inequities.

1990-51 "Incredible Librarian Finally Debuts." *Library Journal* 115 (June 1, 1990):30.
Announces publication of new quarterly, featuring a bilingual superheroine, with a goal to raise readers' consciousnesses about libraries and librarians.

1990-52 Jagusch, Sybilla A. "First Among Equals: Caroline M. Hewins and Anne C. Moore: Foundations of Library Work with Children." Ph.D. diss., University of Maryland, 1990.
Maintains that these women created library work with children as it is today. Also profiles eight women who shared in their work: Caroline Burnite, Mary Dousman, Clara Hunt, Alice Jordan, Frances Olcott, Effie Power, Minerva Sanders, and Lutie Stearns.

1990-53 Jolly, D. Leeann, James W. Grimm and Paul R. Wozniak. "Patterns of Sex Desegregation in Managerial and Professional Specialty Fields, 1950-1980." *Work and Occupations* 17 (February 1990):30-54.
Uses librarianship as an example of a female field in which desegregation is observed as a result of male entry into management. Notes that desegregation is increasing in higher-paying fields but resistance is also higher.

1990-54 King, Edith W. *The Impact of Education on Professional*

Women's Careers in Singapore. American Sociological Association, 1990.

    Uses data from a questionnaire administered during interviews with professional women, including librarians, who are members of the Singapore Association of Women for Action and Research. Solicited responses on changing public policies and their impact on educational opportunities for women.

1990-55 Kniffel, Leonard. "UC/Irvine Faculty Committee Blames Head Librarian for Bias." *American Libraries* 21 (April 1990):278-279.

    Describes committee report which outlines charges of racial and sex bias resulting from interviews with library staff and a survey of library professionals. Report also alleges instances of discrimination for which library director, Calvin Boyer, is held responsible.

1990-56 Kreitz, Patricia A. and Annegret Ogden. "Job Responsibilities and Job Satisfaction at the University of California Libraries." *College and Research Libraries* 51 (July 1990):297-312.

    Studies predominantly female population of librarians and library assistants and examines Allen Veaner's suggestions that blurring of roles contributes to job dissatisfaction. Shows no significant difference between genders in job dissatisfaction.

1990-56a Langerman, Deborah. "Books & Boys: Gender Preferences and Book Selection." *School Library Journal* 36 (March 1990):132-136.

    Discusses and refutes reasons put forward by Ray Nicolle (see **1989-103**) for the reading preferences of boys and girls including Nicolle's speculation that boys lack reading material because librarians are either female or gay.

1990-57 "LC Holds Forum on Affirmative Action." *LC Information Bulletin* 49 (July 16, 1990):264.

    Announces appointment of six candidates for the library's first Affirmative Action Internship Program as a part of its commitment to a more diverse workforce.

1990-58 Learmont, Carol and Stephen Van Houten. "Placements and Salaries, 1988: The Demand Increases." In *The Bowker Annual*, 346-362. New York: Bowker, 1990.

Provides data on salaries and placements, cross-tabulated by sex and geographic area. Analyzes salary differentials between men and women.

1990-59 Learmont, Carol and Stephen Van Houten. "Placements and Salaries, 1989: Steady On." *Library Journal* 115 (October 1990):46-52.

Reports results of 39th annual salary and placement survey of graduates of ALA-accredited library school programs. Includes data by sex. (See also **1990-26b**)

1990-60 Leber, Michelle M. "Pay Equity--A Family Economic Issue" [National Committee on Pay Equity 10th Anniversary Conference]. *Library Personnel News* 4 (Winter 1990):5-6.

Links women's salaries to survival of the family because of the number of single-parent families and the need for two wage-earners in other families.

1990-61 "Let the Honeymoon Begin." *Library Journal* 115 (March 1, 1990):50-56.

Recounts events of 1990 ALA Midwinter Meeting including candidacy of Patricia Glass Schuman for association president; the Committee on the Status of Women in Librarianship's draft policy on sexual harassment; and topics at the LAMA Women Administrators Discussion Group.

1990-62 "The Librarian's Job of the Future." *Library Personnel News* 4 (Spring 1990):18-19.

Quotes Public Library Association President Sarah Long as stating that there will be more women in top library management positions in the year 2000.

1990-62a *Library Education and Leadership: Essays in Honor of Jane Anne Hannigan*, edited by Sheila Intner and Kay Vandergrift. Metuchen, NJ: Scarecrow Press, 1990.

Honors Hannigan, the 1984 Beta Phi Mu award winner, for her contributions to library education, particularly children's and youth services. Includes dedication highlighting her career. (See also **1990-90a**)

Reviews:

Barber, Gary D. *Journal of Academic Librarianship* 17 (November 1991):312.
Ellis, A. *Library Association Record* 93 (December 1991):852.
Gorman, Michael. *Library Journal* 116 (March 15, 1991):121.
Stevens, Norman. *Wilson Library Bulletin* 66:4 (December 1991):96-97.

1990-63 Loughridge, Brendan. "Employment and Career Surveys: Some Reflections on Their Value and Relevance." *Journal of Librarianship* 22 (April 1990):71-90.
 Reviews a selection of surveys of job destinations, career ladders and occupational mobility of former library and information science students in the United Kingdom. Scattered references to data by gender.

1990-64 Maggio, Theresa Griffin and Ron Blazek. "On-campus and Off-campus Programs of Accredited Library Schools: A Comparison of Graduates." *Journal of Education for Library and Information Science* 30 (Spring 1990):315-329.
 Shows no significant gender differences between sites. Females studied were older than males, had more spousal support, less mobility, and were more likely to become employed in school or public libraries. Females showed higher salaries than males prior to receiving MLS degrees, gave fewer speeches and presentations, and authored fewer articles.

1990-65 "Making a Difference." *Library Hotline* 19 (March 5, 1990):2.
 Reports on a *New York Times* article on Barbara Osborne Williams (see **1990-67**), a children's librarian who visits welfare families. Notes that the article "creates a very positive, nontraditional image of a librarian."

1990-66 Marley, Ursula. "Job-Sharing: Compatibility, Commitment, Communication, and Consistency." *Library Association Record* 92 (March 1990):197-204.
   Describes one woman's efforts to secure a job-share as a college librarian. Concentrates on practical issues.

1990-67 Martin, Douglas. "Passing the Word to the Children of the Hotels." *New York Times*, 24 February 1990, 27.
   Describes the work of Barbara Osborne Williams, children's librarian at the Queens Library, who brings library services and materials to homeless children. (See also **1990-65**)

1990-68 Martinez, Ed, Raymond Roney and Judith Harris. "Library Support Staff Salary Survey 1989." *Library Mosaics* 1 (July/August 1990):8-12.

1990-69 Mayer, M. "The Transformation of Librarianship" [editorial]. *Canadian Library Journal* 47 (August 1990):233-235

1990-70 McCaslin, Sharon. "The Displacement of Mary Jones: In the 1890s, Education and Dedication Took a Back Seat to Gender." *American Libraries* 21:3 (March 1990):186-191.
   Reviews the career of Jones, a pioneer of university librarianship, focusing on the problems and discrimination she confronted. Sidebar discusses women's career paths.

1990-71 McReynolds, Rosalee. "The Sexual Politics of Illness in Turn of the Century Libraries." *Libraries and Culture* 25 (Spring 1990):194-217.
   Discusses illness known as "American Nervousness" which afflicted Victorian intellectual women and reviews the occurrence of the disorder among female library staff, the attitudes of library administrators, and the impact that the perception of this illness had on the advancement of women within the profession.

1990-72 Mech, Terrence F. "Academic Library Directors: A Managerial Role Profile." *College and Research Libraries* 51 (September 1990):415-428.

Uses Mintzberg's managerial role typology to study the profiles of 354 directors. Includes characteristics of gender, age, years of library and administrative experience, and others.

1990-73 Meyer, Richard W. "Librarian Salaries: Paid What We're Worth?" *College and Research Libraries News* 51 (June 1990):504-509.

Expresses concern over salary data which frequently lack a frame of reference or systematic analysis. Provides an overview of forces which impact wages, describes efforts librarians have made to improve salaries, and reports on an analysis which indicates that librarians may be paid comparable to teaching faculty. Notes that sex is frequently used as a determinant of salary in statistical comparisons.

1990-74 Miller, Olivia. "A Day in the Life of a Clinical Librarian." *Career Woman* 18 (Fall 1990):28-31.

Discusses responsibilities of the clinical librarian. Notes the opportunities for women that are available in the field.

1990-75 Morris, Beryl. "Surviving the Skills Shortage: Exploring the Options." *Information and Library Manager* 9 (1990):11-22.

Suggests that one strategy to combat skills shortages is to make it easier for women with families to return to work.

1990-76 Nardelli, Sharon A. "The Old Image Problem: What PSLA did about it." *School Library Journal* 36 (November 1990):23-26.

Describes use of balanced mix of sexes to create the video "School Librarian--It's Not a Quiet Corner" designed to dispel persistent stereotypical misconceptions of school librarians as mousy and ineffectual.

1990-77 Olson, Josephine E., Irene Hanson Frieze, and Ellen G. Detlefsen. "Having it All? Combining Work and Family in a Male and a Female Profession." *Sex Roles* 23 (March 1990):515-533.

Attempts to determine if women in a female intensive profession were better able to combine work and family than those in a male intensive profession by comparing the careers and family status of 747 librarians with 449 MBAs. Concludes that groups were about equally likely to have job interruptions; librarians are more likely to have worked part-time; librarians' salaries were much lower but job interruptions and part-time work had a more negative effect on salaries of women in business; and it is probably somewhat more difficult for businesswomen to combine work and family.

1990-78 Passet, Joanne E. "Order Is Heaven's First Law: Itinerant Librarians and Bibliographic Control, 1887-1915." *Library Quarterly* 60 (January 1990):23-43.
Describes the work of librarians who organized collections across the country and notes that two trends--low salaries and the practice of employing untrained people--have influenced the status and image of women in the profession.

1990-79 Passet, Joanne E. "Women Academic Librarians on the Western Frontier, 1900-1920." *Library Quarterly* 60 (1990): 320-336.
Discusses development of western normal schools and land-grant colleges as well as depressed economic conditions in higher education as factors which created opportunities for women in academic librarianship.

1990-80 "Pay Equity: Past Present and Future" [Program at 1990 ALA Conference]. *Library Personnel News* 4 (Fall 1990):50-51.

1990-81 Person, Ruth J. and George Charles Newman. "Selection of the University Librarian." *College and Research Libraries* 51 (July 1990):346-359.
Outlines factors which contribute to a successful search. Notes information in the literature including the predominance of male directors in Association of Research Libraries members between 1933 and 1973.

1990-82 Peterson, Sandra K., Mary I. Vela-Creixell, and Glen A. Zimmerman. *Equality in Librarianship: A Guide to Sex Discrimination Laws.* 2nd edition. Chicago: American Library

Association, 1990.

Discusses equal pay, hiring and promotion, pay equity, pregnancy discrimination, sexual harassment, Title VII complaints, and remedies for sex discrimination.

1990-83 Porter, Exa Lynn. *A Survey on Participative Management Among Texas Community College Reference Librarians*. 1990. ERIC, ED 325 148

Discusses benefits of participative management and tests perceptions on a group of librarians. Of the eighty-one percent who responded, two-thirds were female.

1990-84 *Private Law Libraries: A Survey of Compensation, Operations, and Collections*. 1990 ed. Newton Square, PA: Altman and Weil, 1990.

1990-85 Reeling, Patricia G. "The New Generation of Librarians: What They Are Like and How to Recruit Them." *New Jersey Libraries* (Winter 1990):3-14.

Presents results of a study of Rutgers University MLS students from 1979 to 1989 including prior education and work experience; reasons for choosing librarianship as a career; and post-MLS work preference. Includes impact of gender and personality traits on career decisions.

1990-86 Rees, Alan M. "Human Resources in Ohio Libraries: A Report on a Work in Progress." *Ohio Libraries* 3/4 (July/August 1990):10-11.

Notes contradictory indicators regarding numbers and classifications of library positions needed in the United States and reports on study being undertaken by the Center for the Study of Librarianship at Kent State University of the current marketplace in Ohio. Gender is one category of data to be collected.

1990-87 Robbins, Jane B. "Research in Information Service Practice." *Library and Information Science Research* 12 (April-June 1990):127-128.

Editorial states that one of the causes of problems in information science research is that the field is predominantly female and women, historically, have not been oriented toward a systematic approach to research.

1990-88 Russell, Anne M. "The 25 Hottest Careers." *Working Woman* 15 (July 1990):73-84.
List includes book editor as one of the ten worst careers.

1990-89 Schmidt, Stella. "The Situation of Female Librarians in the USA and West Germany [Die Situation der Bibliothekarinnen in der USA und der Bundesrepublik Deutschland]." *Buch und Bibliothek* 42 (October/November 1990):838-840.
Compares the status of women librarians in the two countries, noting that while there are more women than men in the profession, more men hold administrative positions and receive higher wages. Traces the reason for this disparity to historical developments and current professional and social structures. Notes one major difference in that the legal status of women in the United States is better.

1990-90 Schuman, Patricia Glass. "The Image of Librarians: Substance or Shadow." *Journal of Academic Librarianship* 16 (1990): 86-89.
Discusses the origin of librarian image problems and suggests that the profession focus less on physical stereotypes and more on professional awareness.

1990-90a Schuman, Patricia Glass. "Librarians: Images and Realities." In *Library Education and Leadership: Essays in Honor of Jane Anne Hannigan*, edited by Sheila Intner and Kay Vandergrift, 27-34. Metuchen, NJ: Scarecrow Press, 1990.
Provides background on the development of librarian stereotypes and encourages librarians to promote the profession to increase awareness and improve image. (See also **1990-62a**)

1990-91 "Schuman Wins ALA Presidency." *Library Journal* 115 (July 1990):15-16.
Reports on Schuman's initiatives including pay equity and equal opportunity and notes her contributions to the Feminist Task

Force and to the status of women in the profession.

1990-92 Selsky, Deborah. "Special Libraries' Salary Growth Ahead of Inflation in the 1980's." *Library Journal* 115 (September 15, 1990):36.

Discusses salary structure and growth. Notes that male librarians are routinely paid more than females despite equal positions and experience, however the highest beginning salaries went to women.

1990-93 "Something for Everyone." *Library Hotline* 19 (July 7, 1990):5.

Highlights the American Nudist Research Library which, in addition to its special collections on the history and current practice of nudism, boasts librarians that work in the nude. Notes, "Nowhere is the stereotype of the flour-skinned, bun-haired, starch-dressed librarian more consistently contradicted."

1990-94 Swigger, Keith. "Enrollment Management in the Library School." *Journal of Education for Library and Information Science* 30 (Spring 1990):259-274.

Selected data regarding enrolled populations are analyzed by gender.

1990-95 "Task Force on ACRL and Social Responsibilities." *SRRT Newsletter* 95 (March 1990):6.

Summarizes the work and resulting report from this task force and includes a definition of social responsibility as embracing "a sensitivity to the practice of the profession with respect to the active recruitment, promotion and retention of minorities, women, and special populations."

1990-96 U.S. Bureau of Labor Statistics. *Occupational Projections and Training Data, 1990 Edition*. Bulletin 2351. Washington, DC: U.S. Government Printing Office, 1990.

Table 6 includes occupational employment, 1988, projections for 2000, and selected employee characteristics including sex.

The Bibliography

1990-97 U.S. Center for Education Statistics. *Degrees Conferred in Institutions of Higher Education by Race/Ethnicity and Sex: 1976-77 Through 1986-87.* Washington, DC: U.S. Department of Education, Office of Educational Research and Improvement, Center for Education Statistics, 1990.
    Includes statistics on degrees awarded in library science broken down by sex and race/ethnicity.

1990-97a U.S. Center for Education Statistics. *Digest of Education Statistics 1990,* Thomas D. Snyder, Project Director. Washington, DC: U.S. Department of Education, Office of Educational Research and Improvement, Center for Education Statistics, 1990.
    Includes data for library science degrees by sex of student, 1987-88.

1990-98 U.S. Center for Education Statistics. *Higher Education Act, Title II-B, Library Career Training Program, Abstracts of Funded Projects, 1990.* Washington, DC: U.S. Department of Education, Office of Educational Research and Improvement, Center for Education Statistics, 1990.
    Annual directory of FY90 library education grants to assist minorities, women and economically disadvantaged students.

1990-99 U.S. Congress. House. Committee on House Administration. Subcommittee on Libraries and Memorials. *Underrepresentation of Minorities in Supergrade Positions and Above at the Library of Congress, Hearing . . . April 26, 1990.* Washington, DC: U.S. Government Printing Office, 1990.
    Reports hearings before the Subcommittee on Libraries and Memorials which examine concerns about the underrepresentation of blacks and other minorities in senior-level positions and assesses other affirmative action efforts. Includes statistics by race and gender.

1990-100 U.S. Library of Congress. *Annual Report of the Librarian of Congress, for the Fiscal Year Ending September 30, 1990.* Washington, DC: U.S. Government Printing Office, 1991.
    Includes information about developments including

affirmative action and child care.

1990-101 Vavrek, Bernard. "Assessing Rural Information Needs." In *The Bowker Annual*, 472-478. New York: Bowker, 1990.
Reports results of a national survey on the use of public libraries by adults in rural areas. One finding notes the large percentage of female clientele and suggests that one reason for this finding is that "women may feel more comfortable using the library because the library staff person is usually a woman."

1990-101a Vavrek, Bernard. *Assessing the Information Needs of Rural Americans. Public Libraries.* Washington, DC: U.S. Department of Education, 1990. ERIC, ED 332 721
Reports on a project which investigated rural public library service. Notes that the majority of users are female and speculates that female users may feel more comfortable with libraries since staff persons are usually women.

1990-101b Vavrek, Bernard. *Assessing the Information Needs of Rural Pennsylvanians.* 1990. ERIC, ED 320 590
Reports results of study of rural libraries in Pennsylvania including differences in library use based on gender. Makes recommendation that women be encouraged to lobby on behalf of librarians since they are the primary clientele and staff.

1990-102 Vogel, Sandra. "Women in Libraries." *New Library World* 91 (April 1990):13-14.
Compares membership in the Institute of Information Scientists to membership in the Library Association by gender. Results indicate 48% IIS women and 74% LA women, concluding that women picture themselves as librarians not information scientists.

1990-103 Vogel, Sandra. "Women in Libraries." *New Library World* 91 (July 1990):10-11.
Examines findings of the Institute of Information Scientists' annual Remuneration Survey which are relevant to gender and expresses disappointment that gender factors are ignored in many categories. Chart shows female salaries

consistently lower than male

1990-104 Vogel, Sandra. "The Workforce: Research and Reality." *New Library World* 91 (May 1990):4-6.
    Notes that growth rate of both women's part-time and full-time employment currently outstrips combined growth rate for all male employment. Points out that women may soon find themselves in positions of greater choice with the option to reject low-status positions.

1990-105 Watkins, Heather. "Women in Libraries--Ten Years of Independent Organization in the U.K." *WLW Journal* 14 (Fall 1990):6,8.
    Provides a brief history of Women in Libraries which developed in response to two issues: relatively few women in management positions and lower salaries relative to men's. Notes that membership declined after a peak in 1984, but there are signs of increasing numbers.

1990-106 Watson-Boone, Peter. "Dual Career Couples in Academe." *College and Research Libraries News* 51 (April 1990):292-295.
    Discusses issues involved and describes institutional benefits of a dual-career couples program including reduced systematic bias against recruiting and hiring women. One of the costs of such a program to the individual is the acceptance of different expectations based on gender.

1990-107 Webb, Barbara. "Type-Casting Life with Myers-Briggs." *Library Journal* 115 (June 15, 1990):32-37.
    Discusses applications of the Myers-Briggs Type Indicator and the female tendency towards the "feeler" category. Notes that since librarianship is female intensive, it is unsurprisingly 67% "feeler."

1990-108 "Who Succeeds at Library School?" *Library Hotline* 19 (January 8, 1990):3.
    Announces the results of a University of California at Los

Angeles study of the correlation between 25 factors, including gender, and success in the two-year MLS program.

1990-109 "Women/Gender/Feminist Issues." *Library Journal* 115 (August 1990):38-39.
Reports activities, scholarship, and status of women working within the American Library Association with specific reference to presentations given at the 1990 ALA Annual Conference in Chicago.

1990-110 "Women Managers Bulging in the Middle." *Library Personnel News* 4 (Winter 1990):11.
Summarizes a speech by Marilyn Moats Kennedy sponsored by the Chicago YWCA which addresses several issues relevant to the advancement of women including affirmative action, women's anti-change attitude, skills acquisition, moving up, entrepreneurship, and self-marketing.

1990-111 "Women's Hall of Fame." *Library Journal* 115 (May 15, 1990):178.
Announces induction of librarian Mary Lemist Titcomb into the Maryland Women's Hall of Fame for her work as a pioneer in county library systems and as the originator of what has become the bookmobile.

1990-112 "Women's Rights Backers Debate How Partisan ALA Should Get." *American Libraries* 21 (March 1990):261.
Reviews a discussion at the 1990 ALA Midwinter Conference by the Committee on the Status of Women in Librarianship on whether they should continue to lend ALA's visible political support to future initiatives of the National Organization for Women.

1990-113 Zimmerman, Mary Erb. "Special Libraries Association." In *The Bowker Annual*, 171-174. New York: Bowker, 1990.
Notes approval of petition to form a Women's Issues Caucus to discuss the status of women.

1991 BIBLIOGRAPHY

1991-01 *1990 Salary Survey of Pennsylvania Academic Libraries.* Introduction and Survey Administration by Ronald F. Dow; data compiled by Gordon Fretwell. Harrisburg, PA: Pennsylvania Library Association, 1991.

Includes data for number and average salaries by years of experience, position, and sex.

1991-02 "1991 ALA Awards Recognize Professional Excellence." *American Libraries* 22 (July-August 1991):678, 680.

Announces E.J. Josey as winner of the ALA Equality Award.

1991-02a "1991 ALA Awards Winners." *Library Journal* 116 (July 1991):25.

Announces E.J. Josey as winner of the ALA Equality Award.

1991-02b "1991 ALA Awards Winners." *Wilson Library Bulletin* 66 (September 1991):57.

Announces E.J. Josey as winner of the ALA Equality Award.

1991-03 "Abortion Law Opponents Object, ACRL Sticks with Salt Lake City." *American Libraries* 22 (July-August 1991):684.

Reports objections by Association of College and Research Libraries members to the location of the 1992 conference in Utah because of the state's restrictive abortion laws.

1991-04 *Academic and Public Librarians: Data by Race, Ethnicity, and Sex, 1991.* Chicago: American Library Association, Office for Library Personnel Resources, 1991.

Provides five-year update (see **1986-01**) of data by position, sex, and race/ethnicity.

1991-05 "ALA Highlights." *GLTF Newsletter* 3 (Fall 1991):4-5.
Reports on the annual conference program "Gay and Lesbian Library Service: Exploding the Myths, Dismantling the Barriers."

1991-06 "ALA's Crismond, Cooke Honored for Accomplishments." *American Libraries* 22 (October 1991):912,914.
Cites awards to Eileen Cooke, ALA Washington Office Director, and Executive Director Linda Crismond.

1991-07 Alemna, A. A. "Librarians in Ghana: A Survey of Their Social Origins and Status." *International Library Review* 23 (December 1991):401-411.
Provides demographic data including sex and marital status.

1991-08 Anderson, Felicia B. "Black Women's Oral History Project Interview with Virginia Lacy Jones." *The Georgia Librarian* 28 (Fall 1991):82-85.
Transcribes an interview with Jones, Dean of the School of Library Service at Atlanta University, conducted for the Black Women's Oral History Project of the Schlesinger Library. Discusses her career and contributions towards the improvement of the lives of African Americans and to the development of American society.

1991-09 *ARL Annual Salary Survey, 1991*, compiled by Gordon Fretwell and edited by Sarah M. Pritchard. Washington, DC: Association of Research Libraries, 1991.
Reports professional salaries and analyzes the data by sex including a breakdown of minorities.

1991-10 Barnhart, Linda A. *The Librarian's Stereotyped Image in Mystery Novels, 1980-1990: Has the Image Changed?* ERIC, ED 340 365
Examines the image of 35 librarians as portrayed in 24

novels. Concludes that, in general, librarians' image is more positive than the stereotype and their jobs are seen as interesting. Notes that almost half of the librarians studied are men, and several of them display effeminate traits associated with the male librarian stereotype.

1991-10a Beaudrie, Ronald and Robert Grunfeld. "Male Reference Librarians and the Gender Factor." *The Reference Librarian* 33 (1991):211-213.
Argues for more discussion of the changing role of men in librarianship.

1991-11 Beck, Clare. "Reference Services: A Handmaid's Tale." *Library Journal* 116 (April 15, 1991):33-37.
Argues that gender has shaped the values and practices of reference librarianship and suggests that further sociological research needs to be done on the relationship between gender and the profession, beyond the questions of administration and pay equity.

Letters:

Flexman, Ellen. "Or the Revisionist Librarian?" *Library Journal* 116 (July 1991):8.
Hicks, Jack Alan. "Consenting Professionals." *Library Journal* 116 (June 1, 1991):12-14.

1991-12 Benedict, Marjorie A. "Librarians' Satisfaction with Faculty Status." *College and Research Libraries* 52 (November 1991):538-548.
Found no significant difference in responses by gender to a survey administered in 1982 and again in 1989 of librarians in the State University of New York system. Faculty status was preferred by both groups with women showing a decrease in 1989 in agreement that faculty status benefits outweigh costs.

1991-13 Bergold, Cali, comp. "100 Women Making a Difference." *Today's Chicago Woman* (January 1991):49-53, 56-58.
Includes profile of American Library Association Director

Linda Crismond.

1991-14 Berry, John. "Money, Politics, and Freedom at ALA Midwinter." *Library Journal* 116 (March 1, 1991):50-53.
    Makes brief reference to a forum of American Library Association presidential candidates where Herbert S. White was criticized for not supporting a ban on conferences in states that did not pass the Equal Rights Amendment.

1991-15 Berry, John and Nora Rawlinson. "Program 'Picks and Pans.'" *Library Journal* 116 (June 1, 1991):60-72.
    Previews ALA Annual Conference in Atlanta including programs on gay and lesbian library service, pay equity, feminist presses, women's studies, gender differences in communication, and women's groups within the association.

1991-16 Burhans, Skip. *Serving the Information Needs of the International and Minority Students at the Small College Library: A Librarian's View*. Paper presented at the Annual Meeting of the Central States Communication Association, Chicago, IL, 11-14 April 1991. ERIC, ED 335 714
    Discusses challenges resulting from cultural, linguistic, or socioeconomic differences between international students and "the mostly white, middle class, highly educated (and predominantly female) public service librarians" who work with them. Suggests approaches for overcoming barriers and increasing awareness. Selected allusions to women librarians and gender.

1991-17 Busch, Nancy. "Future Staffing Requirements: Some Considerations." *Wilson Library Bulletin* 65 (May 1991):43-45.
    Discusses future staffing needs of rural libraries and highlights findings of national survey of rural library directors. Composite obtained by combining demographic characteristics is a married white female.

1991-18 Buschman, John and Michael Carbone. "A Critical Inquiry into Librarianship: Applications of the 'New Sociology of Education.'" *Library Quarterly* 61 (January 1991):15-40.
    Seeks to establish that methods of critical inquiry in

education are applicable in studying the library profession. Gender figures into the analysis of status in both professions.

1991-19 Buttlar, Lois. "Analyzing the Library Periodical Literature: Content and Authorship." *College and Research Libraries* 52 (January 1991):38-53.

Analyzes sixteen library periodicals on various characteristics of authors including sex. A total of 1,725 articles were written by 2,072 authors. Despite the fact that librarianship is female intensive, 961 (47.83%) of the authors are male and 1,048 (52.17%) are female. A slow closing of the gap, particularly in special librarianship, is apparent. No differences in the percentages of research-based studies and nonresearch-based writing by sex are evident.

1991-20 "Canadian Plan Raises Concern over Librarians' Status." *American Libraries* 22 (February 1991):125.

News note regarding Canadian Public Service 2000 initiative which proposes reclassification of federal librarians with clerical and secretarial workers. Includes statement from the National Library of Canada expressing concern about several key issues raised by the initiative, including the status of women.

1991-21 Carroll, Frances Laverne and Else Granheim. "Word from an IFLA Fox: An Interview with Else Granheim." *Information Development* 7 (January 1991):12-18.

Reports on interview with Granheim, the first woman president of the International Federation of Library Associations and Institutions in which she discusses the advancement of women in library leadership positions.

1991-22 Caynon, William. "Satisfaction Among Faculties of ALA-Accredited Library Schools." *Journal of Education for Library and Information Science* 31 (Spring 1991):294-313.

Attempts to determine extent to which sex of employee affects job satisfaction and concludes that there is no significant gender difference in attitudes towards work, promotion opportunities, and co-workers. Female administrators are less satisfied than males with pay.

1991-23 Cleary, Jim. "Women Librarians at the Public Library of New South Wales: The First Generation." *Australian Library Journal* 40 (February 1991):3-26.

Reviews careers of three librarians from a historical perspective. Challenges the stereotype of the public librarian and argues that these Australian prototypes were made of sterner material than stereotypical models suggest.

Response:

Editor. "Humble Pie." *Australian Library Journal* 40 (May 1991):167.
Apologizes for several errors and omissions in the publication of Cleary's article and announces the availability of an offprint. Also notes that the article will be published in the Fourth Forum on Australian Library History held September 1989.

1991-24 "Compensation High Priority to Attract and Retain Library Workers." *Library Personnel News* 5 (May/June 1991):1,8.

1991-25 Cornog, Martha and Timothy Perper. "For Sex, See Librarian: An Introduction." In *Libraries, Erotica, and Pornography*, edited by Martha Cornog, 2-35. Phoenix: Oryx, 1991.

Notes that librarianship as a women's profession may be a contributing factor to "why at least some librarians may be drawn to traditional values, particularly in sexuality." (See also **1991-64a**)

1991-26 Cravey, Pamela J. "Occupational Role Identity of Women Academic Librarians." *College and Research Libraries* 52 (March 1991):150-164.

Reports responses to a national survey and provides personal, demographic, and job data. Includes results of a test for orientation to the occupational role and a sex-role orientation test. Concludes that academic librarians have a positive and unique occupational role identity.

1991-26a Darlington, Anne. "Inspire a Lust for Reading." [letter] *Library Journal* 116 (September 15, 1991):8.

Comments on a illustration accompanying an article on the audience appeal of romance fiction and suggests several suggestive captions for a poster promoting library services that could be used with the illustration.

Letter:

Mudick, Kristine E. "Dangerously Suggestive." *Library Journal* 116 (November 1, 1991):10.

Response:

Darlington, Anne. "'Stop Taking It Lying Down.'" *Library Journal* 117 (February 1, 1992):8.

1991-26b DeCandido, GraceAnne A. "The Year in Review, 1990." In *The Bowker Annual*, 12-21. New York: Bowker, 1991.

Makes reference to the *Library Journal* salary survey and wage differences between men and women that the survey finds.

1991-27 Deschatelets, Guy and Josee Saint-Marseille. "Librarians or Managers? Career Profiles of the Directors of Large Francophone Libraries of Canada [Bibliothecaires ou Administrateurs? Profils de Carriere des Directeurs des Grandes Bibliotheques Francophones du Canada]." *Documentation et Bibliotheques* 27 (January-March 1991):25-34.

Presents results of interviews with 10 men and 7 women administrators on their training and career paths. Contributes their success to mobility, professional association activity, and ability to meet demands of their positions.

1991-28 Detlefsen, Ellen Gay and Josephine E. Olson. "Librarian and the Leaver: Who Leaves the Profession." *Journal of Education for Library and Information Science* 31 (Spring 1991):275-293.

Presents data from a follow-up study of MLS graduates from the University of Pittsburgh. Finds that a third are no longer working in libraries. Analyzes demographics, career patterns, and attitudes toward work and sex roles and concludes that the main response for leaving the profession was financially related.

1991-28a Detlefsen, Ellen Gay, Josephine E. Olson and Irene Hanson Frieze. "Women and Librarians: Still Too Far Behind." *Library Journal* 116 (March 15, 1991):37-42.

Based on "The University of Pittsburgh MLS/MBA Study: A Report to Participants" which follows up the 1983 Committee on the Status of Women in Librarianship study by Kathleen Heim and Leigh S. Estabrook. Includes gender comparisons for education, experience, career patterns, administrative positions, career interruptions, salaries, reasons for leaving the profession, and motivations of librarians. (See also **1990-77**)

1991-29 Doak, Elaine M. "Books Were Basics: Guthrie, Oklahoma Territory, Public Libraries, 22 April 1889-23 May 1903." *Journal of the West* 30 (July 1991):35-44.

Notes the involvement of women's clubs in the development of libraries and the work of Margaret Rees, the first full-time librarian in the territory, and Adele Kesler, her successor.

1991-30 Doughan, David. "Women's Libraries Meet in Istanbul." *Library Association Record* 93 (December 1991):831.

Discusses the International Symposium of Women's Libraries and the work of the Women's Library and Information Centre Foundation. Notes that proceedings will be published, an international newsletter begun, and another symposium scheduled for 1994.

1991-30a Engle, Michael. "The Librarian and the Crone--Myth and Reality." *School Library Journal* 37 (January 1991):44.

Discusses the image of the Crone in folklore as it relates to the stereotypical image of librarians. Notes tales in which she is a key figure and encourages librarians to acknowledge "the importance of her presence" as essential to professional development and image.

1991-31 *Fact Book on Women in Higher Education.* Edited by Judith G. Touchton and Lynne Davis. New York: American Council on Education, 1991.

Includes statistical information on women in all areas of higher education with data on number of degrees conferred by sex and level of institution. Also includes historical data from the 1970s and the number and median salary of library deans (most recent data is 1987-88).

1991-32 Finks, Lee. "Librarianship Needs a New Code of Professional Ethics." *American Libraries* 22 (January 1991):84-92.
Makes no direct reference to gender or sex but prompted the responses below.

Letters:

Johnson, Walt. "Prejudices and Our profession." *American Libraries* 22 (July-August 1991):619.
Criticizes Mitchell (below) for biased comments and questions freedom of access to information in Mitchell's library.
Mitchell, Walter W. "Finks' Critics Fuel Disgust." *American Libraries* 22 (May 1991):390-391.
Includes criticism of the American Library Association for "legitimizing such deep, dark sins as homosexuality and lesbianism by recognizing and funding a 'task force' of same" and supporting abortion and pornography.
Ranger, Kim. "Finding Fault with Finks." *American Libraries* 22 (March 1991):217.
Comments on Finks' recommendation that librarians adhere to community standards which suggests that the American Library Association Gay and Lesbian Task Force should disband.

1991-33 Fisher, Edith Maureen. "Modern Racism in Academic Librarianship Towards Black Americans: A California Study." Ph.D. diss., University of Pittsburgh, 1991.
Results of survey questionnaire administered to measure racial attitude and racialistic awareness. Conclusions include finding that gender may affect racialistic awareness. Calls for further research on the perceptions of prejudice and empowerment strategies.

1991-34 Freedman, Janet. "Information for Transformation: The

Perspective of a Library Director." *WLW Journal* 14 (Winter 1991):3-5.

Explores roles of feminist librarians in an academic environment and the application of a feminist management style in one library setting. Encourages women librarians to make connections on campus as well as outside of the campus community. Briefly discusses the impact of automation. Based on paper presented at the National Women's Studies Association conference, Towson, Maryland, June 1989. (See **1989-54**)

1991-34a "From Law to Public Librarianship: Catherine May Fleming, Class of 1990." *Library Journal* 116 (November 1, 1991):48-49.

Chronicles career change of Fleming and notes the influence of her elementary school librarian in encouraging her to use libraries.

1991-35 Garland, Kathleen. "The Nature of Publications Authored by Library and Information Science Faculty." *Library and Information Science Research* 13 (January-March 1991):47-60.

Uses gender as a variable in the prediction of non-scholarly vs. scholarly publications and concludes that it is insignificant.

1991-36 Gasaway, Laura N. "Sexual Harassment in the Library: The Law." *North Carolina Libraries* 49 (Spring 1991):14-17.

Discusses sexual harassment law and liability and the benefits of a harassment-free workplace. Considers the challenge of educating supervisors and employees and developing and enforcing a policy.

1991-37 Gaughan, Tom. "Maybe P.D. James Began This Way." *American Libraries* 22 (April 1991):276.

Editorial discusses librarian Sarah Shoemaker who writes mysteries under the pseudonym S.K. Wolf that feature a reference librarian who is a "delightful, knowing turn on the stereotype." Notes Shoemaker's use of a gender-ambiguous pseudonym because her publisher believes that "men won't buy Ludlumesque thrillers written by a woman."

1991-38 "Gay/Lesbian Concerns." *American Libraries* 22 (May 1991):426.

Announces two publications, a pamphlet "Gays in Library Land: The Gay and Lesbian Task Force of the American Library Association: The First Sixteen Years" by Barbara Gittings (see **1990-41a**) and the book *Gay and Lesbian Library Service* edited by Cal Gough and Ellen Greenblatt (see **1990-40**).

1991-39 "Gays Celebrate New LAPL Programming." *Library Journal* 116 (June 1, 1991):28-29.

Describes programming on gay and lesbian contributions at Los Angeles libraries in June.

1991-40 "GLTF Petitions H.W. Wilson to Include Gay/Lesbian Press." *American Libraries* 22 (April 1991):365.

Reports on Gay and Lesbian Task Force petition to get gay/lesbian periodicals indexed in *Readers' Guide to Periodical Literature*.

1991-41 Goodyear, Mary Lou and William K. Black. "Combating Sexual Harassment: A Public Service Perspective." *American Libraries* 22 (February 1991):134-136.

Discusses harassment between library employees and patrons and between patrons, and outlines Iowa State University's development of a sexual harassment policy in response to concerns.

1991-42 Gothberg, Helen M. "Time Management in Public Libraries: A Study of Public Libraries." *Public Libraries* 30 (November/ December 1991):350-357.

Concludes that women spent more time budgeting, more days away from the library, more time at professional meetings, and were more likely to delegate authority than men.

1991-43 Granger, Dotty. "Acquisition Notes." *Women in Libraries* 20 (July 1991):5-7.

Announces resurrection of *WLW Journal*.

1991-44 Granger, Dotty. *"American Libraries." Women in Libraries* 20 (July 1991):2.

Discusses the downward trend in the coverage of women's issues in *American Libraries* and efforts to effect change.

1991-45 Grosch, Mary and Terry L. Weech. "Perceived Value of Advanced Subject Degrees by Librarians Who Hold Such Degrees." *Library and Information Science Research* 13 (July-September 1991):173-199.

Concludes that when three major indicators are separated by gender, responses by men and women with degrees other than MBAs vary significantly. Confirms that men still represent a higher number of directors.

1991-46 Hanks, Gardner C. "Call for a New Approach Toward Educating a Librarian." *PNLA Quarterly* 55 (Winter 1991):8-10.

Attributes the decline in qualified applicants to increased opportunities for women in fields outside librarianship which offer better pay and career development. Proposed changes in library education to alleviate the problem.

1991-47 Hanson, Roland. "From the Co-Chair." *GLTF Newsletter* 3 (Fall 1991):1-3.

Notes issues confronting the American Library Association Gay and Lesbian Task Force and the need for more participation. Includes announcement for a Female Co-Chair of the Steering Committee and for a Feminist Task Force liaison.

1991-48 Hartse, Merri, Atifa Rawan, and Roger Scanland. "The Evolution of Affirmative Action at the University of Arizona Library." *College and Research Libraries News* 52 (January 1991):7-8, 10-11.

Discusses underutilization of women and minorities at the library prior to 1987 and how the library established goals to increase representation.

1991-49 Heim, Kathleen M. and Anna H. Perrault. "Gender-based Factors Contributing to the Selection of University Administrators." *Journal of Education for Library and Information Science* 32 (Fall/Winter 1991):222-233.

Examines factors related to selection of administrators

with goal of providing a greater understanding of the culture and environment of large research universities so women faculty can be aware of qualities required. Offers strategies for overcoming traditional obstacles.

1991-50 Herubel, Jean-Pierre V. M. "Authorship, Gender, and Institutional Affiliation in Library History: The Case of *Libraries & Culture*." *Behavioral & Social Sciences Librarian* 11 (1991):49-54.
Examines the gender of authorship and institutional affiliation of a scholarly journal. Reveals that more men than women published in library history.

1991-51 Hildenbrand, Suzanne. "Censorship of Feminist Opinions." *Women in Libraries* 21 (November 1991):2.
Concerns the lack of feminist or women's interest material in professional library literature. Notes that historians researching in library literature observe with amazement how little protest is expressed by female librarians over their status and speculates that the phenomenon may be censorship in support of a professional image.

1991-52 Inamdar, N.B. "Planning and Training Workshop for Information Network for Women and Development Studies: A Report." *Herald of Library Science* 30 (January-April 1991):85-88.
Summarizes the workshop including sessions on networking and women's studies and librarianship.

1991-53 "Is 'Genderspeak' the Roadblock to Bridging the Gender Gap?" *American Libraries* 22 (September 1991):717, 719.
Reports on a program sponsored by the American Library Association Committee on the Status of Women in Librarianship at the 1991 American Library Association conference which focused on male-female communication styles.

1991-53a Jackson, Louise and Michael Day. "The Wyoming Literary and Library Association, 1870-1878." *Journal of the West* 30 (July 1991):14-24.
Chronicles the history of the association. Notes the involvement of women and highlights the activities of Eliza Stewart

Boyd, a teacher, and Sarah W. Pease, wife of the Justice of the Peace, who were instrumental in the success of the library.

1991-54 Jenkins, Christine. "Feminism, Pornography, and Libraries." In *Libraries, Erotica, and Pornography*, edited by Martha Cornog, 106-118. Phoenix: Oryx, 1991.

Discusses feminist attitudes and responses towards pornography and the conflict for feminist librarians between concerns for the exploitation of women and censorship. Encourages librarians to acknowledge and confront their views and educate themselves about feminist perspectives on this issue. (See also **1991-64a**)

1991-54a Johnson, Nancy Louise Becker. "Sarah C. N. Bogle: Librarian at Large." Ph.D. diss., University of Michigan, 1991.

Describes life of Sarah Comly Norris Bogle (1870-1932), an academic librarian, public librarian, library school director, and American Library Association executive. Notes her influence on the training of children's librarians, opportunities for African Americans in library school education, the professionalization of librarianship, and the integration of American theory and methods in European, especially French, library school education.

1991-55 Jones, Plummer Alston, Jr. "American Public Library Service to the Immigrant Community, 1876-1948: A Biographical History of the Movement and Its Leaders." Ph.D. diss., University of North Carolina at Chapel Hill, 1991.

Includes biographies of three women leaders of the library movement: Jane Maud Campbell (1869-1947), Eleanor (Edwards) Ledbetter (1870-1954), and Edna Phillips (1890-1968). All were active in the ALA Committee on Work with the Foreign Born and worked with public libraries to provide immigrants with information and guidance.

1991-56 Jordan, Pamela A. "The Librarian Image: A Child's Perspective." M.A. thesis, Kent State University, 1991.

Reports results of a questionnaire administered to fourth graders to measure children's perceptions of librarians based on the assumption that the image is negative and that the negative

The Bibliography

image is more prevalent in boys. Concludes that the negative image was not prevalent and both sexes responded in a strongly positive way.

1991-57 Kirkland, Janice. "Equity and Entitlement: Internal Barriers to Improving the Pay of Academic Librarians." *College and Research Libraries* 52 (July 1991):375-380.

Asserts that women's low sense of personal entitlement and the female majority in academic librarianship combine to give one probable cause of low salaries. Suggests that efforts are needed to raise feelings of entitlement among academic librarians of both sexes.

1991-58 Kirkland, Janice. "The High Cost of Low Salaries: Strong Reasons for Pay Equity." *The Bottom Line* 5 (Spring 1991):11-13.

Argues that gender discrimination keeps salaries low, thus contributing to high turnover, increased recruiting and training costs, interrupted programs, and low morale.

1991-59 Kleiman, Carol. "A Bleak Mother's Day Report." *Chicago Tribune*, 9 May 1991, sec. 3, p. 1-2.

Describes report by the Older Women's League on economic conditions for women and cites librarianship as an example of a low-paying job into which older women are segregated.

1991-60 Kniffel, Leonard. "Minneapolis PL Told to Extend Benefits to Gay Partners." *American Libraries* 22 (November 1991):935.

Reports ruling by the Minneapolis, Minnesota, Civil Rights Department in favor of three lesbian employees of the Minneapolis Public Library who wanted insurance benefits for their partners.

1991-61 Kniffel, Leonard. "UC/Irvine Library Director Resigns During Bias Investigation." *American Libraries* 22 (May 1991):374-375.

Reports resignation of Calvin Boyer under pressure from charges including bias against women and minorities.

1991-62 "Langston Hughes Poem Divides Gays, Blacks at LAPL."
American Libraries 22 (July-August 1991):610-611, 613.
   Reports on withdrawal by City Librarian Elizabeth
Martinez Smith of a poster for Lesbian and Gay History Month
featuring Hughes and his work because of objections by the
African-American community.

Letters:

   Bennett, E. Kenneth. "Sorrow over LAPL Discord." *American
Libraries* 22 (September 1991):702.
   Polacheck, Janet G. "Sorrow over LAPL Discord." *American
Libraries* 22 (September 1991):702.
   Sellen, Betty-Carol. "Outrageous Censorship at LAPL."
American Libraries 22 (October 1991):842-843.

1991-63 Learmont, Carol L. and Stephen Van Houten.
"Placements and Salaries, 1989: Steady On." In *The Bowker
Annual*, 329-343. New York: Bowker, 1991.
   Include data on status of graduates, salaries, and
placements by sex.

1991-63a Leary, Margaret A. "Salary Improvement: Who Must Be
Persuaded?" *AALL Newsletter* 23 (September 1991):474.
   Provides information about salaries of non-director law
librarians. Table compares director and staff salaries by years of
experience and sex for Association of Research Libraries law
libraries.

1991-64 Lee, Frank S. "Lillian Bradshaw and the Dallas Public
Library." *Public Library Quarterly* 11 (1991):39-70.
   Reprint of Ph.D. dissertation (see **1989-78a**). Chapter
entitled "Personal Characteristics and Style" focuses on Bradshaw's
views on "women's issues." A typical expression of her views is "I
don't want a job just because I'm a woman. I want a job because I
damn well do that job and do it better than someone else."

1991-64a *Libraries, Erotica, and Pornography*, edited by Martha
Cornog. Phoenix: Oryx, 1991.

Provides wide range of essays on issues surrounding pornographic materials in libraries and censorship. (See **1991-25**, **1991-54**, and **1991-84**)

Reviews:

Buck, Richard M. *Newsletter on Intellectual Freedom* 40 (July 1991):105-106.
Editors. *Journal of Academic Librarianship* 17 (May 1991):135.
Harter, M. *Library Quarterly* 61 (October 1991):457.
Lanier, D. *Library Resources and Technical Services* 35 (October 1991):489.
Magnuson, Nancy. *Library Journal* 116 (April 1, 1991):162.
McCoy, K. *Voice of Youth Advocates* 14 (August 1991):198.
Merlock, R. *RQ* 31 (Winter 1991):284+.
Pymm, B. *Australian Library Review* 9 (May 1992):26-27 (supp.).
Reference & Research Book News 6 (June 1991):40.
Stevens, Norman. *Wilson Library Bulletin* 65 (April 1991):97.
Weil, M. *Journal of Academic Librarianship* 17 (November 1991):306.

1991-65 Loch-Wouters, Marge. "Children's Cornucopia." *WLW Journal* 14 (Winter 1991):9-11.

Notes that youth workers are in a women's profession within a women's profession and are undervalued and face discrimination. Suggests numerous ways to improve their status including continuing education, professional involvement, involvement in feminist groups, and speaking up to right inequitable situations.

1991-66 Lowe, Michael. *The Business Information Workforce in the United Kingdom*. Aberystwyth, Wales: Department of Information and Library Studies, University College of Wales, 1991.

Finds that the employment of women in business information positions in the private sector is representative of the profession as a whole and that the number of female heads of services is in proportion to the number of females employed. Discusses salary.

1991-67 Luck, Maura. "Gender and Library Work: The Limitations of a Dual Labour Market Theory." In *Working Women: International Perspectives on Labour and Gender Ideology*, edited by Nanneke Redclift and M. Thea Sinclair, 25-41. London: Routledge, 1991.

Examines dual labor market theory as it explains the predominance of women in secondary markets characterized by lower wages and levels of skill, fewer opportunities for promotion, and employment instability. Uses a case study of library workers in a UK university library and concludes that the theory is inadequate to explain women's inferior position in the library workforce. Suggests that the role of part-time work in libraries and in women's lives determines the definition of necessary skills and the high numbers of women in the secondary labor market.

1991-68 Lundberg, Norma June. "The Social Organization of Birth Control Information in Public Libraries." Ph.D. diss., University of Western Ontario (Canada), 1991.

Investigates women's access to birth control information, especially information produced by women and relevant to women's control of reproductive health. Examines how public librarians acquired, organized and provided access. Concludes that "women's knowledge has been marginalized" and several factors had a negative effect on providing access.

1991-69 Mayer-Hennelly, Mary. "She Doesn't Speak My Language!" *Library Personnel News* 5 (September/October 1991):5.

Reports on the program on gender and communications in the workplace sponsored by the American Library Association Committee on the Status of Women in Librarianship at the 1991 American Library Association Annual Conference.

1991-70 McCorkle, Jill. "The Southern Women Writer." *North Carolina Libraries* 49 (Winter 1991):210-211.

Reprints speech sponsored by the North Carolina Library Association Round Table on the Status of Women in Librarianship.

1991-71 McCrady, Ellen. "History of the Abbey Publications." *Library Resources and Technical Services* 35 (1991):104-108.

Traces the evolution of a one-woman enterprise and reveals much about the status of women in preservation and conservation in the 1970s and 1980s.

1991-72 McGilvray, Brenda. "1991 Salary Survey." *Canadian Law Libraries* 16 (October 1991):168-172.

1991-73 McInvaill, Dwight. "Kaycee Hale: The Image of Success." *Wilson Library Bulletin* 65 (January 1991):50-52, 138.

Profiles Hale, Executive Director of the Fashion Institute of Design and Merchandising Museum and Library Foundation, a librarian and former model.

1991-74 Murgai, Sarla R. "Attitudes Toward Women as Managers in Library and Information Science." *Sex Roles* 24 (June 1991):681-700.

Reports results of questionnaire sent to library school students in eleven graduate programs to evaluate their attitudes towards women as managers. Students were chosen because they have already developed adult attitudes towards gender roles and embodied the changing attitudes of coming generations to female administrators. Concludes that a vast majority of respondents think women are as capable as men of being good managers and that traditional attitudes are the greatest impediment to female promotion. Suggests that objective job evaluation, collective management, and studies like this one will help traditionalists change their attitudes towards women administrators.

1991-75 Myers, Marcia J. and Paula T. Kaufman. "ARL Directors: Two Decades of Changes." *College and Research Libraries* 52 (May 1991):241-254.

Examines changes among directorships from 1970 to 1989 including statistics on gender which indicate that in the first year of the study, there were no female directors; by 1989, there were 32. The influx of women into these positions has changed group demographics--the women are younger, have fewer years of service, higher average salaries, and higher budget increases than male counterparts.

1991-76 "New Home for *Women Library Workers*." *American Libraries* 22 (March 1991):242.
Announces resumption of the publication under the auspices of McFarland and Co. beginning with volume fourteen.

1991-77 "News in Brief." *GLTF Newsletter* 3 (Fall 1991):7-8.
Notes development of diversity workshops at the Los Angeles Public Library to promote understanding among employees as a result of the controversy over a Lesbian and Gay History Month display.

1991-78 Oberg, Larry R. "Paraprofessionals: Shaping the New Reality." *Library Mosaics* 2 (May/June 1991):11, 13.
Discusses the status of paraprofessionals in libraries and the need to look at issues which impact them, including pay equity and comparable worth.

1991-79 Olszewski, Ann. "Cleveland's Literacy Lion." *American Libraries* 22 (March 1991):203.
Profiles the career of Eleanor Ledbetter, a branch librarian for the Cleveland Public Library, and her outreach efforts to immigrants in the twenties and thirties.

1991-80 Orlyk, Douglas. "The Stereotypical Librarian?" [letter] *Library Journal* 116 (July 1991):8.
Responds to May 15th issue of *Library Journal* and, in particular, the word "professional." Advocates acceptance of and pride in librarians' professional image.

Letter:

Zordell, Paula Kress. "The 'Worth' of Librarians?" *Library Journal* 116 (October 15, 1991):8, 10.

1991-81 Parker, Sandra. "All Men are Equal (But What About the Rest of Us?)" *Assistant Librarian* (June 1991):84-87.
Discusses progress towards function for equal

opportunities work in the Library Association (UK) and sets out challenges still to be faced.

1991-82 Passet, Joanne E. "Bringing the Public Library Gospel to the American West." *Journal of the West* 30 (July 1991):45-52.
Highlights the experiences of 11 women librarians in the West and their impact on the development of libraries. Notes that "the lives of these westering women challenge" the stereotypical view of the "passive and quiet" librarian.

1991-83 Passet, Joanne E. "Entering the Professions: Women Library Educators and the Placement of Female Students, 1887-1912." *History of Education Quarterly* 31 (Summer 1991):207-228.
Discusses the experiences of early library professionals and the means they developed for other women to enter the profession through higher education. Notes that the first graduates of library schools did not easily acquire positions without compromise.

1991-84 Perper, Timothy. "For Sex, See Librarian: Reprise." In *Libraries, Erotica, and Pornography*, edited by Martha Cornog, 250-298. Phoenix: Oryx, 1991.
Relates responses and attitudes about pornography to librarianship as a historically female intensive occupation and libraries as female-identified institutions. Notes the societal stereotype of librarians as educators and protectors of the minds of women and, particularly, men. (See also **1991-64a**)

1991-85 Peterson, Lorna. "ALA 1899 an All-White Affair." [letter] *American Libraries* 22 (July-August 1991):617.
Responds to article (*American Libraries*, June 1991, p. 566-570) on an early annual conference in Atlanta and cites lack of mention of the controversy surrounding segregation at the conference. Comments that white women's participation was also limited.

1991-86 Pritchard, Sarah M. "ARL 1990 Salary Survey." *ARL: A Bimonthly Newsletter of Research, Library Issues and Action* no. 155 (March 22, 1991):4-5.
Includes table for salary data by sex. Notes that there are

more women directors but that the proportion is still opposite of
the representation in the total workforce of the population
surveyed.

1991-87 Rawlinson, Nora. "Identifying the Enemy." [editorial]
Library Journal 116 (February 15, 1991):114.

Admonishes librarians not to retreat behind bureaucracy
and defensiveness in responding to challenges of the book
American Psycho and notes that, for feminist librarians, "this
particular book tests beliefs in how the first amendment should be
applied."

Letter:

Wilson, Nancy. "As a Feminist and a Librarian." *Library Journal*
116 (April 15, 1991):10.

1991-88 Rawlinson, Nora. "Libraries Order Ellis Novel Despite
Furor." *Library Journal* 116 (January 1991):17.

Notes the publication of *American Psycho* and protests
surrounding it, including the National Organization for Women
boycott. Considers library issues.

1991-89 Reich, Angelika. "The Library: A Satisfying and Fulfilling
Workplace [Bibliothek. Ein zufriedenstellender und erfuellender
Arbeitsplatz.]" *Zeitschrift fuer Bibliothekswesen un Bibliographie* 38
(May/June 1991):201-226.

Reports results of survey of male and female librarians in
administrative positions on their career paths, current positions,
relationships with colleagues, training, and professional activities.
Women perceived themselves as still disadvantaged even though
they hold more administration posts. Most found work satisfying
but wanted more time in which to do their jobs. (See **1991-90**)

1991-90 Reich, Angelika. "Happy in the Library: Results of A
Survey by the Vereins Deutscher Bibliothekare [Gluecklich in der
Bibliothek: ergebnisse des Vereins Deutscher Bibliothekare]."
Mitteilungen der Vereinigung Oesterreichischer Bibliothekare 44
(1991):30-34.

Reports results of survey of library administrators regarding job changes, career paths, and training. Notes that women's career progression is slower and that the highest numbers of women administrators are in public libraries. (See **1991-89**)

1991-91 Reuter, Monika Elizabeth. "The Influence of Technology on Women Librarians' and Library Assistants' Work Experience." Albany, NY: State University of New York at Albany, Department of Sociology, Ph.D. diss., 1991.

Presents sociological research on increasing workforce technology and reports results of study of 62 librarians and library assistants. Concludes that librarians "greeted technology" and thought computers and automation improved job performance. Library assistants thought technology was helpful in completing job assignments, with a small group feeling alienated because technology gave them little opportunity for autonomy and independent judgment. Gives historical background on librarianship and its persistent gender segregation.

1991-91a Riss-Fang, Josephine. "The Women's National Book Association" (in German). *Mitteilungen der Vereinigung Oesterreichischer Bibliothekare* 44 (1991):57-58.

Reports the history and purpose of the Women's National Book Association in the United States.

1991-92 Roseberry, Ann Chamberlain. "Career Helping Relationships for Women in Academic Library Administration: Mentors and Networks." Ed.D. diss., Portland State University, 1991.

Reports results of survey of female academic library administrators which found that 91% had one or more career-helping relationships. Includes detailed study of characteristics of mentors and protegees including group mentoring. Women had in common a willingness to share and to delegate and a commitment to advance and support other women in administration.

1991-93 Schaefer, Mary Ann. "Reviewer's Gender a Factor?" [letter] *School Library Journal* 37 (January 1991):6.

Expresses the view that the gender of a reviewer can affect

his or her opinion of a book, movie, performance or other medium.

1991-94 Schmidt, Karen. "Happy Birthday, Dear Katharine. Happy Birthday to You." *American Libraries* 22 (May 1991):456.

Discusses documents from the American Library Association Archives on the founding of the University of Illinois library school under the leadership of its first director, Katharine Lucinda Sharp.

1991-95 "Sexual Harassment: To Report or Not to Report." *Women in Libraries* 21 (November 1991):1.

Discusses issues and includes a definition of sexual harassment.

1991-96 Sheldon, Brooke E. *Leaders in Libraries: Styles and Strategies for Success*. Chicago: American Library Association, 1991.

Compares leadership characteristics of librarians with corporate and public sector leaders and stresses importance of self-confidence, mentors, and networking. Includes incidents from careers of 60 library leaders.

Reviews:

Editors. *Journal of Academic Librarianship* 17 (November 1991):314-315.
Harmon, Charles. *Booklist* 88 (October 1, 1991):239.
Schad, Jasper G. *Journal of Academic Librarianship* 17 (January 1992):383-384.
Shea, Frances C. *School Library Journal* 37 (December 1991):48.
Stevens, Norman. *Wilson Library Bulletin* 66 (December 1991):97, 133.
Varnet, Harvey. *Library Journal* 116 (August 1991):154.

1991-97 Shields, Theodosia Tramilla. "A Descriptive Study of African American and White Master of Library Science (MLS)...Graduates of the University of Pittsburgh, 1973-1985." Ph.D. diss., University of Pittsburgh, 1991.

Investigates career patterns, lifestyles, and economic status of minority MLS graduates in comparison with white female MLS graduates. Concludes that there was no significant difference in starting salaries; present salaries are higher for African American librarians, but white librarians received more promotions. Major concern named by African American librarians was racial discrimination; majority librarians named sex discrimination.

1991-97a Special Libraries Association. *SLA Biennial Salary Survey*. Washington, DC: The Association, 1991.
Includes salary data by sex for special librarians and information specialists.

1991-97b Squire, Jan S. "Job Satisfaction and the Ethnic Minority Librarian." *Library Administration and Management* 5 (Fall 1991):194-203.
Includes discussion of several studies that include gender as a factor in job satisfaction.

1991-98 Stanyon, Mary. "Classified Men Only?" *New Library World* 92 (March 1991):4-5.
Reflects that the way information is organized can eliminate entire categories of people and muses that classification schemes are patriarchal orders created by males. Advises librarians to question such schemes.

1991-99 Stanyon, Mary. "Flexibility: A Threat or a Promise for Women in the Library Profession?" *New Library World* 92 (January 1991):4-5.
Describes two women library professionals who developed a job-sharing plan to balance maternal and professional commitments.

1991-100 *Statistical Handbook on Women in America*, compiled by Cynthia Taeuber. Phoenix, AZ: Oryx Press, 1991.
Brings together information from various sources to provide a broad range of statistics on women in the United States. Includes data on library school graduates and on librarians in the sections on employment status and educational attainment.

1991-100a Swarte, L., Frank Backer, J.P. Vermeulen, and Carien Karsten. "How Management Functions: Reactions to the Conclusions of a Research Report [Functioneren van directies: Reacties op de Conclusies van een Onderzoek]." *Bibliotheek en Samenleving* 19 (November 1991):381-385.

Presents reactions to a study of students on the deficiencies in public library management in the Netherlands. Points out the need for increased numbers of women in administrative positions.

1991-101 "Trading Places for 11 Years." *Library of Congress Information Bulletin* 50 ((July 14, 1991):267.

Describes a job-sharing experience of two librarians in the Special Events and Public Programs Office.

1991-101a U.S. Center for Education Statistics. *Digest of Education Statistics 1991*, Thomas D. Snyder, Project Director. Washington, DC: U.S. Department of Education, Office of Educational Research and Improvement, Center for Education Statistics, 1991.

Contains a variety of statistics on libraries including data on the sex and race/ethnicity of students awarded degrees in library and archival sciences.

1991-101b U.S. Center for Education Statistics. *Higher Education Act, Title II-B, FY90 Abstracts, Library Career Training Program.* Washington, DC: U.S. Department of Education, Office of Educational Research and Improvement, Center for Education Statistics, 1991.

Reports on library education grants to assist minorities, women, and economically disadvantaged students.

1991-102 deleted

1991-103 U.S. Library of Congress. *Annual Report of the Librarian of Congress for the Fiscal Year Ending September 30, 1991.* Washington, DC: U.S. Government Printing Office, 1991.

Includes information on the affirmative action program and plans for a child care facility.

1991-103a Wallace, Linda. "Librarians Must Learn to Avoid Being Stereotyped--The Findings of an American P.R. Consultant: The Problem of the Librarian's Image Overcome [Bibliothecarissen moeten leren positief met sterotypen om te gaan--bevindingen Amerikannse p.r.-functionaris: imago-probleem valt wel mee]." *Bibliotheek en Samenleving* 19 (January 1991):19-20.

Discusses sources of the negative image of librarians as well as positive public perceptions because of the advances made by women in the workforce. Encourages librarians to look at how they present themselves to the public.

1991-104 Williams, Wilda W. "Librarians Ponder the Effects of Students' Gender and Age on the Future of the MLS--Too Old? Too White? Too Female?" *Library Journal* 116 (September 1, 1991):150-151.

Notes that the demographics of students in library science and the aging of the profession were topics at the 1991 American Library Association conference. Blames the "lack of diversity among MLS students on the failure of the profession to create an image that attracts young people."

1991-105 Williams, Wilda W. "*WLW Journal: News, Views and Reviews for Women and Libraries.*" [review] *Library Journal* 116 (May 1, 1991):113.

Notes that *WLW Journal*, first published irregularly in 1976 by a grassroots organization, Women Library Workers, will now be published quarterly by McFarland.

1991-106 "Women's Interest Group at IFLA." *International Leads* 5 (Winter 1991):7.

Reports on two meetings of the Women's Interest Group at the 1991 Conference of the International Federation of Library Associations and Institutions in Moscow including the group's objectives, officers, and program plans.

1991-107 "Yet Another Good Reason Why Women Can't Be Lawyers." *Legal Reference Services Quarterly* 11 (1991):209.

Notes that two women were refused admission to Harvard Law School in the mid-1870s because it was not considered appropriate for men and women to be in the Harvard Law Library at the same time.

1991-108 Zipkowitz, Faye. "Placements and Salaries 1990: Losing Ground in the Recession." *Library Journal* 116 (November 1, 1991):44-50.

Includes salary data by sex for library school graduates, placements, and salaries.

1992 BIBLIOGRAPHY

1992-01 "1991 ARL Salary Survey Shows Starting Salaries Range from $20,000 to $31,700." *Library Personnel News* 6 (May-June 1992):6.
    Highlights findings from the ARL annual salary survey for university and nonuniversity member libraries.

1992-01a "1992 ALA Awards Winners." *American Libraries* 23 (July/August 1992):607.
    Announces Susan E. Searing as the winner of the 1992 ALA Equality Award.

1992-01b "1992 ALA Awards Winners." *Wilson Library Bulletin* 67 (September 1992):36.
    Announces Susan E. Searing as the winner of the 1992 ALA Equality Award.

1992-02 *ACRL University Library Statistics, 1990-91*, compiled by Denise Bedford. Chicago: Association of College and Research Libraries, 1992.

1992-03 "ALA, AWRT, Capital Cities/ABC Unite Against Sexual Harassment." *American Libraries* 23 (September 1992):700.
    Profiles a public service announcement to combat sexual harassment in the workplace.

1992-04 "ALA Director Crismond Calls It Quits." *Library Journal* 117 (June 1, 1992):17.
    Announces resignation of Linda Crismond, American Library Association Executive Director, suddenly and without explanation.

1992-05 "ALA Director Crismond Quits." *Publishers Weekly* 239 (May 18, 1992):24.

    Announces sudden resignation of Linda Crismond, Executive Director of the American Library Association.

1992-06 "ALA Legal Counsel Warn Press to Back Off." *Library Hotline* 21 (May 25, 1992):1-2.

    Notes that the American Library Association Executive Board cannot discuss the circumstances of Linda Crismond's resignation as the association's Executive Director because of the confidentiality of personnel issues.

1992-07 "ALA Staff Expresses Anger, Need for Trust." *Library Hotline* 21 (May 25, 1992):1-2.

    Reports statement issued by American Library Association staff following the resignation of Linda Crismond, Executive Director, citing "morale and working conditions" at the headquarters as major concerns.

1992-08 *Alternative Library Literature, 1990/1991: A Biennial Anthology*, edited by Sanford Berman and James P. Danky. Jefferson, NC: McFarland, 1992.

    This anthology contains several articles on gay and lesbian topics, including Barbara Gittings' "Gays in Library Land" (see **1990-41a**).

1992-09 "*American Libraries* Cover Photo." *GLTF Newsletter* 4 (Fall 1992):9.

    Notes that the July/August issue of *American Libraries* featured a cover photo of the Gay and Lesbian Task Force contingent in San Francisco's Gay and Lesbian Freedom Day Parade.

1992-10 "*American Libraries* GLTF Cover." *GLTF Newsletter* 4 (Winter 1992):4.

    Includes excerpts of letters sent to *American Libraries* by Stephen J. Stillwell, Jr., Coordinator, American Library Association Social Responsibilities Round Table, and Cal Gough, Gay and Lesbian Task Force member.

1992-11 Anderson, Renee N., John D'Amicantonio, and Henry DuBois. "Labor Unions or Professional Organizations: Which Have Our First Loyalty?" *College and Research Libraries* 53 (July 1992):331-340.

    Reports results of a survey of University of California and California State University librarians in non-management positions about their membership in unions and in professional organizations. Includes analysis by gender, but gender does not seem to influence the choice to join an organization.

1992-12 "Annual Averages." *Employment and Earnings* 39 (January 1992):162-239.

    Contains annual averages for 1991 which include librarians in statistics on "professional specialty occupations." Two tables have specific figures on librarians and library clerks noting percentage of women and their median weekly earnings.

1992-13 "Are You Underpaid?" *Library Personnel News* 6 (September-October 1992):4,7.

    Highlights speakers' presentations at a program at the American Library Association 1992 conference. Speakers proposed some general solutions to the pay-equity problem, recapped what the association has done in this area, and looked at three case studies.

1992-14 *ARL Annual Salary Survey, 1992*, compiled by Gordon Fretwell; edited by Nicola Daval. Washington: Association of Research Libraries, 1992.

    Includes salary differentials by sex for position held and years of experience.

1992-15 "ARL Releases 1991 Salary Stats." *Library Journal* 117 (March 1, 1992):25.

    Notes small increases overall but inequities with regard to sex and race. Also notes that there are still more men in directorships.

1992-16 Baum, Christina D. *Feminist Thought in American Librarianship*. Jefferson, NC: McFarland, 1992.

Based on her dissertation (see **1987-17**). Provides a content analysis of library literature and American Library Association programs, papers, and poster sessions by and concerning women in librarianship. Provides brief background information on the impact of feminism on librarianship from the 19th century forward, stressing the diversity among feminist ideologies and distinguishing between liberal and radical feminism.

Review:

Editors. *Journal of Academic Librarianship* (September 1992):256.
Magnuson, Nancy. *Library Journal* 117 (September 15, 1992):99.

1992-17 Beck, Clare. "Fear of Women in Suits--Dealing with Gender Roles in Librarianship." *Canadian Journal of Information Science* 17 (September 1992):29-39.
Talk given at conference entitled "Librarianship as a Women's Profession: Strategies of Empowerment." Distinguishes between quantifiable progress made by women in librarianship and more subtle gender role issues and looks at the devaluation of work and professionalism of librarians that occurs because it is a female intensive occupation. (See also **1992-59**)

1992-18 Bello, M.A. "The Choice of Librarianship as a Career." *New Library World* 93:1101 (1992):13-18.
Reports on survey done of students registered for the Master of Library Studies programs in two Nigerian universities, Ahmadu Bello University and the University of Ibadan, for a two-year period (1989-90 and 1990-91) to determine the factors motivating them to enter librarianship. Data are grouped into influencing factors, professional factors, and self-expressed values and are analyzed by gender.

1992-19 Berry, John. "The Conference That Wouldn't Stay Put." *Library Journal* 117 (March 15, 1992):36.
Notes that women's rights and ethnic issues disrupted the planning of the 1992 Association of College and Research Libraries conference and how the association reacted with the

formation of a task force.

1992-20 Berry, John. "Crismond Resignation Unleashes Emotional and Legal Reactions." *Library Journal* 117 (June 15, 1992):14-15.

Discusses Linda Crismond's resignation as Executive Director of the American Library Association and the intense comment and speculation which resulted. Highlights statements from the Association's Executive Board, Crismond, and the Association's staff.

1992-21 Berry, John. "No Action on Crismond, Board." *Library Journal* 117 (August, 1992):50-51.

Notes that in spite of heated discussion following Linda Crismond's sudden resignation from the American Library Association, legal counsel advised the Association's Council that the Board acted properly and fairly.

1992-22 Berry, John. "Old Fears and New Targets." *Library Journal* 117 (March 1, 1992):53-54.

Notes range of concerns at the 1992 Association for Library and Information Science Education conference. Includes findings of a study of the Ph.D. pool for library and information science programs and the closing of library schools, quoting Kathleen Heim who noted that "of the 17 programs that were closed, only one was managed by a woman at the time of its closing."

1992-23 Berry, John. "The Right Stuff for ALA." [editorial] *Library Journal* 117 (June 15, 1992):6.

Discusses the probable appointment of Peggy Sullivan as interim Executive Director of the American Library Association following the resignation of Linda Crismond.

1992-24 Berry, John. "The Trouble at ALA." [editorial] *Library Journal* 117 (June 1, 1992):8.

Discusses problems within the American Library Association which affected Linda Crismond's resignation as Executive Director.

1992-25 Berry, John. "What Is ALA's Business?" *Library Journal* 117 (February 15, 1992):100.

    Speculates on the activities with which the Association should concern itself including sexual harassment and discrimination.

1992-26 Berry, John and Francine Fialkoff. "Censorship at H.W. Wilson." *Library Journal* 117 (July 1992):6.

    Discusses the firing of Will Manley, columnist for *Wilson Library Bulletin*, who was dismissed for an offensive column on the sexual behavior of librarians.

1992-27 Berry, John and Francine Fialkoff. "Gay Rights Under the Gun." *Library Journal* 117 (December 1992):6.

    Editorial on anti-gay rights legislation in Colorado, the American Library Association's 1993 Midwinter Meeting in Denver, and activities librarians can participate in to oppose this legislation.

1992-28 Berry, John, Judy Quinn, and Michael Rogers. "Politics, the Media, and the Right to Know." *Library Journal* 117 (August 1992):44-46.

    Highlights of the 1992 American Library Association annual conference including a summarization of Patricia Glass Schuman's presidency. Notes her emphasis on political activism as demonstrated by her President's Program featuring Gloria Steinem and Patricia Schroeder.

1992-29 Bird, Caroline. *Second Careers: New Ways to Work After 50*. Boston: Little, Brown and Company, 1992.

    Cautions librarians over 50 who are attempting to return to librarianship that they "are likely to have suffered from the historic change in the role of women over the course of their lives" and notes that new technology combined with continued low status and salaries may make librarianship a poor economic decision. Suggests special libraries as a place to find better salaries.

1992-29a Bixby, Pamela. "Association of Research Libraries." In *The Bowker Annual*, 172-177. New York: Bowker, 1992.

Notes the 1990 ARL Salary Survey including the increase in the number of women directors.

1992-30 Blazek, Ron and Darlene Ann Parrish. "Burnout and Public Services: The Periodical Literature of Librarianship in the Eighties." *RQ* 32 (Fall 1992):48-59.

Analyzes 49 articles about burnout using content analysis techniques. Identifies sex discrimination as one of 141 factors contributing to burnout as noted in three of the articles.

1992-31 Burrington, Gillian. "Opportunity 2000 and Libraries." *Library Association Record* 94 (October 1992):664-665.

Describes "Opportunity 2000," a campaign to improve women's employment opportunities in many areas, including organizations employing librarians.

1992-32 Buttlar, Lois and William Caynon. "Recruitment of Librarians into the Profession: The Minority Perspective." *Library and Information Science Research* 14 (July-September 1992):259-280.

Reports results of survey of 164 librarians identified as members of minority groups to determine factors influencing their choice of librarianship as a career and to discover effective recruiting techniques to attract minorities to the profession. Respondents across all groups were primarily women.

1992-33 Carmichael, James V. "Women in Southern Library Education, 1905-1945." *Library Quarterly* 62 (April 1992):169-216.

Tackles the subject of the role of women in southern library education, noting that it was an almost exclusively female enterprise until about 1930. Discusses the impact of regional attitudes toward gender, race and class and how the South's impoverished economic climate shaped the way in which library education was adapted to meet regional needs. Finds that "the old girl network" of library school alumnae, community leaders, and even untrained librarians represented a formidable coalition of library advocacy.

1992-34 Chatman, Elfreda A. "The Role of Mentorship in Shaping

Public Library Leaders." *Library Trends* 40 (Winter 1992):492-512.
Reviews the literature on mentoring, including research that includes gender as a variable, and reports results of a survey of directors of large public libraries on mentoring and leadership. Eight of the 38 respondents were women. (See also **1992-106**)

1992-35 "CLA Outstanding Service to Librarianship Award 1992: Hope A. Clement." *Canadian Library Journal* 49 (August 1992):305-306.
Recognizes Clement's 25-year career at the National Library of Canada where she has been Associate National Librarian since 1975, overseeing the development of *Canadiana*, the national bibliography, and the promotion of resource sharing.

1992-36 "Clairol Exec's Personal Mea Culpa." *American Libraries* 23 (October 1992):732.
Notes librarians' reactions to a commercial for Clairol's Nice 'n' Easy hair coloring which showed a woman complaining about her hair by lamenting, "I looked like a librarian."

1992-37 Collins, Janet. "U of T Conference Focuses on Librarianship as a Women's Profession." *Feliciter* (May 1992): n.p.
Describes program sponsored by the University of Toronto's Faculty of Library and Information Science entitled "Librarianship as a Women's Profession: Strategies of Empowerment."

1992-38 "Comments on the Crismond Resignation." *Library Hotline* 21 (May 25, 1992):2,4.
Notes the resignation of Linda Crismond as Executive Director of the American Library Association and the comments it has generated.

1992-39 deleted

1992-40 "Confronting Fundamental Issues and Creating a Framework: Human Resources at the San Francisco Conference." *Library Personnel News* 6 (September-October 1992):1.
Summarizes human resources programming at the 1992

American Library Association Annual Conference. Of note are two programs on rethinking and repositioning librarianship, and a third program entitled "Librarianship: Erosion or Empowerment." Speakers in the first two programs addressed the changing role of librarians, and the third speaker criticized librarians for clinging to the "male model" of a profession.

1992-41 "Crismond Lashes Out; ALA Board Counters." *Library Journal* 117 (June 15, 1992):11.
Notes letter written by Linda Crismond explaining her side of the controversy surrounding her resignation as Executive Director of the American Library Association. Includes highlights of the Association Board's memo to the ALA Council responding to the letter.

1992-42 "Crismond Letter Disputes ALA Board Position." *Library Hotline* 21 (June 8, 1992):1.
Notes that Crismond received a letter from the American Library Association Executive Board "demanding her resignation" and that she "was confused about the abrupt nature of these actions."

1992-43 "Crismond Stands on Her Record." *Library Hotline* 21 (May 25, 1992):1.
Reports conversation between John Berry, editor of *Library Journal*, and Linda Crismond following her resignation as Executive Director of the American Library Association listing some of her accomplishments.

1992-44 "Crismond: Resignation and Response." *School Library Journal* 38 (July 1992):8-9.
Notes that Linda Crismond released a letter to colleagues highlighting her achievements as Executive Director of the American Library Association and expressing her surprise at a vote of no confidence from the Association's Board. Includes Board responses noting inaccuracies in Crismond's statement.

1992-45 "Crismond Resigns." *Wilson Library Bulletin* 66 (June 1992):13.

Announces sudden resignation of Linda Crismond from the position of Executive Director of the American Library Association.

1992-46 DeCandido, GraceAnne. "Gendercide or Accident? The Mis-Education of Girls." *School Library Journal* 38 (April 1992):10-11.

Presents the findings in the study *How Schools Shortchange Girls*, commissioned by the American Association of University Women, and notes lessons for librarians, especially those who serve children and young adults.

1992-47 Deitch, Joseph. "Portrait: Carolyn Clark Morrow." *Wilson Library Bulletin* 66 (January 1992):65-67.

Highlights the work of Morrow in the preservation of materials in the Harvard University library.

1992-48 "Denied Promotion, Male Aide Files Sex Discrimination Suit." *American Libraries* 23 (January 1992):10.

Reports on suit claiming that, on four occasions, library assistant positions were given to less qualified women.

1992-49 Dryden, Sherre. "Susie Bright: On Sexuality, Censorship and Libraries." *Women in Libraries* 21 (June 1992):1.

Profiles a program which the writer notes to be "one of the most exciting and controversial programs Feminist Task Force has presented in years."

1992-50 Dumars, Denise. *"Women Library Workers Journal."* [review] *Library Mosaics* 3 (January/February 1992): 14.

Recommends the publication for women library workers, library book selectors, and public library workers.

1992-51 *E.J. Josey: An Activist Librarian*. Edited by Ismail Abdullahi. Metuchen, NJ: Scarecrow Press, 1992.

Includes essays describing Josey's contributions to librarianship including his efforts to improve the status of women and minorities.

Review:

Washington-Blair, Angela. *Library Journal* 117 (October 15, 1992):106.
Whiteley, Sandy. *American Libraries* 23 (November 1992):876.

1992-52 Elkin, Judith and Clare Nankivell. "Wastage Within the Library and Information Profession: A Report." *Journal of Library and Information Science* 24 (June 1992):71-77.

Reports on a longitudinal study in the UK of the Class of '88 in terms of employment within and outside of the field of library and information science. Indicates differences between men and women in their employment status.

1992-53 deleted

1992-54 Fairchild, Salome Cutler. "Women in American Libraries." *Library Journal* 117 (April 15, 1992): S6,S8.

Originally published in December 1904. Affords a glimpse of the "change of sentiment and practice with reference to the prominence of women in American libraries" by a comparison of three conferences of the American Library Association in 1876, 1893 and 1902.

1992-55 Fialkoff, Francine. "Carol Krueger: A Librarian by Degrees." *Library Journal* 117 (October 15, 1992):34-35.

Describes the experiences of Krueger who worked as a librarian for fifteen years before getting her degree in library science and going to work for the National Library of Medicine.

1992-56 "Fireworks at ALA Conference." *Library Journal* 117 (July 1992):13.

Notes that association politics played a major role at the American Library Association's summer conference as a result of the resignation of Linda Crismond as Executive Director. Action at the conference included a resolution by the ALA Council to censure the Executive Board.

1992-57 Flagg, Gordon. "Rocky Mountain High-Tech: LITA's

Denver Conference." *American Libraries* 23 (November 1992):836-838.
    Includes report on a program at the Library and Information Technology Association conference entitled "Four Women in Automation" featuring Grace Hopper, Henriette Avram, Velma Veneziano, and Barbara Markuson.

1992-58 *Flexible Work Arrangements in ARL Libraries*, compiled by Diane Zabel, Linda Friend, and Salvatore Meringolo. SPEC Kit 180. Washington, DC: Association of Research Libraries, Office of Management Services, 1992.
    Reports results of survey to document practice of flexible work schedules such as flextime and job sharing. Finds that, in libraries responding, women tend to participate in flexible arrangements by a much larger percentage than men. Includes planning documents from a number of research libraries.

1992-59 Frohmann, B. "Librarianship as a Women's Profession--Strategies of Empowerment--13 March 1992 Faculty of Library and Information Science, University of Toronto--Introduction." *Canadian Journal of Information Science* 17 (September 1992):3-4.
    Presents themes of the conference "Librarianship as a Women's Profession: Strategies of Empowerment." Suggests questions linking librarianship as female intensive to changes in roles of libraries, increasing influence of managerial and technical expertise, and commercialization of information control. (See **1992-17, 1992-73, 1992-78,** and **1992-81**)

1992-60 Gaughan, Tom. "Safeguarding the Right to Speculate." [editorial] *American Libraries* 23 (June 1992):420.
    Discusses problems currently facing the American Library Association including issues surrounding the resignation of Linda Crismond as Executive Director.

Letter:

Moffett, William. "Commends Candor on Crismond." *American Libraries* 23 (September 1992):627.

1992-61 Gerhardt, Lillian N. "ALA Executive Director Resigns." *School Library Journal* 38 (June 1992):14.
　　Announces resignation of Linda Crismond as Executive Director of the American Library Association.

1992-62 Glass, Betty. "Is the 'Political Correctness' Backlash Controlling Women's Right to Know? Information Suppression in the Information Age." *Women in Libraries* 21 (June 1992):3.
　　Program description noting speakers and their focus.

1992-63 "GLTF News." *GLTF Newsletter* 4 (Spring 1992):3-5.
　　Includes summary of the January 1992 *Library Journal* article on gay and lesbian library service (see **1992-66a**). Also notes news item regarding allegations of homophobia within the Los Angeles Public Library.

1992-64 "GLTF News." *GLTF Newsletter* 4:3 (Fall 1992): 12.
　　Notes an idea from an article (*Librarians Guild Communicator* 25, January-March 1992, 32) responding to the Los Angeles Public Library Materials Selection Policy as it relates to gay and lesbian issues in the library. Also includes excerpt from letter to Patricia Glass Schuman, President of the American Library Association, responding to a charge of discrimination on the Library/Book Fellows Program.

1992-65 "Go Tell It on the Mountain." *American Libraries* 23 (December 1992):911.
　　Discusses a recent advertisement for a product from Mountain, a software producer, which presents a stereotypical portrayal of a female librarian.

1992-66 Goldberg, Beverly. "ALA's 111th Annual Conference: A San Francisco Subject Sampler." *American Libraries* 23 (June 1992):439-445.
　　Previews several programs of interest to women.

1992-66a Gough, Cal and Ellen Greenblatt. "Services to Gay and Lesbian Patrons: Examining the Myths." *Library Journal* 117 (January 1992):59-63.

Discusses the myths and realities of selecting materials on sexual orientation and AIDS, serving the library needs of gays and lesbians, and access to literature through indexes and reviews. Refers to the work of the American Library Association Social Responsibilities Round Table Gay and Lesbian Task Force and includes sidebar "Campaigning Against Invisibility" by Eric Bryant. (See also **1992-63**)

1992-67 Gregory, Pamela Jeffers. "AALL Salary Survey 1991: Final Report and Results." *AALL Newsletter* 23 (March 1992):703-705.

Includes six tables which contain data by gender on salaries, years of experience, and degrees earned accompanied by text which analyzes the data.

1992-68 Gregory, Pamela Jeffers. "Interim Report: San Francisco Annual Meeting Registration Salary Survey." *AALL Newsletter* 24 (September 1992):14-15.

Provides data collected from attendees at the American Association of Law Libraries' annual conference regarding salary.

1992-69 "Guts, Brains, and Sensitivity or the Ability to Stoop, Lift, and Reach to High Places--What Makes a Good Librarian?" *Library Personnel News* 6 (November-December 1992):4,6.

Reports on two projects aimed at addressing this issue, one concerning changes in the occupational descriptions or profiles of the librarian occupation in two computer-assisted career guidance programs, and the second concerning research on the image and perception of librarians in two inventories--the Strong-Campbell Interest Inventory and the Myers-Briggs Type Indicator.

1992-70 Har Nicolescu, Suzine. "The U.S.A. Experience: Views and Opinions of an Asian American Librarian." Paper presented at the 1992 Conference of the International Federation of Library Associations and Institutions, 1 September 1992.

Examines several issues and problems facing librarians including social issues, diversity, and the economy. Calls for women to "strive not only to survive, but, even more important, to achieve excellence in our profession."

1992-71 Harris, Michael H. "No Love Lost: Library Women vs. Women Who Use libraries." *Progressive Librarian* no. 5 (Summer 1992):1.

Examines the complicity of library women in the production and reproduction of the dominant bourgeois ideology.

1992-72 Harris, Roma. "Information Technology and the De-Skilling of Librarians: Or, The Erosion of a Woman's Profession." *Computers in Libraries* 12 (January 1992):8.

Acknowledges that librarianship is a female intensive profession and discusses the prominent and ever-changing role of automated systems in librarianship and their impact on the overall patterns of library work. Concludes by considering the impact of these realities on the role of women in the field. A version of this paper was presented at Computers in Libraries Canada '91.

1992-73 Harris, Roma. "Librarianship--The Erosion of a Woman's Profession." *Canadian Journal of Information Science* 17 (September 1992):5-17.

Talk given at the conference "Librarianship as a Women's Profession: Strategies of Empowerment." Examines the relationship between the devaluing of female intensive occupations and issues of professional status and image. Questions if librarianship is really a profession and discusses the importance of shared perceptions as a major component in determining what professionalism means. (See also **1992-59**)

1992-74 Harris, Roma. *Librarianship: The Erosion of a Woman's Profession*. Norwood, NJ: Ablex, 1992.

Examines the status of librarianship as a female intensive profession and its relationship to the devaluing of the profession as exemplified in the "de-skilling" of areas of specialization as a result of automation. Assesses librarianship as a profession in the sense of the classic definition and seeks to redefine professionalism in the context of a women's profession.

Review:

Whiteley, Sandy. *American Libraries* 23 (December 1992):951.

1992-75 Heap, Patsy. "Are Women Invisible?" *Assistant Librarian* (July 1992):98-99.
   Provides a further view of the challenges which need to be addressed to enable women to realize their potential in the workplace.

1992-76 Hernandez-Delgado, Julio L. "Pura Teresa Belpre, Storyteller and Pioneer Puerto Rican Librarian." *Library Quarterly* 62 (October 1992):425-440.
   Describes the career of Belpre, the first Puerto Rican librarian hired by the New York Public Library, who was a children's librarian and storyteller.

1992-77 Hiatt, Peter. "Identifying and Encouraging Leadership Potential: Assessment Technology and the Library Profession." *Library Trends* 40 (Winter 1992):513-42.
   Describes the first experimental application of assessment technology to individual professional career development in the field of librarianship. Marks the first use of assessment centers in a predominantly female profession. Explains how assessment technology identifies and improves leadership and management skills, and how assessment centers identify and nurture leadership in the profession of library and information science.

1992-78 Hildenbrand, Suzanne. "A Historical Perspective on Gender Issues in American Librarianship." *The Canadian Journal of Information Science* 17 (September 1992):18-28.
   Talk from conference on "Librarianship as a Women's Profession: Strategies of Empowerment." Discusses how men's leadership in librarianship shaped the writing of its history and how recently written women's library history reinforces the idea that women are responsible for the low status of the profession. Suggests instead that the ratio of women to men is an indication of the profession's low status rather than its cause. (See also **1992-59**)

1992-79 "Honouring NRC's First Librarian." *CISTI News* (July 1992):9.

Notes ceremony in honor of Margaret S. Gill, first librarian for the National Research Council of Canada, who was hired in 1927 and worked until her retirement in 1957.

1992-80 "How They're Seeing Us." *American Libraries* 23 (April 1992):275.
Notes the "image-busting" librarian, Jenny Holding, in the April 1992 *Detective Comics* issue.

1992-81 Howarth, Lynne. "'Add Women and Stir': Panel Summary." *The Canadian Journal of Information Science* 17 (September 1992):40-43.
Presents brief summaries of strategy sessions at the conference "Librarianship as a Women's Profession: Strategies of Empowerment": "The Workplace as Tilted Playing Field," "The Prospects for a Feminist High-Tech," "Whose Education," and "The Glory and Misery of Professional Organizations." (See also **1992-59**)

1992-82 *An Independent Woman: The Autobiography of Edith Guerrier*, edited with an introduction by Molly Matson. Amherst, MA: University of Massachusetts Press, 1992.
Relates the life of librarian Guerrier (1870-1959) who helped develop children's rooms and storytelling at the Boston Public Library and eventually became the first woman supervisor of branch libraries. Also distributed government information in public libraries during World War I.

Reviews:

Gregory, Gwen. *Library Journal* 117 (January 1992):144.
Melvin, P. *Choice* 30 (November 1992):533.
Publishers Weekly 238 (November 29, 1991):37.

1992-83 "International Symposium of Women's Libraries Held at the Women's Library and Information Center, Istanbul, 8-9 October 1991." *Women's Studies International Forum* 15 (1992):PR1-PR3.

1992-84 Jacobson, Frances F. "Gender Differences in Attitudes Toward Using Computers in Libraries: An Exploratory Study." *Library & Information Science Research* 13 (July/September 1992):267-279.

Examines sex differences in library anxiety, computer anxiety, and using computers for library research in 40 academically oriented high school seniors during the course of a year-long intensive library research experience. A gender gap was found to exist in all three areas.

1992-85 Jenkins, Christine and Susan Searing. "Sexual Harassment Series." *Women in Libraries* 21 (September 1992):3.

Announces a possible column in one of librarianship's major journals in which women who have been sexually harassed in the library workplace can anonymously tell their stories.

1992-86 *Job Patterns for Minorities and Women in State and Local Government 1991.* Washington, DC: U.S. Equal Employment Opportunity Commission, 1992.

Includes librarians in the category "Professionals" and library assistants in the category "Paraprofessionals." Breaks down data by sex, race, part-time employment, full-time employment, "new hires employment," and annual salaries.

1992-87 Johnston, Avril. "Cracking the Glass Ceiling." *Assistant Librarian* (June 1992):90-96.

Focuses on the status of women in senior management in library and information services in the United Kingdom. Shows how libraries compare with other organizations and professions in the promotion of women to top jobs and addresses strategies to speed up the process.

1992-88 Kleiman, Carol. *The 100 Best Job$ for the 1990s & Beyond.* Chicago: Dearborn Financial Publishing, 1992.

Speculates that librarians will be in demand in the next twenty-five years because of the new international reliance on the latest information and cites information technology as one of the six most promising fields. Reports on where to find the best-paying librarian jobs and on the status of librarians' salaries.

1992-89 Kniffel, Leonard. "Big Dreams, Fiscal Flatness at ALA Executive Board Spring Meeting." *American Libraries* 23 (June 1992):528-534.
    Includes mention of spousal rights as a topic of discussion as it relates to the United States Information Agency's policies and that body's relationship with the American Library Association.

1992-90 Kniffel, Leonard. [Cover]. *American Libraries* 23 (July/August 1992).
    Controversial photograph of the American Library Association contingent at the San Francisco Gay and Lesbian Freedom Day Parade.

Editorial:

Gaughan, Tom. "The Last Socially Acceptable Prejudice." *American Libraries* 23 (September 1992):612.

Letters:

"*AL*'s Gay Pride Cover: Pro . . . and Con." *American Libraries* 23 (November 1992):840-844.
  Includes 8 letters in favor and 4 against the cover.
Brace, William. "More on Gay Cover-age." *American Libraries* 23 (October 1992):738.
Easley, Janet. "More on Gay Cover-age." *American Libraries* 23 (October 1992):738.
Pearson, Carolyn V. "Gay--and ALA--Pride." *American Libraries* 23 (September 1992):625.
Rasimus, Edward J. "A Call for Constraint." *American Libraries* 23 (September 1992):625.
Sayles, Jeremy. "More on Gay Cover-age." *American Libraries* 23 (October 1992):738.
Thomas, Wendy. "More on Gay Cover-age." *American Libraries* 23 (October 1992):738.
Witt, John M. "Editorial Discretion Advised." *American*

Libraries 23 (September 1992):625.

1992-91 Kniffel, Leonard. "Council, Executive Board, Membership Highlights--San Francisco, 1992." *American Libraries* 23 (July/August 1992):560-564.

Notes request that the International Relations Committee investigate spousal rights practices of government agencies, particularly the United States Information Agency which funds the Library Book Fellows Program.

1992-92 Kniffel, Leonard. "Executive Director Crismond Abruptly Resigns ALA Post." *American Libraries* 23 (June 1992):424.

Reports that Linda Crismond resigned without explanation and that circumstances were unclear but "less than cordial."

1992-93 Kniffel, Leonard. "Peggy Sullivan Accepts Post as ALA Executive Director." *American Libraries* 23 (July/August 1992):543-544.

Announces selection of Sullivan to act as temporary Executive Director of the American Library Association after the sudden departure of Linda Crismond.

1992-94 Kniffel, Leonard. "What Is This Woman Doing? Readers Shed Light on ALA's Attic." *American Libraries* 23 (September 1992):709.

Notes how readers grappled with a picture of a woman in an advertisement for "Library Bureau Patent Diamond Frame Steel Stack," originally printed in an 1899 American Library Association conference program and reprinted in the May 1992 issue of *American Libraries* (see **1992-125**).

1992-95 Kruger, J.A. "Masters and Doctoral Research in Library and Information Science Completed in the Period 1983 to 1990." *South African Journal of Library and Information Science* 60 (March 1992):53-56.

Reports results of study of research projects completed at South African universities, noting the number of projects, men and women involved, and the language of the reports.

1992-96 Larwood, Laurie. "Women Workers as Users of Computer Technology." *Computers in Libraries* 12 (March 1992):38-39.

Examines the impact of computer technology on personnel in female intensive occupations.

1992-97 "Librarianship: Erosion or Empowerment?" *Library Personnel News* 6 (September-October 1992):2,5.

Outlines a speech given at an American Library Association 1992 conference program which proposes that, in attempting to enhance its status by adopting the male models of professionalism, librarians are in danger of losing sight of the values of service delivery that make librarianship unique. Urges a "new" band of female professionalism through a recommitment to service, advocacy for equitable access to information, and activism in addressing employment issues, such as salaries and equity in the workplace.

1992-98 deleted

1992-99 Matthews, Michael D., Charles N. Weaver, and Robert S. Franz. "Perceived Financial Status of Male and Female College Professors." *Psychological Reports* 70 (February 1992):199-202.

Reports analysis of 17 opinion surveys of 138 college professors and 2,761 other professionals, including librarians, regarding their perception of their financial status as compared to their peers. Found that a higher percentage of women college professors viewed themselves as better off than other professionals viewed themselves.

1992-100 McCormick, Edith. "How They're Seeing Us." *American Libraries* 23 (January 1992):17.

Comments on the television situation comedy "Seinfeld" and its recent portrayal of a romance between an errant book borrower and an "attractive NYPL librarian."

1992-101 McCormick, Edith. "How They're Seeing Us." *American Libraries* 23 (June 1992):433.

Notes salute to Margaret Kimmel, Chair of the University of Pittsburgh's Department of Library Science, in the city magazine, *Pittsburgh*.

1992-102 McElderry, Margaret K. "Remarkable Women: Anne Carroll Moore & Company." *School Library Journal* 38 (March 1992):156-162.

Profiles Anne Carroll Moore, one of the small group who pioneered library work with children. Traces her beginnings in library work, and the start of library service for children in New York City, shedding light on the profession and the status of women in the 1930s.

1992-103 "*Money* Magazine Predicts Job Outlook for Librarians, Rates Librarianship as a Career." *Library Personnel News* 6 (May-June 1992):1,2.

The February 1992 issue of *Money* ranked the desirability of one hundred occupations, using seven factors--job satisfaction, quality of work life, earnings, job security, prestige, social value, and ease of entry. The magazine also provided a 1992 outlook and projected fourteen-year growth. Librarianship is ranked twenty-fourth out of one hundred occupations.

1992-104 Moore, Mary J. "Pay Equity Payments--Federal Librarians." *Feliciter* (June 1992):2.

Notes that Canada's federal librarians are finally seeing an increase in their pay equity payments.

1992-105 Moran, Barbara B. "Gender Differences in Leadership." *Library Trends* 40 (Winter 1992):475-91.

Presents an overview of the research on gender differences in leadership, examines the impact of sex stereotyping, looks at organizational effects of various types of leadership, and argues for the acceptance of a diversity of non-gender-linked leadership styles. (See also **1992-106**)

1992-106 Moran, Barbara B., ed. "Libraries and Librarianship: Meeting the Leadership Challenges of the 21st Century." *Library Trends* 40 (Winter 1992).

Presents ten articles on the topic of the changing nature of leadership in libraries with the emergence of electronic global information. Topics address perspectives by various academic disciplines, several research studies, collective leadership, entrepreneurial leadership, gender differences in leadership style, mentoring, assessment centers, leadership training and info-ethics for leaders. (See **1992-34** and **1992-105**)

1992-107 Morgan, Frank B. *Race/Ethnicity Trends in Degrees Conferred by Institutions of Higher Education: 1980-81 through 1989-90*. Washington, DC: U.S. Department of Education, Office of Educational Research and Improvement, Center for Education Statistics, 1992.

Provides statistics on degrees awarded in library science by sex and race/ethnicity.

1992-108 Nankivell, M. Clare. *Equal Opportunities in the Library Profession*. Final Report, March 1992.

Notes the results of an equal opportunities survey and makes several points about gender and salaries. Finds, for example, that between 1988 and 1991, in the United Kingdom, there was evidence to show that there had been an increase in the number of women moving into senior management. Also finds that the proportion of women earning middle management salaries had risen at a higher rate than for men.

1992-109 "New ALA Executive Director Named." *Wilson Library Bulletin* 67 (September 1992):21.

Announces appointment of Peggy Sullivan as interim director of the American Library Association and highlights Sullivan's experience.

1992-110 "New Group Forming for Women's Studies Librarians." *Women in Libraries* 21 (June 1992):5-6.

Notes the formation of a new special interest group for librarians interested in women's studies.

1992-111 "New Push for Gay and Lesbian Programming." *Library Journal* 117 (June 1, 1992):19-20.

Notes the efforts of the Publishing Triangle, an association for gays and lesbians in the publishing industry, to promote Gay and Lesbian Book Month, and Los Angeles Public Library's attempt to do month-long programming.

1992-112 Norman, Sandy. "Will It Work?" *Assistant Librarian* (October 1992):148-155.
Text of the author's presentation at a Library Technology Fair, University of Hertfordshire. Addresses the subjects of women, libraries, information technology, management and employment, particularly barriers to women's progress. Posits that technology may be the vehicle for women to gain at least equal status in the professions.

1992-113 "Not the Big One II." *American Libraries* 23 (September 1992):628-636.
Reports on activities at the American Library Association annual conference including a program on *Librarianship: The Erosion of a Woman's Profession* by Roma Harris, political correctness backlash, and gay/lesbian authors.

1992-114 Parker, Sandra. "Women's Status in Librarianship: The UK Experience." Paper presented at the 1992 Conference of the International Federation of Library Associations and Institutions, 1 September 1992.
Summarizes work done in the United Kingdom since the Library Association established a panel to investigate ways the Association could respond to gender inequities in the profession. Notes that the position of women has improved substantially since 1986 and that the future looks favorable.

1992-115 "Pay Equity." *Women in Libraries* 21 (March 1992):5.
Full text of a February 1992 letter sent to Barbara Griffith of the American Association of University Women by Beryl P. Davey, President of Pay Equity Now, a group of librarians and library workers employed by the city of Omaha, Nebraska.

1992-116 "Pay Equity Now Group Seeks Support." *Library Personnel News* 6 (May-June 1992): 6, 7.
Notes that Pay Equity Now, a group of librarians and library workers employed by the city of Omaha, Nebraska, more

than 80 percent of whom are women, is seeking support for its litigation fund. Background to the issues is provided.

1992-117 Prins, Hans and Wilco de Gier. "Image, Status and Reputation of Librarianship and Information Work." *IFLA Journal* 18 (1992):108-118.

Notes the lack of empirical research on the status and image of librarianship and reports results of study to achieve an accurate description of the problem and identify reasons for its existence. Questionnaire includes reference to librarianship as a female intensive profession. Emphasizes qualitative information due to poor response.

1992-118 Putnam, Kerin E. *Gender and Salary Differentials for Administrative and Professional Staff in Metropolitan Chicago Special Libraries.* May 1992. ERIC, ED 345 883

Reports on study of differences among special librarians at administrative and professional levels in Chicago. Finds that while there are fewer men than women at these levels, women are paid less. Also shows differences in corporate and noncorporate special librarians.

1992-119 Raptis, P. "Authorship Characteristics in Five International Library Science Journals." *Libri* 42 (January-March 1992):35-52.

Reports results of bibliometric study of aspects of authorship from selected international journals in librarianship and information science including gender of author where identifiable.

1992-120 "Rebuttal to Crismond Issued by ALA Board." *Library Hotline* 21 (June 8, 1992):1-2.

Announces the issue of a statement by the Executive Board of the American Library Association to the Association's Council citing concerns with the performance of Linda Crismond as Executive Director and indicating that her resignation was requested. Crismond claimed sex discrimination which the Board determined was groundless.

1992-121 Rothlisberg, Allen P. *Ever Thought of a Library Career?*

Presenting Library/Media Technology as a Positive Career Option. April 1992. ERIC, ED 346 859

    Discusses curriculum offered at Northland Pioneer College (Arizona) and notes that the college is recruiting, among others, housewives reentering the workforce.

1992-122 St. Lifer, Evan and Susan S. DiMattia. "Voters Provide Libraries with Election Day Triumph & Tragedy." *Library Journal* 117 (December 1992):14-16, 18.

    Notes rejection of anti-gay laws in Oregon and passage of gay rights ban in Colorado, site of the American Library Association 1993 Midwinter Meeting.

1992-123 "Salary Winners and Losers." *Working Woman* 17 (January 1992):51.

    Notes that the consumer price index rose 31.3% from 1983 to 1992 and that librarians lost ground with an increase of 28% based on data from the Bureau of Labor Statistics.

1992-124 "San Francisco Conference Program Topics Include Americans with Disabilities Act, Support Staff, Pay Equity." *Library Personnel News* 6 (May-June 1992):3.

    Notes programs and their sponsoring groups. Several programs pertain to the status of the profession, the status of women in the profession, and the changing role of librarians.

1992-125 Schmidt, Karen A. "What Is This Woman Doing?: Creativity at the Library Bureau." *American Libraries* 23 (May 1992):414.

    Features an advertisement for a book stack from Library Bureau that appeared in a 1899 American Library Association annual conference brochure which depicts a female library worker who has "been likened by more than one person to the Grim Reaper." (See **1992-94**)

1992-126 Schmitt, Madelaine M. "A Reluctant Renewal." [letter] *American Libraries* 23 (July/August 1992):552.

    Expresses regret for renewing her membership in the American Library Association since it supports a "liberal political agenda that was (and is) promoted by feminists, homosexuals, and abortion activists."

Letters:

"ALA's Liberal Agenda." *American Libraries* 23 (October 1992):738-740.
Presents seven letters responding to Schmitt's complaints, three in support and four against.

1992-127 "SCOLE and OLPR Complete Study of Support Staff." *Library Personnel News* 6 (May-June 1992):5, 6.
Discusses the results of a study of support staff, with particular attention to issue papers on the role of support staff and librarians and the image of support staff.

1992-128 Scott, Anne Firor. *Natural Allies: Women's Associations in American History*. Urbana: University of Illinois Press, 1992.
Includes discussion of club women as voluntary workers in setting up libraries.

Reviews:

Kuhlman, E. *Choice* 30 (September 1992):208.
New York Times Book Review 31 May 1992, 28.
Stage, Sarah. *The Nation* 255 (August 3, 1992):148-149.
Ulrich, Laurel Thatcher. *New York Times Book Review* 17 May 1992, 11.

1992-129 Shields, Gerald R. "The Determination to Make the Right Things Happen." *Public Libraries* 31 (Jan/Feb 1992):5.
Comments of the use of sexual intimidation and prejudice in the workplace, and specifically, in the library workplace. Notes that librarians have been reluctant to bring the subject of sexual harassment out into the open forum for discussion.

1992-130 Simmonds, Penny. "Women's Events Breakthrough!" *Library Association Record* 94 (June 1992):362.
Describes the program "Smash & Grab . . . Breaking

Through the Glass Ceiling." Addresses issues such as understanding corporate culture, negotiating skills, the role of the feminine manager, career/life planning, image making, and women in professional life.

1992-131 Spencer, Dorothy A. "1992 Salary Survey Published." *MLA News* 247 (August 1992):23.

Highlights the Medical Library Association's 1992 salary survey including compensation, pay equity, and Academy of Health Information Professionals membership.

1992-132 *Statistical Record of Women Worldwide*. Detroit: Gale, 1992.

Includes gender-based data in tables on librarian salaries and placements, earnings, lowest faculty salaries, administrative and clerical support earnings, and librarians in public and academic libraries.

1992-133 Stillwell, Stephen J. "From the Coordinator." *SRRT Newsletter* 106 (December 1992):2.

Comments on the reactions of American Library Association members to the cover of the July/August issue of *American Libraries* and calls for members to take several actions.

1992-134 Streeter, D. "Librarians Have Sex Too." [letter] *Wilson Library Bulletin* 67 (September 1992):12.

Expresses anger over the firing of Will Manley and the unwillingness to recognize that librarians have a sexual identity. One of many letters protesting Manley's dismissal which appeared in *Wilson Library Bulletin*. Included here for its reference to image.

1992-135 Stuart, Thomas and Julia Phipps. "Sexual Harassment Task Force for New York State." *Women in Libraries* 21 (June 1992):6.

Notes the appointment of a special task force to explore the issues of sexual harassment. Encourages libraries which have sponsored or hosted a sexual harassment program, designed pathfinders or special exhibits, or have written specific sexual harassment policies or conducted studies or surveys to contact the Task Force.

1992-136 "Sullivan Appointed ALA Executive Director." *School Library Journal* 38 (July 1992):8.
　　Announces Peggy Sullivan's appointment as the Executive Director of the American Library Association following the resignation of Linda Crismond.

1992-137 Suro, Roberto. "A Woman, a Storefront Library and a Fight for a Better Future." *New York Times* 23 February 1992, 10(N) and 16(L).
　　Features the work of Lucia Rede Madrid whose private library for children in Redford, Texas, brings books and reading to a rural community.

1992-138 Tainton, Madeleine. "Annual Program." *Women in Libraries* 21 (September 1992): 1-2.
　　Reports on the Feminist Task Force's program, "Susie Bright: On Sexuality, Censorship, and Libraries."

1992-139 Tainton, Madeleine. "Meeting Notes from the Coordinator." *Women in Libraries* 21 (September 1992):2.
　　Notes on projected activities, elections, the Feminist Listserv, San Francisco entertainment, and the next authors' breakfast. Projected activities include a Feminist Read and a publisher liaison position.

1992-140 Tainton, Madeleine. "San Francisco Feminist Authors' Breakfast." *Women in Libraries* 21 (September 1992):2.
　　Report on the presentations at this event.

1992-141 Tibbets, Celeste. "Feminist Authors Breakfast." *Women in Libraries* 21 (June 1992):1-2.
　　Includes details about the first "official" breakfast to be held in San Francisco at the 1992 ALA Annual Conference.

1992-142 Tobin, Theresa. "ALA for Feminists." *Women in Libraries* 21 (September 1992):1.

Highlights of the 1992 San Francisco ALA Annual Conference, including the President's Program with Gloria Steinem and Patricia Schroeder; the Feminist Task Force program with sex activist Susie Bright; the Task Force's First Annual Feminist Authors Breakfast; and the Task Force's business meetings.

1992-143 U.S. Bureau of Labor Statistics. *Occupational Projections and Training Data, 1992 Edition.* Washington, DC: U.S. Department of Labor, Bureau of Labor Statistics, 1992.

Includes statistics on librarians broken down by sex and total employment, percent of employment change, and annual average job openings for the years 1990 and 2005.

1992-143a U.S. Center for Education Statistics. *Condition of Education 1992.* Washington, DC: U.S. Department of Education, Office of Educational Research and Improvement, Center for Education Statistics, 1992.

Groups librarians with technical and professional occupations and includes statistics on educational attainment by sex and race/ethnicity.

1992-144 U.S. Center for Education Statistics. *Digest of Education Statistics 1992*, Thomas D. Snyder, Project Director. Washington, DC: U.S. Department of Education, Office of Educational Research and Improvement, Center for Education Statistics, 1992.

Contains a variety of statistics on libraries including data on the sex and race/ethnicity of students awarded degrees in library and archival sciences.

1992-144a U.S. Center for Education Statistics. *Higher Education Act, Title II-B, FY91 Abstracts: Library Career Training Program*, compiled by Yvonne B. Carter and Janice E. Owens. Washington, DC: U.S. Department of Education, Office of Educational Research and Improvement, Library Programs, 1992.

Lists library education grants and sponsoring institutions which offer assistance to women, minorities, and economically disadvantaged students as authorized by Title II-B of the Higher Education Act.

The Bibliography

1992-145 U.S. Library of Congress. *Annual Report of the Librarian of Congress for the Fiscal Year Ending September 30, 1991.* Washington, DC: U.S. Government Printing Office, 1992.

Notes that the Library and various labor organizations agreed on a "new multiyear affirmative action plan" for women, minorities, and people with disabilities. Also briefly discusses a plan to "expedite the resolution of equal employment complaints" and progress on the Library's child-care facility set to open in 1993.

1992-146 Whittlesey-First, Karen. [Excerpt from a letter to Sally Zeckhauser, Vice President for Administration, Harvard University]. *GLTF Newsletter* 4 (Winter 1992):8.

Concerns Harvard's lack of provisions for domestic partner health benefits and urges the university to provide health benefits to gay and lesbian couples.

1992-147 Whittlesey-First, Karen. "Oregon." *GLTF Newsletter* 4 (Fall 1992): 5-6.

Discusses the anti-homosexual measure considered by Oregon. Includes quotes from the library and gay and lesbian press about the impact of the measure on libraries and librarianship.

1992-148 Whittlesey-First, Karen. "San Antonio Author Breakfast." *Women in Libraries* 21 (March 1992):1.

Describes the first Feminist Task Force's author breakfast.

1992-149 Williams, Christine L. "The Glass Escalator--Hidden Advantages for Men in the Female Professions." *Social Problems* 39 (August 1992):253-167.

Studies men's representation in four feminized professions--nursing, elementary school teaching, librarianship, and social work--through indepth interviews. Finds that men entering female professions are often preferred or given fair treatment but face discrimination from outside of their profession.

1992-150 *Women and Librarianship: Newsletter of IFLA Women's Interest Group.* Edited by Mary Biblo. 1 (November 1992).

Reports on the programs and activities of this group, particularly the program from the 1992 conference of the

International Federation of Library Associations and Institutions. Notes the groups plans to seek Round Table status.

1992-151 Zipkowitz, Fay. "Placements and Salaries 1991: Jobs Tight, Salaries Holding." *Library Journal* 117 (October 15, 1992):31-36.

Notes increase in women's salaries over previous year. Includes data on women and men including status of graduates, placements, and full-time salaries.

1992-152 Zipkowitz, Fay. "Placements and Salaries 1990: Losing Ground in the Recession." In *The Bowker Annual*, 357-368. New York: Bowker, 1992.

Notes data by sex on graduates, placements and salaries.

AUTHOR INDEX

AB Bookman's Weekly 1986-19 (review)
Abbott, Andrew 1988-01
Abbott, L.M.C. 1989-105 (review)
Abdullahi, Ismail 1992-51
Abrams, Ann 1989-07 (response)
Albritton, Rosie L. 1990-03
Alemna, A.A. 1991-07
Allanach, David 1988-05
Alloway, Catherine Suyak 1988-102 (review)
Altman & Weil, Inc. 1988-06
Alvarez, Robert S. 1990-04
Alward, Emily 1987-35a (letter)
American Library Association. Committee on Minority Concerns 1987-05, 1990-05
American Library Association. Office for Library Personnel Resources 1987-06, 1989-08
Anderson, A.J. 1987-07, 1987-08, 1987-55 (review), 1989-09
Anderson, Felicia B. 1991-08

Anderson, Rachael K. 1989-10
Anderson, Renee 1992-11
Antler, Joyce 1986-18 (review), 1988-137b (review)
Arrivee, Sally D. 1987-145 (letter)
Artemeeva, E.B. 1986-02
Asheim, Lester 1988-136 (review)
Association of College and Research Libraries. New England Chapter 1987-11, 1988-11, 1989-12, 1990-06a
Association of Theological Schools in the United States and Canada 1986-03, 1987-12, 1988-12
Auld, Lawrence W.S. 1989-13
Austen, G. 1990-03 (review)
Avi 1987-13
Awe, Susan 1988-136 (review)
Azzolina, David S. 1990-40 (review)

Backer, Frank 1991-100a
Bailey, Brenda 1989-16
Bailey, J.F. 1986-20
Bailey, Martha J. 1986-13

Baker, Therese L. 1986-18 (review), 1988-137b (review)
Barber, Gary D. 1989-130 (review), 1990-62a (review)
Barefoot, Martha Bagby 1987-15
Barkman, Donna 1987-16
Barnes, Melvyn 1989-107 (response)
Barnhart, Linda A. 1991-10
Barroso, Maria A. 1989-17
Bate, J. 1989-110 (review)
Baum, Christina D. 1987-17, 1992-16
Baumgaertner, William L. 1986-03, 1987-12, 1988-12
Beaudrie, Ronald 1991-10a
Beck, Clare 1991-11, 1992-17
Becker, Louis 1987-18
Bedford, Denise 1992-02
Bello, M.A. 1992-18
Bender, David R. 1987-19, 1988-30 (letter)
Benedict, Marjorie A. 1991-12
Benedict, Sandra A. 1989-52
Bennett, E. Kenneth 1991-62 (letter)
Bennett, George E. 1988-13
Berger, Patricia Wilson 1990-06d
Bergold, Cali 1991-13
Bering-Jensen, Helle 1988-14
Berlin, Miriam H. 1986-18 (review)
Berman, Sanford 1987-03 (review), 1988-15, 1992-08
Berry, John 1987-20, 1987-21, 1987-22, 1987-23, 1988-16, 1989-18, 1989-19, 1989-20, 1990-07, 1990-07a, 1990-08, 1990-09, 1991-14, 1991-15, 1992-19, 1992-20, 1992-21, 1992-22, 1992-23, 1992-24, 1992-25, 1992-26, 1992-27, 1992-28
Bevacqua, Joanna 1988-40
Biblo, Mary 1992-150
Bierbaum, Esther Green 1988-17
Bird, Caroline 1992-29
Bixby, Pamela 1992-29a
Black, Sophie K. 1988-103 (review)
Black, William K. 1991-41
Blair, K.J. 1986-18 (review)
Blake, Fay M. 1987-26 (review)
Blake, Virgil L.P. 1990-10
Blazek, Ron 1990-64, 1992-30
Bobay, Julie 1988-18a
Bolton, Sandra Lee 1989-21
Bonin, L. 1989-122
Borchardt, Max W. 1987-53 (letter)
Borko, Harold 1986-19 (review)
Boubou, Mohammed 1987-132
Bowron, Albert 1987-24
Brace, William 1992-90 (letter)
Bradley, Kate 1990-11
Brawner, Lee B. 1990-03 (review)

Author Index

Brimsek, Tobi A. 1990-12
Broidy, Ellen 1990-40 (review)
Brophy, P. 1987-43 (review)
Brown, Charles M. 1989-18 (letter)
Brown, Cynthia Farr 1986-18 (review)
Brown, Lorene B. 1989-65a (review)
Brown, Patricia Q. 1990-43a
Bruyns, R.A.C. 1990-13
Bryant, Eric 1990-40 (review), 1992-66a
Bryant, Sue Lacey 1988-20, 1989-22, 1990-14
Buck, Richard M. 1991-64a (review)
Buckland, Michael 1987-25
Bundy, Mary Lee 1987-03, 1987-29
Bunge, Charles A. 1989-23
Burckel, Nicholas C. 1988-103 (review)
Burgan, Mary 1988-137a (review)
Burgin, Robert 1990-15
Burhans, Skip 1991-16
Burns, Grant 1987-84 (letter)
Burns, N. 1987-39 (review)
Burrington, Gillian 1987-26, 1989-24, 1992-31
Burstyn, Joan N. 1986-18 (review)
Busch, Nancy 1991-17
Buschman, John 1991-18
Bustman, Mary J. 1988-21
Butcher, Patricia Smith 1987-143 (review)

Buttlar, Lois 1987-82 (review), 1990-16, 1991-19, 1992-32
Bybee, Howard C. 1988-112a

Cain, Mark E. 1988-22
Caldwell, John 1988-23, 1989-25
Calzonetti, Jo Ann 1987-27
Campbell, Saundra 1989-26
Carbone, Michael 1991-18
Carlson, Pam 1988-96 (letter)
Carmichael, James V., Jr. 1986-10 (letter), 1988-24, 1992-33
Carpenter, Judi 1987-28
Carpenter, Kathryn Hammell 1988-103 (review), 1989-65a (review), 1989-105 (review)
Carpenter, Raymond L. 1988-136 (review)
Carroll, Frances Laverne 1991-21
Carsteens, Timothy 1990-45
Carter, Patricia Anne 1986-18 (review)
Carter, Yvonne B. 1992-144a
Caruso, R.M. 1987-43 (review)
Case, Donald O. 1988-84, 1990-18
Cassell, Kay Ann 1987-29
Catholic Library World 1987-39 (review)
Caynon, William 1991-22,

1992-32
Chadbourne, Robert 1990-19
Chafetz, Janet Saltzman 1987-143 (review)
Chamberlain, Mariam K. 1988-137b
Chambers-Schiller, Lee 1986-18 (review)
Chan, Christina-Sue 1988-51
Chandler, Marjorie O. 1987-160
Chapman, Ellen 1987-56 (letter)
Chasen, Larry 1988-13 (review)
Chatman, Elfreda A. 1992-34
Cheatham, Bertha M. 1987-30, 1989-28, 1990-20b
Chepesiuk, Ron 1988-25
Childers, Thomas 1987-39 (review)
Choi, Jin M. 1988-26, 1989-28a
Clack, Mary Elizabeth 1989-29
Clark, Shirley M. 1987-143 (review)
Cleary, Jim 1991-23
Clifford, Geraldine Jonich 1988-27
Clinefelter, Ruth W. 1989-30
Coady, Reginald 1986-06
Coats, Patricia Boyne 1989-31
Collins, Janet 1992-37
Collins, Sandra 1987-07

Conkling, Diedre 1988-29, 1989-07 (response)
Conlin, Elizabeth A. 1988-30
Connors, Sue 1990-24
Contemporary Psychology 1988-01 (review)
Cornog, Martha 1991-25, 1991-54, 1991-64a, 1991-84
Cothroll, Victoria 1989-09 (letter)
Cottam, Keith M. 1987-33
Coughlin, Caroline 1987-34, 1989-105 (review)
Cowling, Charles V. 1989-77 (letter)
Cravey, Pamela J. 1989-32, 1990-25, 1991-26
Creth, Sheila 1989-56, 1989-112
Curwood, Steve 1987-35
Cutcher, Dan 1988-13 (review)

Dagg, Anne Innis 1988-31
D'Amicantonio, John 1992-11
Danky, James P. 1992-08
Dannreuther, Kathleen 1987-35a
Darlington, Anne 1991-26a, 1991-26a (response)
Daval, Nicola 1992-14
Davis, Donald G. 1989-34
Davis, Lynne 1991-31
Day, Michael 1991-53a
DeCandido, GraceAnne A. 1988-16, 1988-32, 1988-33, 1988-34, 1988-35, 1989-20,

1989-35, 1989-36, 1989-37, 1989-38, 1989-39, 1989-40, 1989-41, 1989-42, 1989-43, 1990-26, 1990-26a, 1990-26b, 1990-27, 1990-28, 1991-26b, 1992-46
de Gier, Wilco 1992-117
Deitch, Joseph 1992-47
DeLoach, Lynda 1988-36
DeLoach, Marva L. 1987-03 (review)
Denny, Mavis 1988-43 (letter)
Deschatelets, Guy 1991-27
DeScossa, C. 1989-65a (review)
Detlefsen, Ellen Gay 1987-22, 1990-29, 1990-77, 1991-28, 1991-28a
Devore-Chew, Marynelle 1988-37
Dewey, Barbara 1986-07
Dewey, Patrick 1989-112 (review)
al-Dhunaybat, Muhammad M. 1988-50a
DiMaggio, Paul 1988-01 (review)
DiMattia, Susan S. 1992-122
Doak, Elaine M. 1991-29
Donath, Ursula 1987-36
Donovan, Mary 1989-45
Doughan, David 1991-30
Dougherty, Richard M. 1987-43 (review)
Dow, Ronald F. 1991-01
Dowell, David R. 1988-39
Doyle, Catherine 1987-07
Doyno, Victor 1987-88

Dryden, Sherre 1990-30, 1992-49
DuBois, Henry 1992-11
Duda, Frederick 1989-46, 1989-47, 1989-56, 1989-112
Dudley, Edward 1987-38
Duffy, Joan R. 1990-30a
Dugger, Linda 1989-151
Dumars, Denise 1992-50
DuMont, Paul F. 1989-48
DuMont, Rosemary Ruhig 1989-48
Duncan, Ann 1987-83 (letter)
Durrance, Joan C. 1990-30b

Eaglen, Audrey 1990-31
Easley, Janet 1992-90 (letter)
Eaton, E. Gale 1988-136 (review)
Eck, Alan 1988-126
Eisenberg, Michael 1989-49
Elder, Terry 1990-33
Elkin, Judith 1992-52
Elliot, Paula 1988-101
Ellis, A. 1990-62a (review)
Emergency Librarian 1990-03 (review)
Emerton, Charles 1987-53 (letter)
Eng, Sidney 1988-40
Engle, Michael 1991-30a
Euster, Joanne R. 1987-43
Everett, Susan Hope 1988-41

Fairchild, Salome Cutler 1992-54

Faragher, John Mack 1988-27, 1988-107, 1988-137
Feinberg, Renee 1987-44
Felice, Clara D. 1987-70
Fenske, Ruth Elizabeth 1987-45
Feye-Stukas, Janice 1989-51, 1990-35
Fialkoff, Francine 1992-26, 1992-27, 1992-55
Fields, Jacqueline P. 1986-08
Fimian, Michael J. 1989-52
Finks, Lee 1991-32
Fisher, David P. 1988-42, 1988-43
Fisher, Edith Maureen 1987-46, 1991-33
Fitch, Donna K. 1990-37
Flagg, Gordon 1987-03 (review), 1988-103 (review), 1992-57
Flexman, Ellen 1991-11 (letter)
Foggin, Carol M. 1988-44
Foster, Connie 1989-109 (review)
Foster, Stephen Paul 1988-13 (review)
Franz, Robert S. 1992-99
Freedman, Janet 1989-54, 1990-38, 1991-34
Fretwell, Gordon 1987-10a, 1989-03, 1989-04, 1989-11, 1990-01, 1990-06, 1991-01, 1991-09, 1992-14
Friedland, Claire 1987-48
Friend, Linda 1992-58
Frieze, Irene Hanson 1990-77, 1991-28a

Frohmann, B. 1992-59
Frye, Michael A. 1990-38a

Gaddis, Dale W. 1987-49
Galler, Anne M. 1987-08
Gamliel, Sandra 1988-126
Gardner, Richard K. 1987-39, 1987-150
Garland, Kathleen 1990-39, 1991-35
Gartanganis, Arthur 1988-45
Gasaway, Laura N. 1989-56, 1991-36
Gaughan, Tom 1988-46, 1988-46a, 1991-37, 1992-60, 1992-90 (editorial)
Geller, Gloria 1988-31 (review)
Gerhardt, Lillian N. 1987-50, 1988-47, 1989-103 (response), 1992-61
Gertzog, Alice 1989-76, 1989-96, 1990-41
Gill, Molly 1986-17 (letter)
Gittings, Barbara 1990-41a
Glass, Betty 1992-62
Glaviano, Cliff 1990-42
Goetsch, Lori A. 1988-48, 1988-103 (review), 1990-43
Goldberg, Beverly 1992-66
Goldhor, Herbert 1988-13 (review)
Goodyear, Mary Lou 1991-41
Gordon, Henry 1990-43a
Gordon, Lynn D. 1988-137 (review)
Gorman, Michael 1990-62a (review)

Gothberg, Helen M. 1987-51, 1991-42
Goudy, Frank William 1987-52, 1988-48a
Gough, Cal 1990-40, 1992-66a
Granger, Dorothy 1989-58, 1991-43, 1991-44
Granheim, Else 1991-21
Grant, Agnes 1988-31 (review)
Green, Joseph 1989-09
Greenblatt, Ellen 1990-40, 1992-66a
Gregory, Gwen 1992-82 (review)
Gregory, Pamela 1989-59, 1989-60, 1992-67, 1992-68
Greiner, Joy M. 1988-49
Grimm, James W. 1990-53
Grosch, Mary 1991-45
Grunfeld, Robert 1991-10a
Gualtieri, Bob 1988-50
Gunn, Arthur C. 1989-61
Guy, Jeniece 1986-01, 1987-117

Hadland, Jeff 1990-33
Hale, Kaycee 1990-44
Halliday, John 1989-152 (letter)
Hamshari, Amr-Ahmad 1988-50a
Hanks, Gardner C. 1991-46
Hannaker, Carmen 1987-53, 1987-53 (letter)
Hannon, Natalie Rodkin 1986-09
Hansel, Patsy 1990-15
Hanson, Roland 1991-47

Harmon, Charles 1989-105 (review), 1989-130 (review), 1990-40 (review), 1991-96 (review)
Har Nicolescu, Suzine 1992-70
Harragan, Betty Lehan 1989-62
Harris, Judith 1990-68
Harris, Michael H. 1988-93 (review), 1992-71
Harris, Roma M. 1987-87, 1988-51, 1988-52, 1988-52a, 1988-118, 1989-64, 1992-72, 1992-73, 1992-74
Hart, Richard 1990-45
Harter, M. 1991-64a (review)
Hartse, Merri 1991-48
Hastreiter, J. 1989-119 (review)
Hayes, Robert M. 1988-13 (review)
Heap, Patsy 1992-75
Hegvik, Robin L. 1989-65
Heim, Kathleen M. 1986-10 (letter), 1987-54, 1987-143 (review), 1988-54, 1988-56, 1988-73, 1988-81, 1988-82, 1988-92, 1988-98, 1988-124, 1989-65a, 1990-42 (letter), 1990-47, 1991-49
Hermann, G.M. 1987-82 (review)
Hernandez-Delgado, Julio L. 1992-76
Herring, Mark Youngblood 1987-55
Herubel, Jean-Pierre V.M. 1991-50

Hiatt, Peter 1992-77
Hibbs, Jack E. 1989-30
Hicks, Jack Alan 1991-11 (letter)
Higginbothan, Barbara 1989-67
Higley, Georgia Metos 1989-67a
Hildenbrand, Suzanne 1987-17 (review), 1989-68, 1989-69, 1991-51, 1992-78
History: Review of New Books 1988-137 (review)
Hole, Carol 1990-48
Hollaway, Pat 1988-53
Holley, Edward G. 1989-70
Holsworth, Pat 1990-49
Hornaday, Ann 1987-56
Howarth, Lynne 1992-81
Howden, Norman 1987-57
Howe, Florence 1988-27, 1988-107, 1988-137
Huber, Bettina J. 1988-137b (review)
Hudson, Phyllis 1988-54
Hulme, Amanda J. 1988-55
Humphrey, E.G 1990-03 (review)
Humphreys, Garry 1988-43 (letter)
Huston, Robert E. 1988-134

Illinois Community College Board 1986-04, 1986-05, 1989-27
Immroth, Barbara 1988-56, 1989-71
Inamdar, N.B. 1991-52
Information Retrieval and Library Automation 1988-136 (review)
Intner, Sheila 1989-68, 1989-119, 1990-62a, 1990-90a
Ivy, Barbara A. 1987-26 (review), 1987-60

Jackal, Susan 1988-31 (review)
Jackson, Louise 1991-53a
Jacobson, Frances F. 1992-84
Jaffe, Martin Elliot 1989-112 (review)
Jagusch, Sybilla A. 1990-52
Jasper, Richard P. 1988-102 (review)
Jayawardene, Marion 1987-26 (review)
Jenkins, Christine 1991-54, 1992-85
Jennings, Kriza A. 1988-58
Jick, Todd 1987-61
Johnson, Nancy Louise Becker 1991-54a
Johnson, Nancy P. 1987-62
Johnson, Stacie 1989-52
Johnson, Walt 1991-32 (letter)
Johnston, Avril 1992-87
Jolly, D. Leeann 1990-53
Jones, Kay F. 1987-63, 1987-64, 1988-60, 1988-61
Jones, Plummer Alston, Jr. 1991-55
Jordan, Pamela A. 1991-56
Josephine, Helen B. 1987-65
Journal of Economic

Literature 1987-82 (review)
JQ: Journalism Quarterly 1989-110 (review)

Karrenbrock, Marilyn H. 1987-66
Karsten, Carien 1991-100a
Katz, Ruth M. 1987-67
Kaufman, Paula T. 1991-75
Kellen, Erin 1987-173 (letter)
Kenady, Carolyn 1989-109
Kendra, William E. 1987-68
Kenney, W. Robert 1988-46a (letter)
King, David E. 1988-102 (review)
King, Edith W. 1990-54
King, Elizabeth J. 1987-69
Kirkland, Janice 1988-73 (review), 1989-69 (letter), 1990-35, 1991-57, 1991-58
Kleiman, Carol 1991-59, 1992-88
Klingberg, Susan 1986-18 (review), 1987-143 (review), 1988-31 (review), 1989-73
Kniffel, Leonard 1989-74, 1990-55, 1991-60, 1991-61, 1992-89, 1992-90, 1992-91, 1992-92, 1992-93, 1992-94
Knowles, Em Claire 1988-73 (review)
Koch, John N. 1987-08
Koichi, Mori 1986-11
Korytnyk, Christine A. 1988-62
Krantz, Les 1988-63

Kreitz, Patricia A. 1990-56
Kroe, Elaine P. 1987-163
Krompart, Janet 1987-70
Krone, Robert 1988-01 (review)
Kruger, J.A. 1992-95
Kuhlman, E. 1992-128 (review)

Labonte, Richard 1990-40 (review)
Lacasse, Francis 1987-132
La Croix, Michael 1990-45
Lam, R. Errol 1990-42
Land, Mary 1988-64
Langerman, Deborah 1990-56a
Lanier, D. 1991-64a (review)
Larwood, Laurie 1992-96
Latham, Joyce M. 1989-75
Lauer, Jonathan D. 1988-65
Lawton, Bethany 1987-35a (letter)
Laynor, Barbara 1987-71
Lazare, Arthur 1988-66
Learmont, Carol L. 1987-72, 1987-73, 1988-67, 1988-68, 1989-77, 1989-78, 1990-58, 1990-59, 1991-63
Leary, Margaret A. 1991-63a
Leather, Deborah J. 1988-69
Leber, Michelle M. 1990-60
Lee, Frank S. 1989-78a, 1991-64
Lefkowitz, Mary 1986-18 (review)
Leonardi, Susan J. 1986-18

(review)
Levering, Mary Berghaus 1987-74
Levy, Claudia 1989-79
Library Hi Tech News 1988-102 (review)
Library Journal 1988-38 (announcement)
Library Science Annual 1986-19 (review)
Little, Jane 1987-77
Loch-Wouters, Marge 1991-65
Lodewycks, Axel 1987-53 (letter)
Looker, E. Dianne 1989-82
Lott, Barbara F. 1988-74
Loughridge, Brendan 1990-63
Louw, Anna 1989-83
Lowe, Michael 1991-66
Luck, Maura 1991-67
Luedtke, Helga 1987-79
Lundberg, Norma June 1991-68
Lynch, Beverly P. 1987-80

MacCann, Donnarae 1989-21, 1989-130
Maggio, Theresa Griffin 1990-64
Magnuson, Nancy 1989-76 (review), 1989-156 (review), 1991-64a (review), 1992-16 (review)
Mahmoud, Donna Seyed 1988-38 (review), 1989-105 (review)
Maller, Mark 1989-115

(letter)
Malone, Cheryl Knott 1987-82
Manley, Will 1987-83, 1987-84
Margolis, Anne 1987-143 (review)
Mark, Rosalyn 1987-84 (letter)
Markowitz, Lois 1990-03 (review)
Markuson, Carolyn 1987-145
Marley, Ursula 1990-66
Marquis, Kathy 1988-75, 1989-85, 1989-86
Marshall, Jane E. 1987-156 (response)
Martin, Clare 1987-85
Martin, Douglas 1990-67
Martinez, Ed 1990-68
Matson, Molly 1992-82
Matte, Carole 1987-132
Matthews, Michael D. 1992-99
May, K. Randall 1990-45
Mayer, M. 1990-69
Mayer-Hennelly, Mary 1991-69
McCaslin, Sharon 1990-70
McCombs, Gillian M. 1988-76, 1989-87
McCorkle, Jill 1991-70
McCormick, Edith 1992-100, 1992-101
McCoy, K. 1991-64a (review)
McCrady, Ellen 1991-71
McCulloch, Deborah 1989-88

Author Index

McElderry, Margaret K. 1992-102
McFarland, Anne S. 1988-77
McFeely, Mary Drake 1986-18 (review)
McGilvray, Brenda 1991-72
McGrath, Lynnley 1989-89
McInvaill, Dwight 1991-73
McIver, G. 1990-40 (review)
McNeer, Elizabeth 1988-78
McNew, Janet 1988-137 (review)
McNutt, Karen L. 1989-82
McReynolds, Rosalee 1988-79, 1990-71
Mech, Terrence F. 1989-90, 1990-72
Mellor, Earl F. 1987-86
Melvin, P. 1992-82 (review)
Meringolo, Salvatore 1990-01, 1992-58
Merlock, R. 1991-64a (review)
Metz, Paul 1989-93
Meyer, Richard W. 1990-73
Miccioli, Gloria 1989-94
Michell, Gillian 1987-87, 1988-52
Mika, Joseph J. 1988-80
Milbrath, Lester 1987-88
Miller, Olivia 1990-74
Minudri, Regina U. 1987-89
Mitchell, Walter W. 1991-32 (letter)
Mitz, Linda 1987-61
Mobley, Emily R. 1989-96
Moen, William E. 1987-45 (review), 1988-54, 1988-56, 1988-73, 1988-81, 1988-82, 1988-92, 1988-98, 1988-124, 1989-65a, 1990-47
Moffett, William 1992-60 (letter)
Montanelli, Dale 1988-103 (review)
Moon, Jeffrey 1987-24 (letter)
Moore, Mary J. 1992-104
Moore, Nick 1987-91
Moran, Barbara B. 1987-92, 1989-56, 1989-98, 1989-99, 1989-100, 1992-105, 1992-106
Morein, P.G. 1987-43 (review)
Morgan, Frank B. 1992-107
Morgan, Paul 1989-101
Morris, A. 1989-119 (review)
Morris, Beryl 1987-93, 1990-75
Morrisey, Locke J. 1988-84
Morrison, Louise E. 1986-12
Moscatt, Angeline 1989-109 (review)
Mudge, Charlotte R. 1987-94
Mudick, Kristine E. 1991-26a (letter)
Munford, W.A. 1990-03 (review)
Murgai, Sarla R. 1987-95, 1991-74
Murphy, Marcy 1986-13
Myers, Marcia J. 1991-75
Myers, Margaret 1987-96, 1990-35
Myllykoski, Tuula 1987-97

Nankivell, M. Clare 1992-52, 1992-108
Nardelli, Sharon A. 1990-76
Neal, James G. 1987-156 (response)
Neenan, Peter A. 1987-92
Nelson, Mary Ann 1988-85
Nelson, Veneese C. 1986-17 (letter)
New Directions for Women 1988-137 (review)
New York Times Book Review 1992-128 (review)
Newcomer, Audrey Powderly 1989-102
Newman, George Charles 1990-81
Ney, Neal J. 1989-130 (review)
Nicolle, Ray 1989-103
Nielsen, Laura 1987-145 (review)
Noel, Tod A. 1987-101
Norman, Nita Vegamora 1989-104
Norman, Sandy 1992-112
Nyhan, Constance W. 1988-105
Nyren, Karl 1987-102, 1987-103

Oberg, Larry R. 1991-78
Ogden, Annegret 1990-56
Ojala, Marde 1989-09
Okko, Marjatta 1986-14
Oleen, Sandra 1987-106
Olson, Josephine E. 1990-29, 1990-77, 1991-28, 1991-28a
Olszewski, Ann 1991-79
Orlyk, Douglas 1991-80
Osburn, Charles B. 1988-102 (review)
Overman, Steven 1989-31
Owens, Janice E. 1992-144a

Pacifico, Michele F. 1987-108
Painter, Frances O. 1989-112 (review)
Panigaburra, Anchalee 1988-91
Para, A. 1989-106
Park, Rosemary 1987-143 (review)
Parker, Jean 1987-55 (review)
Parker, Sandra 1989-107, 1991-81, 1992-114
Parrish, Darlene Ann 1992-30
Parrish, Nancy B. 1987-110
Pasca, T.M. 1989-108
Paskoff, Beth M. 1988-92
Passet, Joanne E. 1988-93, 1990-78, 1990-79, 1991-82, 1991-83
Pastine, Maureen 1989-105 (review)
Patterson, Charles D. 1987-39 (review)
Patterson, Jeanne M. 1987-112, 1987-113, 1987-114
Payne, Judith 1988-96
Pearson, Carolyn V. 1992-90 (letter)
Pearson, Lois R. 1987-118, 1988-97, 1988-97a
Peattie, Noel 1989-110,

Author Index

1989-130 (review)
Pelzer, Adolf 1987-18 (letter)
Pendergrast, Mark 1989-110 (review)
Perkins, Kenneth B. 1988-01 (review)
Perper, Timothy 1991-25, 1991-84
Perrault, Anna H. 1991-49
Perry, Rebecca 1989-07 (letter)
Person, Ruth J. 1990-81
Peterson, Lorna 1991-85
Peterson, Sandra K. 1989-113, 1990-43, 1990-82
Phenix, Katharine 1986-15, 1987-119, 1988-38, 1989-81, 1989-105
Phipps, Julia 1992-135
Pisciotta, Robert A. 1989-102
Pivec, Cathleen S. 1987-53 (letter)
Polacheck, Janet G. 1991-62 (letter)
Porter, Exa Lynn 1990-83
Preer, Jean L. 1989-135
Price, Cheryl A. 1987-120
Prins, Hans 1992-117
Pritchard, Sarah M. 1989-115, 1991-09, 1991-86
Ptacek, Bill 1987-121
Publishers Weekly 1992-82 (review)
Putnam, Kerin E. 1992-118
Pyatt, Sherman E. 1989-117
Pymm, B. 1991-64a (review)

Quill & Quire 1988-31 (review)
Quinn, Judy 1992-28
Quioka-Stanka, W. 1989-119 (review)

Raish, Martin J. 1988-112a
Ramer, James D. 1986-16
Randall, Ann Knight 1987-122, 1988-98
Ranger, Kim 1991-32 (letter)
Raptis, P. 1992-119
Rasimus, Edward J. 1992-90 (letter)
Rawan, Atifa 1991-48
Rawlinson, Nora 1988-16, 1989-20, 1989-118, 1991-15, 1991-87, 1991-88
Ray, Jean Meyer 1987-123, 1987-156 (response)
Redclift, Nanneke 1991-67
Reeling, Patricia G. 1990-85
Rees, Alan M. 1990-87
Rees, Douglas 1987-145 (review)
Reference & Research Book News 1987-39 (review), 1987-55 (review), 1987-82 (review), 1987-143 (review), 1988-102 (review), 1988-137 (review), 1989-76 (review), 1989-130 (review), 1990-03 (review), 1990-40 (review), 1991-64a (review)
Reich, Angelika 1991-89, 1991-90
Reid, Joanne K. 1988-52a
Reinitzer, Sigrid 1987-125

Reuter, Monika Elizabeth 1991-91
Reynolds, Sally Jo 1989-119 (review)
Richards, Diane 1988-101
Richardson, Diana 1987-179
Richardson, John 1990-18
Ricklefs, Dale L. 1987-126
Riddick, John 1989-29
Riggs, Donald E. 1988-102
Riss-Fang, Josephine 1991-91a
Ritchie, Sheila 1987-127
Ritvo, Harriet 1986-18 (review)
Robbins, Jane B. 1987-39 (review), 1990-87
Robbins, Robert J. 1989-103 (response)
Roberts, Brian 1988-37
Roberts, Norman 1988-01 (review)
Rochester, M.K. 1987-43 (review)
Rogers, Michael 1989-42, 1989-43, 1990-27, 1990-28, 1992-28
Rogerson, Holly 1989-76 (review), 1989-109 (review), 1989-110 (review)
Roney, Raymond 1990-68
Rooks, Dana C. 1988-103
Rorvig, Mark E. 1987-61 (letter)
Roseberry, Ann Chamberlain 1991-92
Ross, B. 1988-104
Rothlisberg, Allen P. 1992-121
Rothstein, Samuel 1986-17, 1987-39 (review)
Rowland, Anne E. 1988-46a (letter)
Roy, Loriene 1987-128
Rubin, Angela Battaglia 1987-123
Rubin, Richard Evan 1987-129, 1989-120
Ruse, David 1987-129a
Russ, A.J. 1988-137b (review)
Russell, Anne M. 1990-88
Russell, Thyra Kaye 1987-130

Sabine, Gordon A. 1988-102
St. Lifer, Evan 1992-122
Saint-Marseille, Josee 1991-27
Sanchez, James Joseph 1988-104a
Sanders, Lou Helen Devine 1989-130 (review)
Sanders, Thomas R. 1987-08 (letter)
SantaVicca, Edmund F. 1990-40 (review)
Sapp, Gregg 1987-131
Savage, D.A. 1987-43 (review)
Savard, Rejean 1987-132
Sayles, Jeremy 1992-90 (letter)
Scanland, Roger 1991-48
Scarborough, Katie 1988-105
Schad, Jasper G. 1991-96 (review)
Schaefer, Mary Ann 1991-

93
Schell, B. 1989-122
Schmall, Lorraine 1987-133
Schmidt, Karen 1991-94, 1992-125
Schmidt, Stella 1990-89
Schmitt, Madelaine M. 1992-126
Schuman, Patricia Glass 1987-173 (letter), 1990-90, 1990-90a
Schur, Herbert 1987-179
Schwager, Sally 1988-137 (review)
SciTech Book News 1988-102 (review)
Scollay, Susan 1987-143 (review)
Scott, Anne Firor 1986-10, 1992-128
Scull, Andrew 1988-01 (review)
Searing, Susan E. 1987-134, 1989-123, 1992-85
Seavey, Charles A. 1990-18 (letter)
Seely, Edward 1989-119 (review)
Sellen, Betty-Carol 1991-62 (letter)
Selsky, Deborah 1989-124, 1989-125, 1990-92
Shah, Shaila 1989-127
Shank, Russell 1990-03 (review)
Shaughnessy, Thomas W. 1990-03
Shea, Frances C. 1991-96 (review)

Sheldon, Brooke E. 1991-96
Shields, Gerald R. 1992-129
Shields, Theodosia Tramilla 1991-97
Shiflett, Lee 1988-136 (review)
Shiller, Dan 1990-18 (letter)
Shuman, Bruce A. 1988-80
Sicherman, Barbara 1988-107
Signs 1987-82 (review)
Silver, Linda R. 1987-112, 1987-113, 1987-114, 1987-140, 1988-108, 1988-109, 1989-129
Simeone, Angela 1987-143
Simmonds, Penny 1992-130
Simmons, Adele 1986-18 (review)
Sinclair, M. Thea 1991-67
Sineath, Timothy W. 1988-73a, 1989-80
Slater, Margaret 1987-144
Slinger, Michael J. 1988-110
Smayda, Susan 1988-111
Smith, Catherine 1986-17a
Smith, Eldred 1987-03 (review)
Smith, Elizabeth Martinez 1988-112
Smith, Nathan M. 1988-37, 1988-112a
Snyder, Thomas D. 1987-161, 1988-127, 1991-101a, 1992-144
Sochen, June 1986-18 (review)
Sokoloff, Natalie J. 1989-131

Solomon, Barbara M. 1986-18
Somerville, Mary 1987-145, 1988-113
Soper, Mary Ellen 1989-119 (review)
Spacks, Patricia Meyer 1986-18 (review)
Spaulding, Frank H. 1987-146
Special Libraries Association 1988-114, 1989-132, 1991-97a
Spencer, Dorothy A. 1992-131
Spillman, Nancy Z. 1988-63 (review)
Squire, Jan S. 1991-97b
Stafford, Audrey A. 1987-147
Stage, Sarah 1992-128 (review)
Stanyon, Mary 1991-98, 1991-99
Starr, Carol 1988-115
Stern, Joyce D. 1987-160
Stevens, Norman D. 1987-03 (review), 1987-39 (review), 1987-43 (review), 1988-13 (review), 1988-102 (review), 1988-103 (review), 1988-117, 1988-136 (review), 1989-76 (review), 1989-110 (review), 1989-119 (review), 1989-133, 1989-134, 1990-40 (review), 1990-62a (review), 1991-64a (review), 1991-96 (review)

Stielow, Frederick J. 1987-03, 1987-29
Stillwell, Stephen J. 1992-133
Stinchcombe, Arthur L. 1988-01 (review)
Stone, Elizabeth W. 1989-135
Streeter, D. 1992-134
Stuart, Thomas 1992-135
Sturm, Rebecca 1987-148
Stuttaford, Genevieve 1988-137 (review)
Sullivan, Peggy 1987-149, 1987-150
Suro, Roberto 1992-137
Sussex, Gay 1987-151
Swan, John 1987-43 (review)
Swarte, L. 1991-100a
Swigger, Keith 1990-94

Taeuber, Cynthia 1991-100
Tague, Jean 1988-118, 1989-64
Tainton, Madeleine 1989-137, 1992-138, 1992-139, 1992-140
Tallman, Johanna E. 1986-19
Tarin, Patricia A. 1988-96 (response)
Tate, Thelma 1989-138
Terblanche, F. 1990-03 (review)
Theron, J.C. 1987-39 (review)
Thistlethwaite, Polly 1988-120, 1988-121
Thomas, Wendy 1992-90

Author Index

(letter)
Thompson, Patricia J. 1988-31
Tibbets, Celeste 1992-141
Tidball, M. Elizabeth 1987-143 (review)
Tilley, Christine M. 1987-26 (review), 1988-122, 1988-123, 1989-139
Tjoumas, Renee 1990-10
Tobin, Theresa 1992-142
Tolbert, Pamela S. 1988-01 (review)
Tolson, Stephanie D. 1989-119 (review)
Touchton, Judith G. 1991-31
Treiman, Donald J. 1987-156
Trelles, O.M. 1986-20
Trezza, Alphonse F. 1987-03 (review)
Tucker, John Mark 1989-34
Turner, Bryan S. 1988-01 (review)
Turner, Philip M. 1988-124

Ulrich, Laurel Thatcher 1992-128 (review)
U.S. Bureau of Labor Statistics 1988-126, 1990-96, 1992-143
U.S. Center for Education Statistics 1987-157, 1987-158, 1987-159, 1987-160, 1987-161, 1987-162, 1987-163, 1988-127, 1988-127a, 1988-128, 1989-142, 1989-143, 1989-144, 1990-97, 1990-97a, 1990-98, 1991-101a, 1991-101b, 1992-143a, 1992-144, 1992-144a
U.S. Congress. House. Committee on Education and Labor. Subcommittee on Employment Opportunities. 100th Congress 1987-164
U.S. Congress. House. Committee on House Administration. Subcommittee on Libraries and Memorials 1990-99
U.S. Congress. House. Select Committee on Children, Youth, and Families. 99th Congress 1986-20a
U.S. Congress. Senate. Committee on Governmental Affairs. Subcommittee on Federal Services, Post Office, and Civil Service. 100th Congress 1987-166
U.S. Employment Standards Administration 1989-141
U.S. Library of Congress 1987-167, 1988-129, 1990-100, 1991-103, 1992-145
U.S. Office of Personnel Management 1987-168
University Press Book News 1988-01 (review)

Van Beresteijn, E.A. 1987-169
Vandergrift, Kay 1990-62a, 1990-90a

Van House, Nancy A. 1987-170, 1988-130
Van Houten, Stephen 1987-72, 1987-73, 1988-67, 1988-68, 1989-77, 1989-78, 1990-58, 1990-59, 1991-63
Varnet, Harvey 1990-03 (review), 1991-96 (review)
Vasi, John J. 1987-43 (review)
Vatanen, Pirjo 1988-131
Vavrek, Bernard 1990-101, 1990-101a, 1990-101b
Vela-Creixell, Mary I. 1990-82
Verdin, Jo Ann 1987-80
Vermeulen, J.P. 1991-100a
Via, Barbara J. 1988-21
Vlasova, A. 1988-132
Vogel, Sandra 1989-146, 1989-147, 1989-148, 1990-102, 1990-103, 1990-104

Walker, Luise E. 1988-133
Wall, Tom 1988-13 (review)
Wallace, Linda 1989-150, 1991-103a
Walsh, Margaret 1986-18 (review)
Walsh, W. Bruce 1988-134
Walters, Daniel L. 1986-21
Washington, Nancy 1988-26
Washington-Blair, Angela 1992-51 (review)
Watkins, Heather 1990-105
Watson-Boone, Peter 1990-106
Watstein, Sarah Barbara 1989-07 (response)
Wavle, Elizabeth 1990-40 (review)
Weaver, Charles N. 1992-99
Webb, Barbara 1990-107
Webreck, Susan J. 1986-22
Weech, Terry L. 1991-45
Weil, M. 1991-64a (review)
Weinberg, Belle 1988-104a
Welch, Jeanie M. 1989-151
Weldon, Jean 1987-172
Wemett, Lisa C. 1987-145 (letter)
Whisner, Mary 1988-80 (letter)
White, Herbert S. 1987-39 (review), 1987-173, 1987-173 (response), 1988-135, 1989-152, 1990-18 (discussion)
Whitehead, D. 1990-03 (review)
Whiteley, Sandy 1992-51 (review), 1992-74 (review)
Whittick, M.H. 1989-119 (review)
Whittlesey-First, Karen 1992-146, 1992-147, 1992-148
Wiegand, Wayne A. 1987-39 (review), 1988-01 (review), 1988-13 (review), 1988-136 (review), 1989-153
Williams, Christine L. 1992-149
Williams, Robert V. 1989-76 (review)
Williams, Wilda W. 1991-104, 1991-105
Williamson, Edgar 1989-

117, 1989-154, 1989-155
Williamson, Josephine B. 1989-117, 1989-155
Wilson, Nancy 1991-87 (letter)
Wilson, Thomas D. 1988-55
Wilson Library Bulletin 1988-73 (review), 1988-102 (review)
Winter, Michael F. 1988-136
Witt, John M. 1992-90 (letter)
Wood, Frances 1987-179
Wood, Linda M. 1988-112 (letter)
Woodsworth, Anne 1989-158
Wozniak, Paul R. 1990-53

Yoo, Jakyung 1988-139

Zabel, Diane 1992-58
Zhdanova, T.A. 1986-02
Zimmerman, Glen A. 1990-82
Zimmerman, Judy 1989-160
Zimmerman, Mary Erb 1990-113
Zipkowitz, Faye 1991-108, 1992-151, 1992-152
Zordell, Paula Kress 1991-80 (letter)

SUBJECT INDEX

Abortion movement 1989-07, 1989-137, 1989-157, 1990-112, 1991-03
Academic achievement 1990-18
Academic libraries 1986-01, 1986-07, 1987-09, 1987-10a, 1987-11, 1987-24, 1987-35, 1987-43, 1987-69, 1987-88, 1987-123, 1988-07, 1988-08a, 1988-09, 1988-11, 1988-18a, 1988-21, 1988-22, 1988-23, 1988-26, 1988-40, 1988-46, 1988-50a, 1988-54, 1988-65, 1988-78, 1988-133, 1988-139, 1989-02, 1989-03, 1989-04, 1989-11, 1989-12, 1989-25, 1989-28a, 1989-30, 1989-35, 1989-36, 1989-98, 1989-99, 1989-100, 1989-117, 1989-151, 1990-01, 1990-06, 1990-06a, 1990-56, 1990-70, 1990-72, 1990-79, 1990-81, 1990-106, 1991-01, 1991-04, 1991-09, 1991-12, 1991-16, 1991-26, 1991-31, 1991-34, 1991-48, 1991-49, 1991-57, 1991-75, 1991-86, 1991-92, 1992-01, 1992-02, 1992-11, 1992-14, 1992-15, 1992-58, 1992-99
Achievement need 1989-139

Acquired Immune Deficiency Syndrome (AIDS) 1989-20, 1992-66a
Administrators 1986-13, 1987-07, 1987-08, 1987-09, 1987-14, 1987-20, 1987-24, 1987-49, 1987-50, 1987-53, 1987-63, 1987-92, 1987-104, 1987-112, 1987-113, 1987-114, 1987-120, 1987-123, 1987-175, 1988-17, 1988-31, 1988-39a, 1988-40, 1988-46a, 1988-49, 1988-77, 1988-78, 1988-88, 1988-89, 1988-97a, 1988-106, 1988-112a, 1988-133, 1988-137b, 1989-05, 1989-11, 1989-18, 1989-19, 1989-39, 1989-40, 1989-43, 1989-64, 1989-74, 1989-83, 1989-90, 1989-98, 1989-99, 1989-100, 1989-102, 1989-158, 1990-04, 1990-13, 1990-15, 1990-19, 1990-20, 1990-20b, 1990-26a, 1990-46, 1990-53, 1990-62, 1990-70, 1990-72, 1990-81, 1990-89, 1990-99, 1990-105, 1990-110, 1991-06, 1991-13, 1991-17, 1991-27, 1991-31, 1991-34, 1991-49, 1991-61, 1991-64, 1991-74, 1991-75, 1991-86, 1991-89, 1991-90, 1991-92,

Subject Index

1991-100a, 1992-04, 1992-05,
1992-06, 1992-07, 1992-20,
1992-21, 1992-23, 1992-24,
1992-38, 1992-41, 1992-42,
1992-43, 1992-44, 1992-45,
1992-56, 1992-60, 1992-61,
1992-79, 1992-87, 1992-92,
1992-93, 1992-108, 1992-109,
1992-118, 1992-120, 1992-136

Admissions 1988-35

Advertising 1989-15, 1989-118, 1992-03, 1992-65, 1992-94, 1992-125

Affirmative action 1986-01,
1986-06, 1987-02, 1987-04,
1987-33, 1987-90, 1987-100,
1987-124, 1987-167, 1988-72,
1988-80, 1988-116, 1988-129,
1989-56, 1989-142, 1990-28,
1990-42, 1990-55, 1990-57,
1990-99, 1990-100, 1990-110,
1991-48, 1991-61, 1991-103,
1992-145

Ahmadu Bello University
(Zaria, Nigeria) 1992-18

Alabama 1990-37

Alaska 1990-33

Allensworth Colony
(California) 1987-46

Ambition 1987-95

American Association of Law
Libraries 1988-06, 1992-67,
1992-68

American Association of
University Women 1992-46

American Libraries 1987-18,
1991-44, 1992-09, 1992-10,
1992-90, 1992-133

American Library
Association 1987-149, 1987-171, 1988-03, 1988-04, 1989-05, 1989-07, 1989-15, 1989-18, 1989-19, 1989-20, 1989-37, 1989-39, 1989-40, 1989-43, 1989-74, 1989-95, 1989-116, 1989-137, 1989-157,
1990-02, 1990-06d, 1990-07,
1990-08, 1990-09, 1990-20b,
1990-26a, 1990-32, 1990-109,
1990-112, 1991-06, 1991-13,
1991-14, 1991-15, 1991-85,
1992-04, 1992-05, 1992-06,
1992-07, 1992-13, 1992-20,
1992-21, 1992-23, 1992-24,
1992-25, 1992-28, 1992-38,
1992-40, 1992-41, 1992-42,
1992-43, 1992-44, 1992-45,
1992-54, 1992-56, 1992-60,
1992-61, 1992-66, 1992-89,
1992-90, 1992-91, 1992-92,
1992-93, 1992-97, 1992-109,
1992-113, 1992-120, 1992-122, 1992-124, 1992-126,
1992-136

American Library
Association. Association of
College and Research
Libraries 1990-95, 1992-02,
1992-19

American Library
Association. Association of
College and Research
Libraries. Women's Studies
Section 1988-02, 1989-36,
1991-03, 1992-62

American Library
Association. Black Caucus
1990-22

American Library Association. Committee on Minority Concerns 1987-05, 1990-05

American Library Association. Committee on Pay Equity 1988-94, 1988-95

American Library Association. Committee on the Status of Women in Librarianship 1987-32, 1987-60, 1987-64, 1987-122, 1988-15, 1989-71, 1990-09, 1990-17, 1990-43, 1990-61, 1990-112, 1991-53, 1991-69

American Library Association Equality Award 1987-04a, 1987-06a, 1987-37, 1987-40, 1988-12a, 1988-137a, 1989-06a, 1989-13a, 1989-150a, 1990-01a, 1990-06b, 1990-06c, 1991-02, 1991-02a, 1991-02b, 1992-01a, 1992-01b

American Library Association. Library Administration and Management Association. Women Administrators Discussion Group 1989-06, 1990-49, 1990-61

American Library Association. Library Information and Technology Association 1992-57

American Library Association. Office for Library Personnel Resources 1987-05, 1987-18, 1987-122, 1989-08

American Library Association. Social Responsibilities Round Table 1987-171, 1988-15

American Library Association. Social Responsibilities Round Table. Feminist Task Force 1988-29, 1988-91, 1988-115, 1988-121, 1989-05, 1989-14, 1989-33, 1989-55, 1990-22, 1990-30, 1990-34, 1990-38, 1992-49, 1992-138, 1992-139, 1992-140, 1992-141, 1992-142, 1992-148

American Library Association. Social Responsibilities Round Table. Gay and Lesbian Task Force 1988-08, 1989-44, 1990-41a, 1991-05, 1991-40, 1991-47, 1992-09, 1992-10, 1992-27, 1992-90

American Nudist Research Library 1990-93

American Psycho 1991-87, 1991-88

Animals 1989-133

Association for Library and Information Science Education 1986-15, 1987-22, 1988-10, 1992-22

Association of Research Libraries 1987-10a, 1988-07, 1988-08a, 1988-46, 1989-02, 1989-03, 1989-11, 1990-06, 1990-81, 1991-09, 1991-75, 1992-01, 1992-14, 1992-15, 1992-58

Subject Index

Association of Women Working in Libraries (Germany) 1987-79
Associations 1992-11 (*see also* Organizations and names of specific associations)
Athletes 1988-57
Australia 1988-122, 1989-88, 1989-139, 1991-23
Austria 1987-125
Authority 1987-105, 1987-111, 1987-140, 1988-108
Authors 1987-66, 1989-154, 1989-155, 1990-16, 1990-45, 1991-19, 1991-37, 1991-50, 1991-70, 1991-93, 1992-119

Balancing work and family life 1987-51, 1987-71, 1987-173, 1988-20, 1989-23, 1989-24, 1989-29, 1989-159, 1990-77, 1991-99
Barker, Tommie Dora 1988-24
Belpre, Pura Teresa 1992-76
Berman, Sanford 1988-15, 1989-06a, 1989-13a, 1989-150a
Berry, Louise 1990-36
Beta Phi Mu 1990-62a
Bibliographic instruction 1989-35
Bibliographies 1988-85, 1989-34, 1989-45, 1989-59, 1989-105
Bingham, Rebecca 1989-58
Biography 1986-19, 1987-108, 1987-148, 1987-150, 1988-24, 1989-67a, 1990-52, 1991-08, 1991-53a, 1991-54a, 1991-55, 1991-64, 1992-47, 1992-55, 1992-76, 1992-79, 1992-82, 1992-102, 1992-137
Birth control 1991-68
Birth name 1989-66
Boaz, Martha 1987-39, 1987-150
Bogle, Sarah C.N. 1991-54a
Book reviews 1991-93
Books 1989-101, 1989-124
Boston Public Library 1992-82
Boyd, Eliza Stewart 1991-53
Boyer, Calvin 1990-28, 1990-55, 1991-61
Bradshaw, Lillian 1989-78a, 1991-64
Brazil 1989-17
Bright, Suzie 1992-49, 1992-138
Broidy, Ellen 1989-35
Bureaucracy 1989-89
Burnout 1988-112a, 1989-38, 1992-30
Burrington, Gillian 1988-123

Cain, Del 1987-147
California 1990-35
California State University system 1992-11
Campbell, Jane Maud 1991-55
Canada 1986-17, 1987-24, 1987-94, 1988-118, 1992-35
Canadian Library Association 1992-35
Career break 1988-44, 1990-77, 1991-28a

Career change 1986-08, 1991-34a, 1992-29
Career choice 1988-130, 1989-31, 1990-30a, 1992-18, 1992-32, 1992-69
Career feminism 1989-36
Career interest inventories 1988-134, 1992-69
Career ladders 1987-21, 1987-53, 1987-54, 1987-92, 1987-127, 1987-178, 1988-17, 1988-18a, 1988-40, 1988-49, 1988-55, 1988-77, 1988-78, 1988-82, 1988-110, 1988-118, 1989-59, 1989-60, 1989-62, 1989-64, 1989-67, 1989-90, 1989-99, 1989-102, 1989-148, 1989-158, 1990-13, 1991-27
Career opportunities 1986-08, 1987-26, 1987-64, 1987-128, 1988-55, 1988-123, 1989-29, 1989-62, 1990-63, 1990-74, 1991-17, 1991-46, 1992-121
Career planning 1987-93, 1987-95, 1987-128, 1988-77, 1988-122, 1989-64, 1989-148, 1990-88, 1992-77
Career satisfaction 1987-56, 1987-127, 1988-55, 1988-130, 1989-62, 1990-63, 1991-28a, 1992-52
Career strategies 1987-25, 1987-177, 1988-77, 1988-78, 1988-118, 1988-123
Case, Donald O. 1988-10
Cataloging 1987-57, 1989-68, 1989-69, 1989-119
Censorship 1989-108, 1989-122, 1991-54, 1991-64a, 1991-87, 1991-88, 1992-49, 1992-138
Centre for Research, Education and Information on Women (Germany) 1987-36
Certification 1987-147
Child care 1987-01, 1987-31, 1987-34, 1987-75, 1987-76, 1987-107, 1987-135, 1987-137, 1988-32, 1988-106, 1989-20, 1989-42, 1990-100, 1991-103, 1992-145
Child development 1989-31
Children 1990-30a
Children's library services 1987-13, 1987-121, 1987-128, 1987-145, 1988-56, 1988-113, 1989-26, 1989-67, 1989-103, 1990-38a, 1990-52, 1990-62a, 1990-65, 1990-67, 1991-65, 1992-46, 1992-76, 1992-82, 1992-102, 1992-137
Chilton Book Company 1987-153
China 1988-74
City government 1989-92, 1990-33
City University of New York 1988-40
Civil rights 1987-15
Clairol 1992-36
Classification 1991-98
Clement, Hope A. 1992-35
Cleveland Public Library 1991-79
Club women 1988-132, 1989-135, 1991-29, 1992-128
Cognitive processes 1988-26
Collaboration 1989-155

Subject Index

Collections 1989-101
Collective bargaining 1988-28
College and Research Libraries 1989-93
College students. *See* Women college students
Colleges 1987-11, 1987-35, 1988-11, 1989-12, 1990-06a
Colorado 1992-27, 1992-122
Columbia University School of Library Services 1986-11, 1988-35
Comic strips 1988-70, 1988-71, 1990-51, 1992-80
Coming out 1988-08
Communication 1989-21
Communication styles 1986-22, 1987-07, 1987-08, 1989-140, 1991-53, 1991-69
Community college libraries 1986-04, 1986-05, 1989-27, 1990-83
Community colleges 1986-04, 1986-05, 1988-28, 1989-27
Comparable worth 1987-25, 1987-62, 1987-65, 1987-96, 1987-156, 1987-166, 1987-168, 1988-39, 1988-48a, 1988-50, 1988-69, 1989-46, 1989-47, 1991-78
Compensation packages 1989-46, 1989-47
Competence 1987-87, 1988-51
Competitive behavior 1987-57
CompuServe 1990-21
Conferences 1987-01, 1987-31, 1987-138, 1987-153, 1987-156, 1988-02, 1988-04, 1988-32, 1988-36, 1989-15, 1989-20, 1989-33, 1989-37, 1989-42, 1989-57, 1989-116, 1989-156, 1990-08, 1990-09, 1990-49, 1990-61, 1990-109, 1990-112, 1991-03, 1991-05, 1991-14, 1991-15, 1991-53, 1991-85, 1991-106, 1992-13, 1992-17, 1992-19, 1992-22, 1992-28, 1992-37, 1992-40, 1992-49, 1992-54, 1992-56, 1992-57, 1992-59, 1992-62, 1992-66, 1992-70, 1992-73, 1992-78, 1992-81, 1992-97, 1992-113, 1992-122, 1992-124, 1992-138, 1992-140, 1992-141, 1992-142
Connecticut 1988-53, 1988-111, 1990-36
Content analysis 1987-17, 1989-49, 1992-16
Continuing education 1987-93, 1987-125, 1988-17
Contraception 1991-68
Contracts 1988-28
Cooke, Eileen 1991-06
Cost of living 1992-123
Crismond, Linda 1989-43, 1989-74, 1990-06b, 1990-20b, 1990-26a, 1991-06, 1991-13, 1992-04, 1992-05, 1992-06, 1992-07, 1992-20, 1992-21, 1992-23, 1992-24, 1992-38, 1992-41, 1992-42, 1992-43, 1992-44, 1992-45, 1992-56, 1992-60, 1992-61, 1992-92, 1992-93, 1992-120, 1992-136

Cromwell, Emma Guy 1987-148
Crones 1991-30a
Cuyahoga County Public Library (Ohio) 1987-30, 1987-118, 1987-141, 1987-142, 1988-97

Deans 1987-21, 1990-20, 1990-46
Deferential behavior 1987-104, 1987-111, 1987-140
Degrees 1987-157, 1987-158, 1987-160, 1987-161, 1988-45, 1988-127, 1988-128, 1989-142, 1989-143, 1990-97, 1990-97a, 1991-31, 1991-100, 1991-101a, 1992-107, 1992-143a, 1992-144
Demographic characteristics 1988-126, 1990-96, 1992-143
Demographic measurements 1988-22, 1989-64, 1990-29, 1990-64, 1991-07, 1991-17, 1991-28, 1991-75
Deskilling 1992-72, 1992-73, 1992-74
Detlefsen, Ellen Gay 1987-22
Devaluation 1992-17, 1992-72, 1992-73, 1992-74
Dewey, Melvil 1986-11
Directories 1988-38, 1989-08, 1989-44, 1989-53, 1989-81
Discrimination laws 1987-133, 1988-85, 1989-09, 1991-60, 1992-27, 1992-122, 1992-147
Diversity 1988-96, 1989-75, 1989-84, 1991-104
Doctoral degrees 1988-135, 1992-22
Dolan, Mary Anne 1989-36
Donlon, Patricia 1990-19
Dougherty, Richard 1989-58
Dressing for success 1987-77
Dual career couples 1990-106

Economic theory 1989-129
Editors 1990-88
Educational attainment 1988-137b, 1989-27, 1989-82, 1989-124, 1991-100
Employee benefits 1989-159, 1991-60
Employee development 1987-45, 1988-44
Employment opportunities 1986-19, 1987-57, 1988-21, 1988-137b, 1989-152, 1990-29, 1992-52, 1992-86, 1992-88
Employment patterns 1987-72, 1987-73, 1987-179, 1988-03, 1988-14, 1988-63, 1988-67, 1988-68, 1988-126, 1989-77, 1989-78, 1989-88, 1990-58, 1990-59, 1990-96, 1991-08, 1991-63, 1992-52, 1992-86, 1992-88, 1992-143, 1992-151, 1992-152
Employment practices 1986-06, 1986-17a, 1987-104, 1988-85, 1989-145, 1990-99
Enrollment in library school 1990-94
Equal employment opportunity 1986-06, 1987-

Subject Index

14, 1987-15, 1987-33, 1987-40a, 1987-41, 1987-42, 1987-53, 1987-136, 1987-167, 1988-80, 1988-116, 1988-129, 1988-136, 1989-56, 1989-107, 1989-141, 1991-81, 1991-103, 1992-31, 1992-75, 1992-108, 1992-114, 1992-145

Equal rights amendment 1987-55, 1991-14

Equity at Issue 1987-05

Ethics 1991-32

Ethnic groups 1988-98, 1988-128, 1989-70, 1992-86, 1992-107

Eubanks, Jackie 1989-110

Evaluation criteria 1986-07, 1990-10

Examinations 1989-13

Expectations 1989-82

Faculty 1986-04, 1986-05, 1986-16, 1987-70, 1987-159, 1987-163, 1988-65, 1988-73a, 1988-119, 1989-30, 1989-66, 1989-80, 1990-39, 1990-70, 1991-12, 1991-22, 1991-35, 1991-49, 1992-99

Family income 1990-60

Family responsibility 1989-09, 1989-41, 1990-77

Fear of success 1989-139

Federal assistance programs 1987-162, 1988-127a, 1989-144, 1990-98, 1991-101b, 1992-144a

Federal employment 1987-166, 1987-177

Female intensive occupations 1986-08, 1986-09, 1986-18, 1986-21, 1987-13, 1987-36, 1987-38, 1987-52, 1987-54, 1987-56, 1987-62, 1987-102, 1987-105, 1987-111, 1987-120, 1987-121, 1987-125, 1987-132, 1987-140, 1987-143, 1987-145, 1987-151, 1987-156, 1987-164, 1987-169, 1987-170, 1988-01, 1988-13, 1988-14, 1988-17, 1988-18, 1988-25, 1988-27, 1988-34, 1988-39, 1988-48, 1988-52, 1988-54, 1988-56, 1988-66, 1988-72, 1988-92, 1988-93, 1988-102, 1988-105, 1988-108, 1988-113, 1988-134, 1988-136, 1988-137a, 1989-16, 1989-17, 1989-22, 1989-26, 1989-31, 1989-50, 1989-54, 1989-58, 1989-68, 1989-69, 1989-72, 1989-94, 1989-123, 1989-125, 1989-131, 1989-133, 1989-139, 1989-153, 1990-11, 1990-20a, 1990-24, 1990-38a, 1990-48, 1990-53, 1990-71, 1990-77, 1990-87, 1990-89, 1990-101, 1990-101a, 1990-101b, 1990-104, 1991-10a, 1991-19, 1991-20, 1991-25, 1991-26, 1991-46, 1991-59, 1991-65, 1991-67, 1991-83, 1991-84, 1991-104, 1992-12, 1992-17, 1992-29, 1992-37, 1992-59, 1992-71, 1992-72, 1992-73, 1992-74, 1992-81, 1992-96, 1992-97, 1992-117, 1992-130, 1992-132, 1992-149

Feminism 1986-15, 1987-17, 1989-35, 1989-115, 1992-16
Feminist writing 1987-17, 1992-16
Feminists 1986-15, 1989-116, 1990-08
Fiction 1987-106, 1990-24, 1991-26a
Financial aid. *See* Student financial aid
Fleming, Catherine May 1991-34a
Flexible work schedules 1987-47, 1988-44, 1989-24, 1989-29, 1990-66, 1992-58
Folk culture 1991-30a
Forecasting 1987-60, 1988-82, 1988-105, 1988-126, 1989-124, 1990-96, 1992-72, 1992-73, 1992-74, 1992-88, 1992-143
Foreign students 1991-16
Frauenforschungs-bildungs-und-informationszentrum 1987-36
Freedom of information 1991-68, 1992-62
Funding 1987-23, 1987-63

Gay and Lesbian Freedom Day Parade (San Francisco) 1992-09, 1992-10, 1992-90, 1992-133
Gay men 1988-66, 1990-10a, 1990-27, 1990-40, 1991-38, 1991-39, 1991-60, 1992-08, 1992-27, 1992-63, 1992-64, 1992-66a, 1992-111, 1992-122, 1992-146, 1992-147

Gender differences 1986-04, 1986-05, 1986-13, 1987-09, 1987-11, 1987-24, 1987-28, 1987-44, 1987-49, 1987-53, 1987-54, 1987-61, 1987-63, 1987-72, 1987-73, 1987-80, 1987-86, 1987-87, 1987-88, 1987-91, 1987-95, 1987-113, 1987-114, 1987-127, 1987-129, 1987-144a, 1987-157, 1987-158, 1987-159, 1987-160, 1987-161, 1987-163, 1987-168, 1987-173, 1987-175, 1987-179, 1988-03, 1988-06, 1988-11, 1988-21, 1988-22, 1988-23, 1988-26, 1988-33, 1988-37, 1988-39, 1988-45, 1988-49, 1988-50a, 1988-51, 1988-60, 1988-62, 1988-63, 1988-66, 1988-67, 1988-68, 1988-73a, 1988-82, 1988-98, 1988-99, 1988-103, 1988-110, 1988-114, 1988-118, 1988-125, 1988-126, 1988-127, 1988-128, 1988-130, 1988-139, 1989-02, 1989-10, 1989-12, 1989-18, 1989-48, 1989-59, 1989-60, 1989-63, 1989-65, 1989-77, 1989-78, 1989-83, 1989-90, 1989-94, 1989-97, 1989-98, 1989-99, 1989-102, 1989-111, 1989-117, 1989-120, 1989-125, 1989-132, 1989-140, 1989-141, 1989-142, 1989-148, 1990-01, 1990-04, 1990-05, 1990-06, 1990-06a, 1990-10, 1990-12, 1990-13, 1990-15, 1990-18, 1990-28a, 1990-29, 1990-37, 1990-38a, 1990-

Subject Index

39, 1990-43, 1990-45, 1990-47, 1990-56a, 1990-58, 1990-59, 1990-62, 1990-63, 1990-64, 1990-81, 1990-85, 1990-92, 1990-102, 1990-103, 1990-105, 1990-107, 1990-108, 1991-11, 1991-12, 1991-22, 1991-26b, 1991-35, 1991-42, 1991-45, 1991-49, 1991-50, 1991-53, 1991-56, 1991-63, 1991-63b, 1991-69, 1991-86, 1991-89, 1991-90, 1991-93, 1991-97a, 1991-98, 1991-108, 1992-01, 1992-14, 1992-15, 1992-52, 1992-58, 1992-67, 1992-68, 1992-84, 1992-86, 1992-99, 1992-105, 1992-108, 1992-118, 1992-132, 1992-151

Gender roles 1987-173, 1991-10a

Germany 1990-89

Ghana 1991-07

Gill, Margaret S. 1992-79

Gilligan, Carol 1990-31

Girls 1990-31

Graduate degrees 1987-28, 1987-147, 1987-157, 1987-158, 1987-160, 1987-161, 1987-168, 1988-45, 1988-127, 1988-128, 1989-141, 1989-142, 1989-143, 1990-43a, 1990-97, 1990-97a, 1990-101a, 1990-108, 1991-31, 1991-45, 1991-100, 1991-102, 1992-107, 1992-143a, 1992-144

Graduate education 1986-14, 1987-21, 1987-22, 1987-150, 1987-179, 1988-10, 1988-17, 1988-35, 1988-82, 1988-105, 1988-122, 1989-63, 1989-65a, 1989-113, 1989-119, 1990-18, 1990-64, 1991-94, 1991-104, 1992-33

Granheim, Else 1991-21

Grants 1987-162, 1988-127a, 1989-144, 1990-100, 1991-101b, 1992-144a

H.W. Wilson Co. 1991-40, 1992-26

Hale, Kaycee 1991-73

Hannigan, Jane Anne 1990-62a

Harris, Michael 1986-15

Harvard Law Library 1991-107

Harvard University 1992-47, 1992-146

Health hazards 1987-103

Heim, Kathleen 1987-04a, 1987-06a, 1987-37, 1987-40, 1988-99, 1990-20, 1990-46

Hewins, Caroline M. 1990-52

Higher education 1986-07, 1987-73a, 1987-123, 1988-22, 1988-31, 1988-107, 1989-30, 1989-45, 1989-73, 1989-80, 1989-82, 1989-123, 1990-54, 1990-72, 1990-79, 1990-81, 1990-106, 1991-26, 1991-34, 1991-48, 1991-57, 1991-83

Hiring policy 1987-07, 1987-18, 1988-41, 1989-152

History 1986-10, 1986-11, 1987-15, 1987-64, 1987-79, 1987-108, 1987-148, 1987-149, 1987-169, 1988-27,

1988-35, 1988-90, 1988-93, 1988-107, 1988-132, 1989-34, 1989-135, 1989-136, 1990-41a, 1990-78, 1990-79, 1991-23, 1991-29, 1991-51, 1991-53a, 1991-82, 1991-83, 1991-94, 1991-107, 1992-33, 1992-54, 1992-78, 1992-79, 1992-82, 1992-102, 1992-128
Homeless 1990-65, 1990-67
Hughes, Langston 1991-62
Human resources 1989-84, 1989-112, 1990-86, 1992-40
Humor 1989-75

Illinois 1986-04, 1986-05, 1987-130, 1989-25, 1989-27
Illness 1987-61, 1990-71
Image 1987-58, 1987-77, 1987-131, 1987-144, 1987-153, 1988-05, 1988-43, 1988-57, 1988-64, 1988-70, 1988-71, 1988-76, 1988-79, 1988-84, 1988-87, 1988-96, 1988-101, 1988-112a, 1988-117, 1989-16, 1989-32, 1989-42, 1989-49, 1989-72, 1989-75, 1989-87, 1989-91, 1989-94, 1989-118, 1989-134, 1989-149, 1989-150, 1989-160, 1990-20a, 1990-21, 1990-24, 1990-25, 1990-26, 1990-36, 1990-30a, 1990-30b, 1990-44, 1990-51, 1990-63, 1990-65, 1990-67, 1990-76, 1990-78, 1990-90, 1990-90a, 1990-93, 1990-113, 1991-10, 1991-26a, 1991-30a, 1991-34a, 1991-37, 1991-56, 1991-73, 1991-80, 1991-82, 1991-103a, 1991-104, 1992-17, 1992-36, 1992-65, 1992-69, 1992-80, 1992-94, 1992-100, 1992-117, 1992-125, 1992-134
Immigrants 1991-55, 1991-79
Indexes 1991-40
Industrial Society, Pepperell Unit (UK) 1987-85, 1987-93
Influence 1991-34a
Information dissemination 1986-21, 1987-134, 1989-54, 1989-89, 1989-156, 1990-38, 1991-68, 1992-59, 1992-62, 1992-82
Information science 1988-73a, 1988-81, 1988-82, 1989-149, 1990-87, 1992-59, 1992-95
Information services 1987-138, 1989-71, 1989-88, 1989-89, 1989-104, 1989-136, 1989-138, 1989-156, 1990-47, 1990-101, 1990-101a, 1990-101b, 1991-11
Inner city 1989-104
Institute of Information Scientists (UK) 1990-102, 1990-103
International Federation of Library Associations and Institutions 1987-59, 1987-138, 1987-155, 1989-156, 1991-21, 1991-106, 1992-70, 1992-114, 1992-150
International Symposium on Women's Libraries (Istanbul) 1991-30
Internships 1990-57
Interviews 1986-17a

Japan 1989-66
Job advertisements 1987-18, 1989-63
Job descriptions 1987-10, 1987-16
Job discrimination 1987-14, 1987-18, 1987-112, 1987-113, 1987-114
Job evaluation 1986-07, 1987-10, 1987-156, 1989-109
Job market 1987-57, 1987-72, 1987-73, 1987-91, 1987-128, 1987-145, 1988-30, 1988-67, 1988-68, 1988-113, 1989-01, 1989-67, 1989-77, 1989-78, 1989-114, 1990-58, 1990-59, 1990-86, 1991-63, 1991-108, 1992-151, 1992-152
Job placement 1987-72, 1987-73, 1988-67, 1988-68, 1989-77, 1989-78, 1990-58, 1990-59, 1991-63, 1991-108, 1992-151, 1992-152
Job recruitment 1986-16, 1987-18, 1987-121, 1988-47, 1988-54, 1988-56, 1988-73, 1988-81, 1988-92, 1988-98, 1988-99, 1988-124, 1988-135, 1989-39, 1989-40, 1989-65a, 1989-119, 1990-23, 1990-47, 1990-85, 1992-31, 1992-32
Job satisfaction 1987-44, 1987-56, 1987-80, 1987-88, 1988-18a, 1988-103, 1990-37, 1990-56, 1991-22, 1991-89, 1991-90, 1991-91, 1991-97b
Job sharing 1987-130, 1988-18a, 1990-66, 1991-99, 1991-101
Job standards 1987-10

Job training 1989-119, 1992-31
Jones, Kay 1987-147
Jones, Mary 1990-70
Jones, Virginia Lacy 1991-08
Josey, E.J. 1991-02, 1991-02a, 1991-02b, 1992-51

Kennedy, Marilyn Moats 1990-110
Kent State University Center for the Study of Librarianship 1990-86
Kesler, Adele 1991-29
Kimmel, Margaret 1992-101
Kolb's Learning Style Inventory 1989-28a
Krueger, Carol 1992-55

Labor market 1987-170, 1988-30, 1989-01, 1990-104, 1991-67
Labor practices. *See* Unfair labor practices
Labor unions 1992-11
Lamar University 1989-151
Language 1991-53, 1991-69, 1991-98
Law libraries 1988-06, 1988-30, 1989-59, 1990-84, 1992-67, 1992-68
Lawsuits 1987-35, 1987-102, 1987-103, 1987-118, 1987-141, 1987-142, 1988-97, 1989-28, 1991-60, 1992-48
Leadership 1987-20, 1987-24, 1987-32, 1987-149, 1987-171, 1988-102, 1989-43, 1989-58, 1989-74, 1989-76, 1989-96,

1989-98, 1989-136, 1990-03, 1991-21, 1991-73, 1991-94, 1991-96, 1992-34, 1992-77, 1992-105, 1992-106
Leadership roles 1987-16, 1988-16, 1988-49, 1988-76, 1989-70, 1989-87, 1990-02, 1990-36, 1990-41
Leadership skills 1987-16, 1990-03, 1990-41, 1991-74, 1991-96
Learning differences 1988-26, 1989-28a
Ledbetter, Eleanor 1991-55, 1991-79
Leita, Carole 1989-110
Lesbian and Gay History Month 1991-62, 1991-77
Lesbian Archive 1989-127
Lesbians 1988-66, 1990-10a, 1990-27, 1990-40, 1990-41a, 1991-38, 1991-39, 1991-40, 1991-60, 1992-08, 1992-27, 1992-46, 1992-63, 1992-64, 1992-66a, 1992-111, 1992-122, 1992-147
Libraries & Culture 1991-50
Library and Information Science Students' Attitudes, Demographics, and Aspirations Survey 1989-65a, 1990-47
Library Association (UK) 1987-40a, 1987-41, 1987-42, 1987-129a, 1987-151, 1989-97, 1989-107, 1989-147, 1990-102, 1991-81, 1992-31, 1992-114
Library Association of Australia 1987-53, 1987-138, 1987-155, 1989-156
Library of Congress 1987-50, 1987-75, 1987-76, 1987-98, 1987-99, 1987-100, 1987-107, 1987-135, 1987-136, 1987-137, 1987-167, 1988-86, 1988-106, 1988-116, 1988-129, 1988-138, 1989-39, 1989-40, 1990-100, 1991-101, 1991-103, 1992-145
Library schools 1986-14, 1986-16, 1987-21, 1987-159, 1988-73a, 1988-105, 1989-80, 1990-13, 1990-64, 1990-85, 1990-94, 1990-108, 1991-22, 1991-35, 1991-83, 1991-94, 1992-18, 1992-22, 1992-32, 1992-95
Library science 1987-21, 1987-39, 1987-143, 1988-31, 1988-73a, 1988-81, 1988-82, 1988-137, 1989-66, 1989-80, 1989-113, 1989-119, 1990-43a, 1992-95
Library workers 1987-47, 1987-98, 1987-99, 1987-136, 1988-50, 1988-74, 1991-67, 1991-78 (*see also* Paraprofessionals; Support staff)
Literature 1987-131, 1988-76, 1989-103, 1991-10
Local government 1992-86
Los Angeles (California) 1987-65
Los Angeles Public Library 1990-07a, 1991-62, 1991-77, 1992-63, 1992-64, 1992-111

Subject Index

Louisiana State University 1990-20, 1990-46

Madrid, Lucia Rede 1992-137
Male intensive occupations 1986-09, 1988-27, 1989-131, 1990-77
Management 1987-54, 1987-95, 1987-125, 1987-173, 1988-39, 1989-48, 1989-83, 1989-112, 1989-127, 1990-110, 1991-100a
Management practices 1987-08, 1987-20, 1987-120, 1987-171, 1988-49, 1988-109, 1991-61
Management styles 1987-07, 1988-49, 1988-109, 1989-18, 1989-54, 1989-74, 1989-140, 1990-15, 1990-83, 1991-34, 1991-74
Management training 1987-93, 1990-03
Manley, Will 1992-26, 1992-134
March for Equality/Women's Lives 1989-07, 1989-20, 1989-137, 1989-157
Maryland Women's Hall of Fame 1990-111
Massachusetts 1987-35
Maternity benefits 1987-94, 1987-124, 1988-06, 1989-56, 1989-65
Medical libraries 1989-10, 1989-102
Medical Library Association 1992-131
Meetings 1989-140

Memory 1987-134
Men 1988-84, 1990-48, 1991-10a, 1992-149
Mental health 1987-61, 1990-71
Mentors 1988-78, 1989-96, 1990-15, 1991-92, 1991-96, 1992-34
Minneapolis Public Library 1991-60
Minnesota 1987-65, 1989-51, 1990-35, 1990-50
Minority employment 1987-05, 1988-03, 1988-25, 1988-72, 1988-98, 1990-05
Minority experience 1987-178, 1989-61, 1990-99
Minority groups 1987-67, 1987-162, 1988-98, 1988-128, 1989-96, 1989-141, 1989-144, 1990-05, 1990-42, 1990-97, 1990-98, 1990-99, 1991-16, 1991-48, 1991-101b, 1992-32, 1992-39, 1992-51, 1992-86, 1992-107, 1992-143a, 1992-144, 1992-144a
Moen, William E. 1988-99
Montgomery County Department of Public Libraries (Maryland) 1987-04, 1987-90
Moore, Anne C. 1990-52, 1992-102
Morrow, Carolyn Clark 1992-47
Mothers working outside the home 1987-71
Motivation 1988-50a, 1989-139, 1990-85, 1991-28a
Myers-Briggs Type Indicator

1990-107, 1992-69

National Library of Ireland 1990-19
National Research Council of Canada 1992-79
Netherlands 1987-169, 1990-13, 1991-100a
New England 1987-11, 1988-11, 1989-12, 1990-06a
New York Public Library 1989-39, 1989-40
Nicolle, Ray 1990-56a
Nonverbal communication 1988-37
North Carolina 1987-15
North Carolina Library Association. Round Table on the Status of Women in Librarianship 1991-70
Norton, Ethel Hall 1987-46
Nudity 1990-93

Occupational attitudes 1986-21, 1988-76, 1988-134, 1989-65a, 1989-67, 1989-82, 1990-37, 1990-47, 1990-108, 1991-89, 1991-90
Occupational mobility 1987-129, 1987-177, 1988-110, 1988-124, 1989-59, 1989-60, 1989-64, 1989-120, 1990-13, 1990-14, 1990-63, 1990-110, 1991-27
Occupational patterns 1986-01, 1988-23, 1988-107, 1989-10, 1989-25, 1989-82, 1990-77, 1991-04, 1991-28, 1991-83
Occupational roles 1987-45, 1989-32, 1990-72, 1991-26
Occupational sex segregation 1986-18, 1987-26, 1987-62, 1987-121, 1987-145, 1988-56, 1988-89, 1988-93, 1988-108, 1989-13, 1989-68, 1989-69, 1989-92, 1989-129, 1989-146, 1991-59, 1991-67
Occupational status 1986-03, 1986-21, 1987-12, 1987-58, 1987-86, 1987-105, 1987-11, 1987-128, 1987-140, 1987-147, 1987-165, 1988-12, 1988-21, 1988-30, 1988-136, 1989-01, 1989-67, 1989-68, 1989-69, 1989-73, 1989-87, 1989-92, 1989-113, 1989-138, 1991-20, 1991-65, 1991-67, 1991-100, 1992-78
Occupational stress 1987-61, 1989-23, 1989-52, 1991-91, 1992-30
Occupational trends 1988-30, 1988-105, 1988-126, 1989-01, 1989-75, 1990-88, 1990-96, 1992-143
Ohio 1987-112, 1987-113, 1987-114, 1988-77, 1990-86
Ohio Women Librarians (OWL) 1987-14, 1987-104, 1987-105, 1987-111, 1987-112, 1987-113, 1987-114, 1987-140, 1987-175, 1988-77, 1988-88, 1988-89, 1988-109, 1989-28
Older women 1991-59, 1992-29
Oregon 1992-122, 1992-147
Organizations 1987-19, 1987-149, 1988-38, 1988-66, 1989-

Subject Index

08 (*see also* Associations and names of specific organizations)
Organizing 1989-71
Osborne, Nancy 1989-110

Paraprofessionals 1989-106, 1990-56, 1991-78 (*see also* Library workers; Support staff)
Paretsky, Sara 1990-09
Part-time employment 1987-71, 1988-21, 1990-66, 1990-77, 1991-67, 1991-101
Patriarchy 1987-105, 1987-111, 1987-140, 1988-16, 1988-90, 1988-108, 1988-109
Pay equity 1987-23, 1987-27, 1987-35, 1987-52, 1987-65, 1987-68, 1987-70, 1987-89, 1987-102, 1987-110, 1987-115, 1987-116, 1987-117, 1987-123, 1987-125, 1987-156, 1987-166, 1988-16, 1988-25, 1988-50, 1988-61, 1988-94, 1988-95, 1988-120, 1989-29, 1989-51, 1989-79, 1989-109, 1989-113, 1989-151, 1990-35, 1990-50, 1990-60, 1990-80, 1990-82, 1991-22, 1991-57, 1991-58, 1991-78, 1992-104, 1992-115, 1992-116, 1992-131
Pease, Sarah W. 1991-53a
Pennsylvania 1989-04, 1989-111, 1990-01, 1990-101b, 1991-01
Perception 1987-87, 1987-145, 1988-37, 1988-51, 1988-52, 1988-84, 1988-101, 1992-17, 1992-69
Periodicals 1987-66, 1988-15, 1989-14, 1989-33, 1990-27, 1991-50 (*see also* names of specific periodicals)
Personality traits 1986-22, 1988-42, 1988-76, 1989-96, 1990-85
Phillips, Edna 1991-55
Play 1989-31
Political activism 1987-03, 1987-29, 1989-130, 1990-112, 1992-126
Political spouses 1987-151
Pornography 1987-84, 1991-25, 1991-54, 1991-64a, 1991-84
Power 1987-59, 1987-138, 1987-155, 1988-109, 1989-36, 1989-71, 1989-88, 1989-156
Pregnant workers 1987-124, 1988-20, 1989-09, 1989-56, 1989-65
Preservation 1991-71, 1992-47
Pritchard, Sarah 1989-36
Profanity 1987-08
Professional awards 1987-48, 1987-139, 1987-174, 1987-176, 1988-10, 1991-06, 1992-35 (*see also* American Library Association Equality Award)
Professional development 1987-92, 1988-17, 1988-44, 1990-57, 1991-46
Professional education 1986-14, 1987-25, 1988-55, 1989-

80, 1989-82, 1990-63, 1990-94, 1991-46, 1991-83, 1991-100
Professional occupations 1989-45
Professional status 1986-09, 1987-22, 1988-13, 1988-14, 1988-52, 1989-30, 1989-49, 1989-80, 1989-106, 1989-117, 1989-118, 1989-152, 1990-41, 1990-90, 1990-90a, 1991-12, 1991-18, 1991-20, 1991-28a, 1992-17, 1992-72, 1992-73, 1992-74, 1992-97, 1992-117, 1992-124
Professional women's groups 1988-38, 1989-37, 1989-53, 1989-81, 1990-109, 1991-15 (*see also* names of specific organizations)
Professionalism 1986-21, 1992-97
Progressive Librarians Guild 1990-23
Promotions 1990-77, 1991-74
Psychological factors 1989-122, 1991-57
Psychological testing 1989-52
Public libraries 1986-01, 1987-14, 1987-46, 1987-49, 1987-87, 1987-92, 1987-104, 1987-112, 1987-113, 1987-114, 1987-129, 1987-169, 1988-49, 1988-77, 1988-96, 1989-90, 1989-120, 1989-133, 1990-04, 1990-48, 1990-101, 1990-101a, 1990-101b, 1990-111, 1991-04, 1991-17, 1991-23, 1991-29, 1991-42, 1991-55, 1991-79, 1991-82, 1991-100a, 1992-34
Public Library Association 1987-121, 1990-62
Public officials 1989-92, 1990-33
Public speaking 1987-85
Publications 1987-89, 1988-48, 1988-62, 1989-93, 1989-117, 1989-154, 1989-155, 1990-16, 1990-39, 1990-43, 1990-45, 1991-19, 1991-35, 1991-38, 1991-50, 1991-51, 1992-119 (*see also* names of specific publications)
Publishing industry 1987-139, 1987-174, 1987-176, 1991-71, 1992-111

Quality of work life 1987-88

Race class and gender studies 1989-131, 1991-33, 1991-97
Racial discrimination 1987-18, 1988-04, 1988-80, 1988-96, 1989-145, 1990-55, 1990-99, 1991-61
Racism 1987-109, 1987-122, 1988-50, 1988-58, 1988-72, 1988-91, 1988-112, 1988-115, 1988-121, 1990-30, 1991-85
RAND Corporation 1988-96
Randall, Margaret 1989-33
Reading 1989-124, 1990-48, 1990-56a
Reentry women 1988-44, 1989-24, 1990-75, 1992-121
Rees, Margaret 1991-29

Subject Index

Reference services 1988-51, 1988-52, 1991-11
Regan, Muriel M. 1989-72
Regional studies 1989-154, 1989-155
Repression 1987-134
Research 1987-64, 1987-119, 1987-154, 1988-48, 1988-61, 1989-98, 1989-99, 1989-136, 1989-139, 1989-153, 1990-10, 1990-39, 1990-45, 1990-87, 1991-11, 1991-18, 1991-35, 1991-50, 1991-51, 1992-14, 1992-15, 1992-78, 1992-95, 1992-105, 1992-119, 1992-149
Research libraries 1986-13, 1987-09, 1987-10a, 1987-11, 1987-24, 1988-07, 1988-09, 1988-11, 1988-22, 1988-46, 1988-78, 1989-02, 1989-03, 1989-11, 1990-06, 1991-09, 1991-75, 1992-02, 1992-14
Richardson, John V. 1988-10
Risk-taking behavior 1989-96, 1989-122
Role models 1987-20, 1988-76, 1990-31, 1991-73
Rugge, Sue 1988-41
Rural areas 1990-101, 1990-101a, 1990-101b

Saudi Arabia 1987-69
Scholarship 1988-49, 1988-62, 1988-110, 1989-21, 1989-93, 1989-117, 1990-39, 1990-45, 1990-109
Scholarships 1987-02
School libraries 1988-124, 1990-76
Schroeder, Patricia 1992-28

Schuman, Patricia Glass 1990-07, 1990-34, 1990-61, 1990-91, 1992-28, 1992-64
Scott, Anne F. 1986-10
Selection procedures 1986-17a
Self-concept 1986-21, 1987-58, 1988-76, 1988-79, 1989-32, 1989-87, 1989-122, 1989-134, 1990-90, 1990-90a (see also Image)
Sellen, Betty-Carol 1989-33, 1990-01a, 1990-06b, 1990-06c
Sex discrimination in education 1988-31, 1989-45, 1991-107
Sex discrimination in employment 1987-14, 1987-18, 1987-25, 1987-30, 1987-35, 1987-102, 1987-103, 1987-104, 1987-118, 1987-133, 1987-141, 1987-142, 1987-171, 1988-04, 1988-28, 1988-31, 1988-80, 1988-84, 1988-90, 1988-97, 1988-123, 1989-23, 1989-29, 1989-45, 1989-145, 1990-35, 1990-53, 1990-55, 1990-70, 1990-71, 1990-82, 1990-98, 1991-61, 1991-74, 1992-30, 1992-48, 1992-129, 1992-149
Sex stereotypes 1987-79, 1987-83, 1987-105, 1987-131, 1987-144, 1987-145, 1987-172, 1988-15, 1988-42, 1988-43, 1988-51, 1988-64, 1988-79, 1988-87, 1988-108, 1988-117, 1989-15, 1989-42, 1989-75, 1989-94, 1989-103, 1989-

118, 1989-134, 1989-150,
1989-160, 1990-20a, 1990-21,
1990-24, 1990-25, 1990-26,
1990-30a, 1991-10, 1991-10a,
1991-23, 1991-37, 1991-84,
1992-17, 1992-36, 1992-65,
1992-105
Sexism 1987-83, 1988-112,
1989-14, 1989-33, 1989-108,
1991-26a, 1991-98
Sexual equality 1987-154,
1989-21
Sexual harassment 1987-124,
1987-133, 1988-80, 1989-56,
1990-61, 1990-82, 1991-35,
1991-41, 1991-95, 1992-03,
1992-25, 1992-85, 1992-129,
1992-135
Sexuality 1991-25, 1991-54,
1991-64a, 1991-84, 1992-26,
1992-49, 1992-134, 1992-138,
1992-142
SHARE Directory 1989-33,
1989-128, 1990-23
Sharp, Katharine Lucinda
1991-94
Shoemaker, Sarah 1991-37
Silence 1987-134
Silver, Linda R. 1987-30,
1987-118, 1987-141, 1987-142, 1988-97, 1989-28
Singapore Association of
Women for Action and
Research 1990-54
Single mothers 1989-09
Sipapu 1989-110
Smith, Elizabeth Martinez
1990-07a, 1991-62
Social attitudes 1991-16,
1992-32
Social construction of gender
1988-90, 1992-17
Social movements 1990-95,
1992-128
Socialization 1987-45
Society of American
Archivists 1987-108, 1988-35, 1988-75, 1989-85, 1989-86, 1989-91
Sociology of knowledge
1991-18
Sophiea, Laura 1988-57
South Africa 1992-95
Soviet Union 1988-132
Special libraries 1988-30,
1988-92, 1989-01, 1990-92,
1991-66, 1992-118
Special Libraries Association
1987-58, 1987-146, 1988-32,
1989-42, 1989-132, 1990-44,
1990-113
Spouse support 1992-89,
1992-91, 1992-146
Standards 1987-23
State employment 1986-06,
1989-51, 1992-86
State government 1990-33
State libraries 1986-06
State University of New
York, Albany 1988-119
State University of New
York, Buffalo 1989-136
Statistics 1986-01, 1986-03,
1986-04, 1986-05, 1986-13,
1986-16, 1986-20a, 1987-06,
1987-09, 1987-10a, 1987-11,
1987-12, 1987-19, 1987-24,
1987-28, 1987-63, 1987-64,
1987-66, 1987-73, 1987-86,

1987-89, 1987-112, 1987-113, 1987-114, 1987-119, 1987-127, 1987-129a, 1987-132, 1987-146, 1987-157, 1987-158, 1987-159, 1987-160, 1987-161, 1987-163, 1987-164, 1987-168, 1987-175, 1987-179, 1988-03, 1988-06, 1988-07, 1988-09, 1988-11, 1988-12, 1988-14, 1988-21, 1988-22, 1988-23, 1988-31, 1988-35, 1988-45, 1988-63, 1988-66, 1988-74, 1988-81, 1988-98, 1988-107, 1988-114, 1988-126, 1988-127, 1988-133, 1989-03, 1989-04, 1989-11, 1989-12, 1989-25, 1989-27, 1989-59, 1989-60, 1989-77, 1989-78, 1989-83, 1989-93, 1989-100, 1989-114, 1989-125, 1989-141, 1989-142, 1990-01, 1990-02, 1990-06, 1990-06a, 1990-12, 1990-29, 1990-33, 1990-47, 1990-58, 1990-59, 1990-73, 1990-84, 1990-96, 1990-96a, 1990-97, 1990-98, 1990-101a, 1990-102, 1990-103, 1990-108, 1991-01, 1991-04, 1991-09, 1991-31, 1991-63b, 1991-75, 1991-86, 1991-100, 1991-101a, 1992-01, 1992-02, 1992-12, 1992-14, 1992-15, 1992-30, 1992-67, 1992-68, 1992-86, 1992-107, 1992-132, 1992-143, 1992-143a, 1992-144, 1992-151

Status of women 1986-02, 1987-18, 1987-29, 1987-36, 1987-38, 1987-60, 1987-67, 1987-79, 1987-93, 1987-108, 1987-119, 1987-123, 1987-145, 1987-172, 1988-48, 1988-52, 1988-61, 1988-89, 1989-26, 1989-34, 1989-39, 1989-40, 1989-83, 1989-84, 1989-105, 1989-113, 1990-78, 1990-89, 1990-109, 1990-113, 1991-51, 1991-66, 1992-51, 1992-54, 1992-70, 1992-71, 1992-75, 1992-112, 1992-124

Steinem, Gloria 1992-28

Stimpson, Catharine 1990-09

Strikes 1988-120

Strong-Campbell Interest Inventory 1992-69

Student financial aid 1987-162, 1988-127a, 1989-144, 1990-98, 1991-101b, 1992-144a

Students 1986-14, 1988-81, 1988-82, 1988-122, 1988-130, 1990-13, 1990-18, 1992-18, 1992-121

Sullivan, Peggy 1992-23, 1992-93, 1992-109, 1992-136

Support staff 1988-69, 1990-37, 1991-78, 1992-127 (*see also* Library workers; Paraprofessionals)

Support systems 1987-98, 1987-99, 1987-135, 1987-136, 1987-137, 1988-86, 1988-106, 1988-138, 1989-23, 1989-143, 1990-99, 1991-103, 1992-145

Surveys 1986-16, 1987-129, 1987-132, 1987-144, 1987-146, 1987-179, 1988-07,

1988-51, 1988-61, 1988-65, 1988-82, 1990-29, 1990-44, 1990-83, 1990-103, 1991-12, 1991-56, 1991-89, 1991-90, 1992-117

Tallman, Johanna 1986-19
Technology 1988-112a, 1988-139, 1989-48, 1989-63, 1991-91, 1992-57, 1992-59, 1992-72, 1992-73, 1992-74, 1992-84, 1992-96, 1992-112
Tenure 1988-119
Test bias 1989-52
Texas 1990-83
Texas Library Association 1987-126
Thompson, R. Roosevelt, Jr. 1989-84
Time management 1987-51, 1991-42
Titcomb, Mary Lemist 1990-111
Turnover rates 1987-129, 1989-120, 1991-58

Unfair labor practices 1989-09
United Kingdom 1987-25, 1987-91, 1991-66, 1992-52, 1992-87, 1992-108
University of California at Irvine 1990-28, 1990-55, 1991-61
University of California system 1992-11
University of Ibadan (Ibadan, Nigeria) 1992-18
University of Illinois Graduate Library School 1991-94
University of Montreal Library School 1987-132
University of Pittsburgh 1988-46a, 1992-101
University of Toronto 1992-37
University of Western Ontario 1988-52a
Unpaid employment 1987-82
Upward mobility 1986-09, 1988-47, 1988-82, 1989-62, 1992-87, 1992-130
Utah 1991-03

Value systems 1991-11, 1991-25
Vereinigung Bibliothekarischarbeitender Frauen 1987-79
Vermont 1990-35
Video display terminals 1987-103
Virginia 1988-39a, 1988-46a, 1988-97a
Volunteer work 1987-82, 1989-135, 1992-128

Wage discrimination 1987-17, 1987-62, 1987-104, 1987-112, 1987-113, 1987-114, 1988-39, 1988-95, 1988-111, 1989-26, 1992-16
Wage earning mothers 1987-47, 1987-71, 1988-32, 1990-66, 1990-75
Wage gap 1987-09, 1987-14, 1987-23, 1987-49, 1987-56, 1987-62, 1987-63, 1987-72, 1987-112, 1987-113, 1987-

114, 1987-123, 1987-127, 1987-175, 1988-09, 1988-14, 1988-18, 1988-21, 1988-33, 1988-34, 1988-39, 1988-46, 1988-66, 1988-94, 1988-95, 1988-111, 1988-114, 1989-02, 1989-03, 1989-04, 1989-10, 1989-11, 1989-22, 1989-29, 1989-59, 1989-60, 1989-65, 1989-111, 1990-06, 1990-28a, 1990-43, 1990-89, 1990-103, 1990-105, 1991-57, 1991-58, 1992-67, 1992-68

Wages 1986-03, 1986-20a, 1987-09, 1987-10a, 1987-11, 1987-12, 1987-23, 1987-24, 1987-49, 1987-63, 1987-64, 1987-72, 1987-73, 1987-86, 1987-102, 1987-103, 1987-112, 1987-113, 1987-114, 1987-119, 1987-120, 1987-123, 1987-127, 1987-145, 1987-147, 1987-156, 1987-159, 1987-163, 1987-164, 1987-170, 1987-175, 1988-06, 1988-07, 1988-09, 1988-11, 1988-12, 1988-18, 1988-21, 1988-30, 1988-33, 1988-34, 1988-36, 1988-39, 1988-46, 1988-47, 1988-48a, 1988-53, 1988-54, 1988-60, 1988-61, 1988-65, 1988-66, 1988-73a, 1988-102, 1988-105, 1988-111, 1988-114, 1988-137a, 1989-01, 1989-02, 1989-03, 1989-04, 1989-11, 1989-12, 1989-13, 1989-16, 1989-24, 1989-30, 1989-50, 1989-59, 1989-60, 1989-65, 1989-77, 1989-78, 1989-80, 1989-109, 1989-111, 1989-113, 1989-114, 1989-121, 1989-125, 1989-132, 1989-151, 1989-152, 1990-01, 1990-06, 1990-06a, 1990-12, 1990-28a, 1990-29, 1990-33, 1990-35, 1990-43, 1990-50, 1990-58, 1990-59, 1990-60, 1990-64, 1990-73, 1990-77, 1990-78, 1990-84, 1990-92, 1990-103, 1991-01, 1991-09, 1991-24, 1991-26, 1991-26b, 1991-28a, 1991-31, 1991-57, 1991-58, 1991-63, 1991-63b, 1991-75, 1991-86, 1991-97a, 1991-108, 1992-01, 1992-12, 1992-14, 1992-15, 1992-29, 1992-67, 1992-68, 1992-86, 1992-88, 1992-99, 1992-108, 1992-118, 1992-123, 1992-151

Washington (state) 1987-65

Washington Post 1989-15

Weibel, Kathleen 1988-12a, 1988-137a

Williams, Barbara Osborne 1990-65, 1990-67

WLW Journal 1988-15, 1991-43, 1991-76, 1991-105, 1992-50

Wolf, S.K. 1991-37

Wolfreston, Frances 1989-101

Women college students 1988-35, 1991-107

Women in Libraries (UK) 1990-105

Women in Libraries 1988-15, 1989-33

Women Library Workers

1989-110
Women of color 1987-46, 1987-178, 1989-61, 1991-08
Women's clubs. *See* Club women
Women's colleges 1987-69
Women's groups 1989-38
Women's history 1988-93, 1989-61, 1989-70, 1989-100, 1989-136, 1989-153, 1990-70, 1990-71, 1990-78, 1990-79, 1991-08, 1991-29, 1991-53a, 1991-82, 1991-83, 1991-94
Women's Information and Referral Exchange (Australia) 1989-89
Women's movement 1987-17, 1987-29, 1987-57, 1987-84, 1989-115, 1992-16
Women's National Book Association 1987-48, 1987-74, 1987-139, 1987-174, 1987-176, 1991-91a
Women's rights 1989-07, 1989-20, 1989-152, 1989-157, 1990-112, 1992-19
Women's studies 1989-35, 1989-54, 1989-123, 1991-52, 1992-110
Woodsworth, Anne 1988-46a
Work alienation 1991-91
Work hazards 1987-103
Work history 1989-64, 1990-29
Workplace 1989-36, 1989-86, 1992-75
Workshops 1989-85, 1989-91, 1991-52
Wyoming Literary and Library Association 1991-53a

Yates, Ella Gaines 1988-39a, 1988-46a, 1988-97a